D1351674

SAILOR IN A RUSSIAN FRAME

SAILOR
IN A
RUSSIAN
FRAME

Cdr. ANTHONY COURTNEY

JOHNSON

LONDON

ANTHONY COURTNEY © 1968

First published 1968

S.B.N. 85307 010 5

MADE AND PRINTED IN GREAT BRITAIN BY
MORRISON AND GIBB LIMITED, LONDON AND EDINBURGH
FOR JOHNSON PUBLICATIONS LTD
11/14 STANHOPE MEWS WEST, LONDON, S.W.7

CONTENTS

PART ONE

PART TWO

PART THREE

Contents

PART FOUR

EPILOGUE

APPENDICES

INDEX

ILLUSTRATIONS

TO
ELISABETH

who never trusted bears

FOREWORD

by

Dr. Donald Johnson, Chairman of Johnson Publications Ltd., and former M.P. for Carlisle.

I feel privileged, as Commander Courtney's publisher and with his approval, to be writing this Foreword to the chequered story which he has to tell, the general outlines of which are familiar to the nation as a whole.

As a politician, Commander Courtney is an enigma to many people. An almost swashbuckling indiscretion, combined with a sterling sense of patriotism and immense courage, both political and moral—these are not the hallmarks of the politician as he exists today, whether in actuality or in the public mind.

The answer to our conundrum is that we must surely judge our author, not so much as the politician in which capacity he became known, but as the sailor which, both in his title and throughout the book, he rightly insists that he is—a sailor who has wandered into politics and who applies his own sense of values to the political scene. A by no means welcome intruder into the political scene of today!

It is generally known that this book has been delayed by an action for defamation of character but with the decision of the Court in favour of our author in the case, *Courtney v. Constantine*, in March, 1968, comment is now free. It is difficult, however, to comment without a feeling of the ridiculous at the extent of the obloquy which in some quarters has descended on our author's head. What more natural than that a widowed sailor (as was proved in the aforementioned case) should in the course of his travels take a pretty woman friend to a hotel bedroom? The photograph of Zina facing page 129 can be left to speak for itself. Or maybe this is altogether *too* natural for our permissive society?

9

*   *   *

This Foreword would end this point, were it not that I have other associations with Commander Courtney. As I was, so was he one of the series of M.P.'s whose dispute with his constituency Association Executive has ruffled the serene façade of Conservative Party politics in recent years. Former Parliamentary colleagues, abstainers on the Profumo Debate, he and I have undergone similar experiences, in as much as in each case our political associations have terminated in a successful action for defamation in the Law Courts.

In similar fashion to Commander Courtney, I entered Parliament following a lifetime as a doctor, with professional values and professional principles as my guidance. I was, alas, no more welcome than he was when I attempted to apply these to the political situation at the time of the Profumo crisis in 1963.

And, of course, I met a similar fate. As I have read the final part of Commander Courtney's story that concerns his dealings with the Harrow East Conservative Association I have found myself, line by line, sentence by sentence, with a sense of *déjà vu*. All this happened in East Harrow, but it also happened in Carlisle three hundred miles away.

So, in Commander Courtney's story, character assassination by the Russians is followed by further character assassination at home—one totalitarian institution reacts in sympathy with another, so it seems, to destroy the lone voice.

Commander Courtney, at any rate, cannot be swept under the carpet and we shall doubtless hear more of him. In the meantime he gives us a story of courage and tenacity and one that is heartening to all those who still have the will to resist the enemy both without and within the gates.

DONALD McI. JOHNSON.

London, 1968

PART ONE

1. FORMATIVE YEARS

I REALLY believe it all started one summer's morning in 1917 when the telegraph boy, that bird of evil omen in those wartime days, delivered a telegram to my mother in the garden of our house on the Surrey/Sussex border. It was from my father, from whom we had not heard for more than three months, to tell us that he had safely arrived at Aberdeen and what he needed most of all was a hot bath. This had been the latest and most anxious of his periodic visits to Petrograd for, as we knew from what he told us, to the perils of U-boats and the other hazards of war there was now added a ferment within Russia herself which might at any time flare into revolution or civil war. To us children our father seemed to be something of a crusader even though, for reasons which were never entirely clear to us, he was not in uniform, like other children's fathers, away being shot at by Germans at the Front. It seemed that the Russians were in desperate need of machines of certain kinds which my father alone could give them, things which made the guns with which our brave allies were helping Haig and Jellicoe (Kitchener, alas, had been drowned on his way to visit them) to win the War. He called them machine-tools.

All this deeply impressed me as a boy of nine, but my imagination was kindled most of all by the presents which my father used to bring back with him. There were beautifully-carved wooden toys, bears and wolves which could be made to perform ludicrous antics, and illustrated books of fairy-tales, illuminated in blue and gold, whose princes and princesses far outshone anything we had previously found in the hag-ridden pages of Grimm or the wishy-washy stories of Hans Christian Andersen. But these stories were locked away in page after page of the beautiful Russian script, and not even my father's careful translation, whenever he could be badgered into

13

reading to us, was satisfactory. I determined that when I grew up I would speak and read Russian myself. All this helped to paint for me a mental picture of this far-off, lovely land, which really came to life when my father sat down at the piano and sang Russian folk-song after folk-song, Ukrainian songs, military songs, "romances" (which I did not like then and have not liked since), The Song of the Haulers on the Volga and The Song of the Flea. He had a good light baritone voice and could imitate a Russian infantry regiment singing *Lebedushka* on the march, with a crashing chorus which took our old Broadwood out of its prim English self and which set an indelible seal, with tingling all up the spine, on the mind of his young son.

This time my father brought bad news from the country of my dreams. Defeatism, hunger and mutiny were undermining the Provisional Government and he had witnessed terrible scenes of mob-violence and apparently aimless cruelty against harmless individuals. By chance, while in Petrograd, he had run across a childhood friend, Sasha Kropotkina, the daughter of a Russian exile, old Prince Kropotkin, who had lived close to my grandfather's home in Bromley. Sasha had returned to her native land and was married to an influential member of the Bolshevik party, which was feverishly active in the capital. She told him that a shortage of bread would inevitably lead to rioting, that the military could no longer be relied on to intervene against the hungry masses, and that it was this situation which would at last make it possible to overthrow the Menshevik régime and to establish in its stead their life's dream, Government by Councils of Workers and Peasants —the Soviets. She urged my father to leave Russia while the frontier remained open. Business was inevitably at a standstill and time must elapse before it could be re-established under the new conditions. Meanwhile it would be indiscreet, and could be dangerous, for a foreigner to remain in the country while the Russians put their house in order. *Rasplata*—the reckoning—had arrived. It seems that my father's Jewish partner, by the name of Weinberg, agreed with this view, though he probably had no option, and having wound up the business to the best of his ability in the chaotic conditions prevailing, my father found his way with difficulty through Finland to Bergen and thence by ship to Aberdeen. He was never to see his beloved Russia again.

A schoolboy, particularly in wartime, makes much of his father's background and achievements, and at my school in Lee-on-Solent his adventures lost little in the telling. In particular, a chance contact of his with the monk Rasputin some years previously was magnified into a national court intrigue that owed a good deal to *The Prisoner of Zenda*—still one of my favourite books. After all, there was always the awkward and unacknowledged fact that my father was not in uniform like all the rest. It was an easy step, therefore, to associating him, and by implication myself, with a romantic and mysterious background closely associated with the crumbling Tsarist Empire, and this in turn impelled me to reinforce my almost unassailable position among my school-mates by an intensive study of *Hugo's Russian Course, Part* I. I found then, as I have found since, that an assumption of expertise in an uncommon language is very seldom challenged. It is a gambit, furthermore, which is by no means confined to speakers of Russian.

Four years later, a gangly red-headed naval cadet, acutely self-conscious in his new Gieves uniform, joined the Royal Naval College Dartmouth, and embarked on an intensive period of disciplinary, character and physical training for which he has never ceased to be grateful, and which was to stand him in good stead in the trials which awaited him. Dartmouth was a major experience, representing as it does the most formative four years of my life. We were driven hard— sometimes so hard that weaker brethren fell by the wayside— but the end product of the machine was to form the backbone of the Navy in the Second World War, and in its conduct of that affair the sometimes-maligned system under which the Royal Navy College of those days operated received its ultimate justification. I have returned once or twice to Dartmouth, with oddly mixed feelings. The smell of the gym still brings back fear of the boxing-ring, the cadets' bathroom the awful anticipation of "three cuts" after rounds. But for me the personalities of the men whom we followed and imitated still pervade the atmosphere, Gresham Nicholson and "Shorty" Butlin, our Term Lieutenants, Hubert Brown, Michael Lewis, Hughes, Marten and "P.T.H.", who crammed both knowledge and respect for learning into our heads, also the incomparable Blake Term, Chief Petty Officer, who was father and mother to us all. It was a time in which to put away childish dreams, but underneath the thickening naval veneer there remained a set purpose from earlier years, which was that, somehow and sometime, I must re-establish my father's connection with Russia and tie my future life in some way to that great, unhappy, far-off country.

* * *

Two and a half years at sea as a cadet and midshipman in big ships, cruisers and destroyers included an unforgettable six months in the battle-cruiser *Renown* in which the Duke and Duchess of York sailed for the opening of the newly-built Australian Federal Houses of Parliament at Canberra. Calls at the Canary Islands and Jamaica, followed by the passage of the Panama Canal and on via the Marquesas and Fiji brought us to New Zealand and finally to Australia, where I exercised a midshipman's prerogative by falling in love seriously for the first time. She was a lovely, tennis-playing, fair-haired Australian, and as a grandmother many times over she still remains nearly my oldest friend. The return to England, jaded and exhausted by the wonderful hospitality which we had experienced everywhere, was via Mauritius, Aden, Port Said, Malta and Gibraltar. It had been a unique experience to have seen the world under these conditions, and it needed a hard year back with the Battle Cruiser Squadron to bring us, officers and ship's company alike, once again up to the Fleet standard of sea-going efficiency.

After a period ashore doing courses at Greenwich and Portsmouth, where boxing and Rugby football took up a good deal of my time, I was appointed to the China Station as Sub

(1) Laying-up the Colour of *H.M.S. Lancaster*: 1932

(2) R.N. Heavyweight: 1926 to 1936

Lieutenant of *H.M.S. Cornwall,* and it was here that my Russian thinking, which had lain dormant for so long, began to re-emerge, through the first tenuous contacts with Russian *émigrés* and Russian associations in the Far East. Visits to Dalny and Port Arthur stimulated my reading of the history of the Russo-Japanese War, while a journey to Mukden in Manchuria and several spells in Shanghai brought me into contact with many delightful girls in the White Russian clubs and cabarets, most of whom, I remember, seemed to have it in common that they possessed "brothers in the Imperial Guards". Here was a real incentive to improve my Russian, and Tatiana Sabline, who worked at a night-club known as "The Tavern", was delightfully co-operative.

It was at this time that I entered for the first time for the competitive Examination in Russian, held by the Admiralty each year, and to my surprise and delight won a small prize. I had also met two men who were to exercise some influence over my future life. The first was a delightful bachelor member of the Diplomatic Service, Jack Greenway, known to his naval friends as "the Crab", who spoke some Russian and was addicted to travel by "grey-funnel line", in other words to taking passage with his friends in H.M. Ships. The second was Derek Wyburd, Junior Watchkeeper in the *Cornwall* and some four years senior to me. Jack had spent two years as a Secretary in the British Embassy in Moscow and he had many a good story to tell about life among the Muscovites. I was particularly intrigued by the method which he said he had used to get rid of a particularly obnoxious Russian employee. He had simply written "Voronov—100 roubles" on a piece of paper, blotted it quickly and carefully and then destroyed the original. According to the story his *bête noire* had disappeared as if by magic!

After a year in China and a short Physical Training Course at Portsmouth, I was appointed Lieutenant in *H.M.S. Malaya,* then junior private ship in the 2nd Battle Squadron, Atlantic Fleet. It was in the *Malaya* that I went through the traumatic experience of the Invergordon mutiny of 1931. *Malaya* was a West Country ship, and we were particularly lucky in some of our officers, with the result that we experienced practically no trouble and emerged with a reputation as a "clean ship". The incident was widely attributed at the time to Communist subversion, and it served to heighten my curiosity about the "Soviet Fatherland", hostile and remote, which had played, it seemed, such a part in inflicting a terrible blow to the morale and prestige of the Service which I loved so much. For a second —and then for a third time I received prizes and a commendation in the Annual Examination for the Russian language. As a Lieutenant of two years seniority it was time to consider Specialization—qualification as a specialist officer in Gunnery, Torpedo, Navigation, Signals or Anti-Submarine. I had already applied separately in response to an Admiralty Fleet Order calling for volunteers to qualify as Interpreter in Russian, with the added attraction of a six months' preliminary course at London University before proceeding abroad to learn the language with a family. Derek Wyburd had already been selected for this course and was due to go on for the second part of it to Tallinn, the Tsarist Reval, in Esthonia, where there was a sizeable colony of White Russians, and a number of officers from all three Services studying the language. Quite a number of them returned to England with Russian wives. In due course my application went in to specialize in Signals and Wireless Telegraphy, and I was told that, having qualified reasonably well in my examination for Lieutenant with two First-Class Certificates, it was probable that I would be selected. But there was only just time to fulfil my language ambitions, and with the help of my Captain, G. W. Hallifax, who wrote strongly on my behalf to the Admiralty, I achieved my object, though Their Lordships, in granting the application, pointed out that I already knew too much Russian to justify the six months course at London University, but that I could immediately proceed abroad on nine months' language leave. It was my first experience of Treasury parsimony.

But where to go?

Tallinn was so full of language students that it would be just about as useful to study Russian in "The Goat". Prague, from all accounts, was mainly German-speaking and a dead loss.

Beloved Shanghai was much too far away. The Soviet Union was as yet barred to Service language students. I bethought myself of Jack Greenway, now First Secretary at the British Legation in Bucharest, and a letter to him brought an enthusiastic response. Bucharest he wrote, was full of *émigré* Russians, tumbling over themselves to teach me the language.

That was a sad time in my family circle, for my father was very ill with cancer, and I knew that when I left this time I should never see him again.

2. LEARNING RUSSIAN

ON an evening in the autumn of 1933 I arrived in the British Legation at Bucharest, where I was met by Jack Greenway and made welcome by the Minister and his wife, Michael and Mary Palairet, and their two delightful children, Anne and Anthony.

The impact of these pleasant surroundings in a Balkan capital on a young sailor straight from sea was considerable, and not very favourable to the serious business in hand. True, I wrote exercises, read books and had two hours' tuition every day with a reasonably competent Russian teacher, but as the weeks ebbed away I began to realize that at this rate I should never learn enough Russian to qualify as an interpreter at the end of my period of language study.

All the same, my knowledge of Russian was evidently sufficient to satisfy one particular local requirement, and it was in this way that I first came in contact with our Secret Intelligence Service. The representative in Roumania had been deprived of his Russian-speaking assistant at a difficult time, and for a few weeks I was pressed into service. It was an instructive period, in which I formed a considerable affection for the tight-lipped, inconspicuous little man who directed the activities of British Intelligence in that part of the world.

There were other excitements. I was in the Legation when news came through that Duca, the Roumanian Prime Minister, had been assassinated by a member of the Iron Guard, a Nazi-orientated organization which was steadily increasing its influence in Roumanian politics. I put on my coat and went off at once through the snow to the bar of the Athenée-Palace Hotel, always a hotbed of uninhibited political gossip. Predictably, one of the less temperate members of the Cantacuzen family was holding forth at the top of his voice to a group which included more than one newspaperman. His general line was that Duca, the francophile middle-of-the-roader had only received his deserts, and my ears pricked when he added that de Hauteclocque, First Secretary at the French Legation, might be next on the list for treatment of a similar kind.

Back at our Legation Michael Palairet was drafting a long telegram to the Foreign Office, but at my news he put on his silk hat and went straight off to see the French Minister. It was perhaps due to this warning that de Hauteclocque continued, until he died just after the war, to ornament the ranks of the French Diplomatic Service.

It was with a heavy heart that I said goodbye to my Bucharest friends and set out for Kishinev, the capital of the former Russian province of Bessarabia, incorporated since 1918 in the Kingdom of Roumania. Apparently it was an outlandish spot, so much so that no-one I met in Bucharest had ever been there. After a tedious train journey, enlivened by the intense curiosity of my fellow-passengers, I arrived at two in the morning in an old-fashioned Russian droschky at the Hotel Londonskaya, where I ate my first *Chicken Kievskaya* to the strains of a first-class Roumanian orchestra, and was eaten in my turn for the rest of the night by voracious Bessarabian bedbugs. Kishinev, despite strong attempts at Roumanization, had remained in essence a Russian provincial town of some 100,000 inhabitants. Pushkin had not been impressed by the amenities of the town to which he was exiled, but my first impressions were more favourable. In particular, the Russian language, which was to be heard on all sides, showed me that I had come to the right place at last. I had a letter to a Madame Sukhomlinova, and soon fixed up to have lessons with her husband, an enormous bald Russian, cousin of the former Tsarist Minister for War, but the most vital problem was accommodation with a Russian family, as it was imperative to escape as soon as possible from the terrible Londonskaya.

Accordingly, on the day following I presented myself at a long, low single-storey house in the main street, the Alexandrovskaya, to a large Jewish lady who, I soon realized, considered herself to be the leading social figure in Kishinev. She was the wife of a Liberal Senator who had been formerly a member of the Petrograd Duma; her name was Xenia Iliynitchna Synadino. I drank tea with *varenye** in the Russian style, was introduced to her husband, old Panteleimon Viktorovitch, his son Viktor of about 22 and a nice daughter Sasha of 19. Mutual inspection having proved satisfactory, terms were agreed and I moved the same evening into the comfortable Synadino house, where I was to stay for over seven months.

I realize now how immensely fortunate I was to have lighted on Kishinev for a proper grounding in the Russian language, Russian customs and the Slav mentality. The family spoke beautiful Russian, and Xenia Iliynitchna had a lovely voice with which she sang by heart an immense variety of Russian songs to her own accompaniment on the piano. Viktor was away most of the time in Bucharest, but Panteleimon Viktorovitch, when at home, was always anxious to discuss international affairs, and skating, walking and games with Sasha and her girl-friends all helped to give me an insight into the ordinary lives of these charming Russian people. There were other families, Krupenskys and Tsankos and a kind and hospitable community of Russian Christian Scientists who made me welcome in their homes. Inevitably I fell in love with an attractive divorcée, considerably older than myself, Tamara Yurievna Yeshchinskaya, who was an enchanting companion to the young British naval officer, so far from home.

I also found a new and excellent tutor. Roman Niedzelsky was a Russian of Polish origin who had formerly lived in the

* *varenye*; a sweet, very liquid home-made jam.

Ukraine. He had fled with his family a few years previously, swimming the river Dniester under fire from the Red frontier guards with his small daughter clinging to his shoulders. He was deeply interested in international affairs and was convinced that a main objective of British policy was the seizure of the Russian oilfields in the Caucasus. "When that happens," he used to say, "I shall return to my country and fight against you, even though the Bolsheviks may shoot me afterwards." He was a fine teacher of Russian, and I owe much to him and to his kindly family.

But my necessary concentration on things Russian had its drawbacks, for I ran foul of the Roumanian authorities, and this began to be reflected in a noticeable coolness on the part of the Military Governor, General Canciulescu. Situated only twelve miles from the Soviet frontier, along the river Dniester, Kishinev was a cauldron of intrigue and international espionage, which was right above the head of a young Englishman there to learn Russian and enjoy himself. It seemed inconceivable to me in those days that my letters should be actually intercepted and opened by the Roumanian Political Police, the *Sigurantza*, but the facts of Balkan life were borne in on me unmistakably by three experiences. In the first place I discovered for certain that my belongings were being regularly searched. Secondly, I and others sometimes heard the screams of the unfortunates being interrogated in the *Sigurantza* headquarters further up the Alexandrovskaya. And finally, being addicted to long walks with a rucksack full of food and lesson-books, I eventually found myself under arrest by the Roumanian frontier guards for being in a prohibited zone close to the frontier. The subsequent interview at Police headquarters was not very pleasant.

In my comparative innocence it was only slowly that I became aware of the clandestine activities which were centred in Kishinev. The Poles were active, it seemed, under the direction of Colonel Jan Kowalewski, the Military Attaché, whom I had met in Bucharest. The French, too, had a young and active Consular staff which seemed scarcely justified by the importance of Kishinev itself. But there were other and stranger characters such as Michael Flemmer, who carried a fountain-pen-type tear-gas gun (imported from Chicago) and once invited me to take a trip with him into Soviet Russia across the ice from Akkerman.

It seems that in the early months of 1934 the Roumanian Cabinet decided that I was to be expelled from the country. As I was, in their view, clearly engaged in espionage of some sort and had not taken the authorities into my confidence it was too dangerous for the Roumanians to allow matters to remain as they were. In point of fact I was neither qualified nor competent to take any hand in such activities. I had a shrewd suspicion that our Secret Intelligence people had an active representative in Kishinev, but I never discovered who he was, nor did I try to do so. Fortunately the British Minister in Bucharest had his ear to the ground, and I was both mystified and delighted when he and Mary invited themselves up to Kishinev, to stay with me for the Russian Easter celebrations. The Minister's moral support was sufficient for its purpose, and I stayed.

Finally, in June 1934, I said goodbye to many dear friends in my now reasonably fluent Russian and started back by train across Europe with a small eight-year-old English boy under my wing. The Tsanko family had discovered him, the son of an English father some years dead and a Roumanian mother, who was persuaded to let the boy leave with me to take up his English heritage. A passport from the Consul at Galatz, help from the Legation in Bucharest and a cable to the National Children's Home in England enabled this to be done, and when I last heard from him Charles Wells was doing well in the radio business in London. But I never knew what became of his poor mother.

After an intensive few weeks of examination-cramming by that master of his craft, Professor Raffi, I attended the Civil Service Commission and passed my examination as a Russian Interpreter, First Class, for which I received the princely sum for those days of £150, all of it already spent in advance to meet the expenses of my time in Roumania. I had acquired, not just a knowledge of Russian, but a wider and deeper knowledge of the people and their mentality from my Turgeniev-like existence in the Alexandrovskaya. I had spent eight months in what was perhaps the last remaining piece of old Russia.

3. PREWAR INTERLUDE

ON my return to England I learned that I had been accepted for the Long Course in Signals and Wireless Telegraphy, and was appointed as First Lieutenant of *H.M.S. Sardonyx* at Portsmouth to fill in time before joining the Signal School. It gave me the chance of a new experience, qualifying to fly at Eastleigh Aerodrome, and by the end of the year I had done my tests and received my pilot's "A" licence.

I never made much of a Signals Officer, and in retrospect it was probably a mistake for me ever to have specialized in this branch, which demanded then, as it does now, a completeness of concentration which does not allow of an absorbing outside interest such as I had already acquired in my studies of Russian. To the rest of the Navy our branch had what would currently be described as something of a "grouse-moor" image. The Long Course (S) was notoriously the most intensive and complex of all the specializations, and the fact that we described our tie, of blue and grey diagonal stripes, as representing "blue blood and grey matter" did not particularly endear us to the rest of the Service.

It so happened that at the end of 1934, or thereabouts, the ban was at last lifted on visits by officers of the Armed Forces to Soviet Russia, and this was a chance too good to miss. In the summer leave period of 1935, therefore, with a naval friend, Lt. Cdr. Wyburgh Thruston, who afterwards lost his life in *H.M.A.S. Sydney* in the Pacific, I found myself travelling Third Class with a party of Friends of the Soviet Union on board the Soviet ship *Kooperatsiya*, bound for Leningrad. With us, travelling First Class, were Patrick Blackett and his wife, also paying their first visit to the Soviet Union. Patrick was himself a former naval officer, and during the whole journey we greatly enjoyed swapping our impressions with his own pinkish ones, and with those of his wife, which were a very distinct red.

As we passed through the Kiel Canal the strains of the *Internationale*, hurriedly organized by the Friends on the fo'c's'le, competed with the *Horst Wessel Lied* sung in a clear treble by a party of Hitler Youth on the bank. A Russian deck-hand played Solveig's song on a guitar with a delicacy of touch and a rapt intensity of feeling that I remember to this day. Comrades of the First Class vied with Comrades from the Third in composing a eulogy of welcome to the Soviet Father-land, which it fell to me, as the solitary Russian-speaker among them, to declaim on their behalf before a bored assembly of officers and ship's company. My spirits rose as we entered the Gulf of Finland and passed Kronstadt on our port beam before entering the Morskoi Kanal which leads to modern Leningrad. And that evening I introduced Wyburgh in the lounge of the Astoria Hotel to the correct way of drinking vodka. He was certainly a willing pupil. There were two nice-looking girls sitting at the bar, and I suggested that we might redeploy our forces, move across and intercept. "I'd like nothing better," said Wyburgh, looking pensively towards them, "and I feel as sober as a judge, but the fact is, Tony, I just can't stand up!"

From Leningrad by train to Moscow, on to Kiev and Kharkov and back to Leningrad we travelled with our charming but rather eccentric English companions, and at last my knowledge of Russian really came into its own. To the exasperation of our Intourist guides we broke away whenever we could from the bear-led organized parties. We made notes, took photographs, asked awkward questions, chivvied officials and generally behaved rather stupidly, for I at least had not yet learned the need for discretion and patience if one is to obtain either usefulness or pleasure out of a visit to modern Russia, even to the pre-purge Russia of 1935. Nevertheless I had made my first real contact with the Soviet Union, and despite the frustrations and the inefficiency of much of our experience I now knew that the country and its people still held much of the charm that had captivated my father in pre-Revolutionary days. On our return we composed a lengthy report on what we had seen, from ships in the Neva to prices in the open market at Kiev, which was duly forwarded to the Admiralty by the Commander-in-Chief, Portsmouth.

This visit, and the report which followed it, had a decisive effect on my whole naval career, for at the end of the Long Course I was sent for by the Captain of the Signal School who told me that, instead of a seagoing Signals appointment, I was to be lent to the Naval Intelligence Division at the Admiralty for six months to re-write the Russian Intelligence Report, which was badly in need of revision.

I enjoyed every moment of my six months at the Admiralty, particularly as I was one of the most junior officers ever appointed to that establishment. The work was fascinating and the subject close to my heart, while the helpfulness and support of the Naval Intelligence Staff from the Director, Rear-Admiral J. A. G. Troup, downwards, were a continual delight. It fell to me to conduct the first Soviet Naval Attaché, Engineer-Flagman Antsipo-Chikunsky into St. Paul's on the occasion of the Funeral Service for King George V and on an unforgettable occasion I met and accompanied Marshal Tukhachevsky and the Soviet Military Attaché in London, General Putna, both of whom were subsequently shot during the Red Army purge.

It was during this period, too, that I made a good friend of Georgi Alexandrovitch Astakhov, the First Secretary of the Soviet Embassy in London, who stayed with me at the Royal Naval Barracks, Portsmouth and came as my guest aboard my old ship, the destroyer *Sardonyx*, to the Coronation Review at Spithead. As the *Victoria and Albert* passed through the lines a mile or so away from our humble position we dutifully cheered ship and then returned to our gin in the wardroom.

"You English," said Georgi Alexandrovitch rather intensely as he descended the steel ladder, "how sure you are of yourselves!"

In those days British and Russians discussed politics with a freedom which I have never experienced since, and I have

26

always believed that he, as I, was convinced that a community of interest vis-à-vis the rising power of Nazi Germany must force England and the Soviet Union into some kind of a military alliance for the sake of pure survival. Georgi Alexandrovitch soon afterwards left to take up an appointment as Press Attaché in Berlin, where he was instrumental in the early exchanges which led to the conclusion of the Molotov-Ribbentrop pact. I have never been able to renew contact with my former friend, who is now dead, and I should have liked to have reminded him of those conversations of prewar days. He was a good man and a patriotic Russian. Had we been allowed to meet again it could only have been to the benefit of our two countries.

By 1937 Their Lordships, in their wisdom, had decided that I must go to sea, if I were not to be sidetracked into specialized Russian affairs, and I therefore went for two years as Flag Lieutenant and Signals Officer to the Admiral Commanding 3rd Cruiser Squadron, flying his flag in *H.M.S. Arethusa* in the Mediterranean. "Nutty" Wells was not the easiest of Admirals to serve, and it was a strange "cuddy" that for some time included the Admiral, Philip Vian, his Flag Captain, Jasper Parrott, his Secretary, myself and Noël Coward, enjoying himself, as always with the Navy, and gathering material which he put to good use in *In Which we Serve*.

It was the period of the Spanish Civil War, and on so-called Non-Intervention patrol we were frequently bombed, with the utmost impartiality, by Italian aircraft operating on behalf of General Franco from Majorca, and by Russian aircraft supporting the Government forces and based near Barcelona. It was at Almeria, on a visit to see the wounded sailors from the mined *H.M.S. Hunter*, that I had the experience of drinking sherry in the wardroom of the *Jaime I* with the Spanish Admiral, his officers and the red-rosetted sailors of the "Ship's Committee". Though I did not know it at the time, for he took care to steer clear of us, there was at Almeria a Soviet Naval Attaché by the name of Golovko, whom I was to meet and work with many years later when he became Commander-in-Chief of the Soviet Northern Fleet at Polyarnoe.

A cruise up the Black Sea to Constanza enabled me to renew my old contacts with Roumania, though I failed to get as far as Kishinev.

It was at this time that I met and fell in love with Elisabeth, then working as Secretary to the Defence Security Officer in Malta; we were married at St. Mark's, Alexandria, at the end of the Munich crisis in 1938. My best man was also a Signalman. We had been ordered to call briefly at Malta for oil at the height of the crisis, but wireless silence was in force and I could get no word to my fiancée to tell her to meet me. However, the Signals Trades Union was equal to the emergency, and as we sighted the Port War Signal Station a message came through by light—"Arethusa Flag Lieut. from Fleet Signal Officer. Your baggage is waiting on the jetty." And so she was.

4. FROM HALIFAX TO ARCHANGEL

IN April, 1939, I returned to England with my wife, and found myself in October, 1939, on my way across the Atlantic in *H.M.S. Resolution* as Signal Officer to the Rear-Admiral Commanding, 3rd Battle Squadron, later to become the North Atlantic Escort Force, based on Halifax, Nova Scotia. It was the western end of the Battle of the Atlantic, and represented a vital sector of the British war effort. During this period I made friends with many French officers who visited the port in various warships, and I had the intense sadness of witnessing the effects of the fall of France on these fine ships and their companies. It was a dreadful thing to be sent, one day, as I was, to see Battet, a personal friend and Captain of the *Emile Bertin* to tell him that the Admiral had observed that he had raised steam, and to inform him that, should he attempt to sail without permission, the forts at the entrance to the harbour had been given orders to open fire.

My time at Halifax was an interesting period, complicated by Canadian domestic politics, but my heart was no longer in this end of the war after 22nd June, 1941, when news came through that the Wehrmacht had invaded Russia.

By the middle of October the Admiralty had acted, and I was on my way back to the country which still fascinated me so much, this time to take up the post of Deputy Head of the Naval Mission in Moscow. Fortified by promotion to the acting rank of Commander, which was considered essential for the job, I travelled north to Kirkwall and joined *H.M.S. Kenya*, Captain Michael Denny, flying the flag of Rear-Admiral Harold Burrough, who was senior officer in command of the covering force for convoy PQ 3. The Admiral had a family connection with the Russians, as it was a forbear of his, Stephen Burrough, who gave his name to the Kara or Burrough Strait dividing the mainland from Novaya Zemlya, which he discovered in the sixteenth-century. Another Burrough, furthermore, had fought in the English squadron alongside the Russians at the battle of Navarino. For this reason he took a special interest in five Russian airmen who were taking passage in the ship after visiting the United States on a purchasing mission. The senior officer was Colonel Mikhail Mikhailovitch Gromov, a charming and cultured Russian, an accomplished horseman, a breeder of fox-terriers and the second Soviet aviator, after Chkalov, to fly across the North Pole. With him were the four men of his crew, Yumashev, Baidukov, Gordienko and Leonchenko, whom I was able to get to know intimately in the weeks ahead.

Despite bad weather we sailed for Iceland, where the convoy was assembling, and in their anxiety to get home the Russians, desperately bored in their unfamiliar surroundings, simply could not understand the reason for the delay. The wardroom food in the *Kenya* was bad even by wartime standards, so on Russian insistence I went ashore and bought a whole sheep in order that they might entertain their hosts in something like their accustomed style. The Captain's galley having been taken over for the purpose, the Russians cooked huge quantities of *shashlik*,* and Siberian *pelemeny*,** which were eaten by the Admiral, the Captain and a number of guests

* *shashlik*; Caucasian dish on skewers.
* * *pelemeny*; mincemeat, boiled in balls of dough. A Siberian dish. Stored outside under the snow during winter.

at a gargantuan feast, washed down with gin in the absence of vodka. It was a strange and notable occasion. The passage to Murmansk was made in the worst weather conditions ever experienced by many of us on board. The high seas even detonated mines in our own minefields, so close at one point that we thought we had been torpedoed. It was probably not only the Russians who thought that their last hour had come, but it was none the less gratifying when I groped my way by the light of an electric torch (the whole after part had gone "off the board") down to my charges in the stern cabins, to find Gordienko on his knees, obviously interceding with his Maker. It was an interesting example of reversion to type under stress of war.

Throughout the worst of the gale Colonel Gromov remained on the bridge, quite unaffected by seasickness and taking a lively personal interest in all that was going on. He told me afterwards that it had been one of the greatest experiences of his life. For the Russians it was undoubtedly a very severe ordeal, but their cheerfulness and patience impressed us all. Their relief at the sight of the grey, forbidding Murman coast was almost comical. It must have been in much the same spirit that Ivan the Terrible's first Ambassador to the Court of St. James, with his suite, had arrived back home in Archangel with Captain Richard Chancellor four centuries earlier.

At last the eternal games of "Preference" came to an end, the final *yelochki** were recorded on the score-card, and as the first Russian launch came alongside in the Kola Inlet they were away. I had made five good friends, and was sorry to see them go. One point about them had struck us all, which was the difference in physique and facial features between Gromov and Yumashev on the one hand, and the remaining three on the other. This difference was the clearest evidence of the survival of an aristocratic strain in the midst of proletarian revolution, and the Russians themselves were certainly conscious of it.

The Soviet sailors, who tend to look upon surface warships simply as mobile gun-platforms suitable for bombardment

* *yelochki*; miniature fir-trees, used for scoring in Russian card games such as "Preference".

operations, were delighted with the *Kenya's* broadside of twelve 6″ guns, and this, together with Admiral Burrough's long-standing family connection, with which we made tremendous play, produced one remarkable result which was not to be repeated throughout the whole course of the war. After much discussion, the Soviet Commander-in-Chief of the Northern Fleet was persuaded, through Admiral Burrough's diplomatic charm and persistence, to authorize a combined Anglo-Soviet operation consisting of a sweep down the Norwegian coast by a mixed force consisting of *H.M.S. Kenya*, two Soviet and two British destroyers. Both the plan and the communication organization were primitive in the extreme and though, for reasons on which I need not enlarge, no German shipping was encountered, the operation was crowned by a bombardment of Vardö, which pleased our Russian allies enormously. For my part I was given the job of British liaison officer in the Russian flagship, the *Gremyashchi*, Captain Fokine, and it was strange, unnecessary and exhausting to have to conform to the Russian habit of remaining at action stations continously throughout the operation. It was even stranger to come down from the bridge at 3 a.m. after securing alongside at Polyarnoe to find a tremendous celebration party in full swing in the wardroom. It was not apparently considered necessary to refuel and by 5 a.m., with the best will in the world, and even supposing that we had restocked with fuel and ammunition, it would have been quite impracticable to have taken either of the Soviet destroyers to sea.

A couple of weeks at Polyarnoe, the former Port Alexandrovsk, gave me my first experience of working with the Soviet naval staff, and I was not sorry when I was sent in one of the British minesweepers to Archangel, where certain signal problems needed my attention before I finally proceeded south to join the British Mission in Moscow.

At Archangel, the early onset of winter, which had created such havoc with the German Armies at the Front, posed special problems. The Russians had assured us that they would be able to keep Archangel open for merchant ships throughout the winter, but it already seemed doubtful whether convoy QP 4 would be able to get away through the ice. I was therefore sent on board the icebreaker *Lenin* as a matter of urgency to supervise the breaking-out of the convoy. I joined her at night, alongside the wharf at Bakaritsa, and we sailed within the hour. The ice downriver was already solid from shore to shore, and the swift arrival of the heavy frosts made it seem that the Russians would very soon be able to lay the railway extension across the ice into Archangel town. Crowds of hurrying figures on the ice, even at that late hour, turned the Dvina into a public highway. But there were ships to be got out and the three great propellers of the icebreaker were soon driving us downstream. It was a scene worthy of a seventeenth-century Dutch painter to see the *Lenin* breaking her way out, brilliantly lit despite the ever-present risk of air attack, with masthead searchlights shining on the ice ahead as men, women and children, shapeless in their padded *fufaiky** and laden with bundles of all kinds, often pulling sledges, struggled frantically to cross the river ahead of the smoking monster, which was shattering the Arctic silence with the crashing rumble of its advance.

The next two weeks were a nightmare. The *Lenin* was commanded by a magnificent Arctic sailor, Captain Khramtsov, who was handicapped by a continual shortage of coal and by the presence of a particularly obnoxious commissar called Alexandrov whose total ignorance of the sea was only matched by his capacity to interfere. Luckily his attentions were diverted by the ship's doctor, an attractive young woman in khaki, and the pursuit of his quarry kept him mercifully clear of the bridge for the greater part of the time. Having taken our toll of the coal of the merchant ships, leaving some of them with barely sufficient to reach Seidisfjord in Iceland, we succeeded finally in reaching clear water, and returned thankfully to Archangel. It had been an unforgettable experience, and hard work on a diet of *passé* cod, black bread and tea had brought me down nearly a stone in weight. I had made another friend on board the icebreaker, Captain Byelousov, and I learnt to respect the fine professional qualities of the front rank of

* *fufaiky*; short winter jackets.

(3) Wedding reception in *H.M.S. Arethusa*: Alexandria, 1938

(4) 30 Military Mission: Moscow, 1942

Soviet Arctic seamen. I was put ashore on the ice two miles off Molotovsk in company with a companion, Boris Ward, and it was a bleak welcome that we received from a hostile sentry, who marched us to the nearest command post. But we found refuge in one of the ships which had missed the convoy, and I shall never forget the cups of English tea and the steak and kidney pudding with which we were regaled, in a British merchant ship still fast in the ice alongside.

Our train into Archangel stopped finally, for no apparent reason, at the junction of Isakagorka, but an approach to the local commander of the N.K.V.D., The People's Commisariat for Internal Affairs, succeeded in retrieving the engine, on which we trundled proudly into the city. From smokestack to buffers the engine was covered by our fellow-passengers, like bees on a honeycomb, and as the honoured foreign guest I was jammed in the driver's cabin right against the firebox, roasting on one side and with twenty degrees of frost in the open air on the other. It was a splendidly typical introduction to life in the country of my choice. This was my first direct contact with the Russian Secret Police, and the memory of that N.K.V.D. officer's courtesy and helpfulness remains with me to this day.

5. WARTIME MOSCOW

AT this time the Russians, perennially suspicious even of their allies, were holding up visas, which had stopped me from going south to Moscow, but at last I was able to proceed, and with my two wireless ratings I arrived in Moscow after a six-day journey from Archangel in an unheated Russian train.

By the end of January, when I arrived in Moscow, the British Naval Mission, headed by Admiral Miles, had arrived back in the capital after the panic evacuation of the entire diplomatic corps to Kuibyshev the previous October. The Mission was a small one, consisting of the Admiral, his Secretary, Geoffrey Palmer, one Russian-speaking staff officer, namely myself, and a small communications staff. It was part of a larger Military Mission, containing a sizeable R.A.F. element under Group-Captain Cheshire, the whole being under the command of General Mason Macfarlane. The General had been a highly successful prewar British Military Attaché in Berlin, and it may well have been thought that this fact would predispose the Russians in his favour. As usual, however, London completely misjudged the Soviet reaction. In the Russian view the General must have been a very competent Intelligence Officer to have held his prewar appointment in Berlin—and it followed that his position as "Head of Mission" in Moscow was obviously a cloak for activities on behalf of the "British Intelligence Service". We were all sorry when the General left us in May, 1942, to be succeeded by Admiral Miles.

I look back on my time in Moscow as one of the most interesting and fruitful periods of my life, largely due to the personality of my Admiral, who was kind and forbearing to a degree, and who realized the advantage to be gained by having at his right hand a Russian-speaking officer on whom he could rely to interpret, not just the language, but the customs and mentality of the difficult world in which we were called upon to operate.

It is a measure of Admiral Miles's character and of the power of his personal example as a representative of his country that I believe that the Russians developed a greater liking and respect for him than for any other diplomatic or Service representative whom they encountered during the war. Had he stayed with us longer, the same might also have been said of the Hon. Joe Maclay, the British War Transport representative in charge of shipping affairs at Archangel.

In dealing with the Russians we sailors possessed certain advantages. In the first place we were the only Service which could be seen to be giving tangible help to their country, fighting for its life. Secondly we were a very small, but competent, Mission, for which reason we were spared some of the endemic Russian suspicion of foreigners, even Allies, which was reflected in the eternal battle with Narkomindel, the People's Commissariat for External Affairs, over entry visas.

This advantage was reinforced by the fact that the Red Navy, for long the Cinderella of the Soviet Armed Forces, relied on us to support them in the bitter inter-service conflicts within the Defence Council. We were soon told when the Red Army dug a tank-trap right across the only usable Naval Aerodrome in the vicinity of Moscow, without so much as a "by your leave", although there was nothing that we could do about it.

In Moscow there existed an atmosphere of suspicion and mistrust in which our Army and Air Force colleagues were quite unable to get nearer to the Defence Commissariat than the "Otdyel", a kind of political/military post office. And yet at the same time the Admiral and I were able to call at short notice on the Soviet Admiralty and be received personally by the People's Commissar, Admiral Kuznetsov. It was remarked, as a measure of the confidence that the Russians had in us, that at many of these conferences the only interpreter present was myself, a situation which would have been unthinkable at any other Angle-Soviet meeting of those days.

Another odd commentary on our special naval relationship with the Russians was the fact that, in order to avoid the embarrassment of walking around Moscow in British uniform I used frequently to "go ashore" in the local garb of khaki blouse and long leather boots. The N.K.V.D. watch-dogs who manned the sentry-boxes outside our flat were visibly delighted when Anton Vasilievitch, alias *Gospodin Komander*, presented himself for their inspection before vanishing into the teeming crowds of wartime Moscow.

My work involved continual and close contact with the principal naval liaison officer, Captain (2nd Rank) Eleazar Alexandrovitch Zaitsev, who soon became a close personal friend. His standard official rejoinders of "I have nothing against that proposal" or "I shall do everything which is within my competence" were typical of the official side of our dealings. But it was the oblique Slav comments on a great variety of matters, in hours of gossip, often lubricated by vodka and sweet biscuits, which made up the substance of our relationship, and these conversations involved a real effort of memory to record and pass on subsequently to my Admiral.

Zaitsev fondly considered himself to be the only channel of information reaching me on a variety of subjects, and it was with unconcealed astonishment that he sometimes found that I was as well informed as he was. On enquiring how I had heard about such and such an event the reply was more or less standard. "My dear Eleazar Alexandrovitch, you told me that two days ago, when you were drunk." There was rarely any comeback. One day, while walking to the Mission, I sighted Zaitsev's chauffeur emerging from the *Voentorg*, a kind of Soviet Army and Navy Stores, with a naval monkey-jacket over his arm on which was one thick stripe. He did not observe me. At my next routine meeting with Zaitsev, sitting at his desk with the usual four stripes on his sleeve I congratulated him formally on his promotion. Zaitsev was aghast.

"How did you know?" he said, with real anxiety in his voice.

"Oh, easy," I replied, "just a tip from the British Intelligence Service."

On more than one occasion we were surprised and a little disconcerted to discover how much the Russians seemed to know about our naval affairs. On one occasion, at a meeting with the Soviet naval staff, they named the exact figure of German U-boats which had been sunk up to that date—a figure which was naturally kept highly secret. Despite our denials, at the same meeting they appeared convinced that we had actually captured a U-boat. Our denial was made in good faith, for the fact that U 110 had been captured by *H.M.S. Aubretia's* escort group on 9th May, 1941, was kept such a close secret until long after the end of the war that it does not even appear in the official history of the war at sea. But it seems certain that the Russians knew of it within two months of the occurence.

In the discussion of our mutual naval problems the Soviet naval staff were very conscious of their inexperience and of the inadequacy of their efforts in assisting the safe passage of the Arctic convoys. They may have been influenced by a wish to show that there was one department at least in which they excelled when one day the People's Commissar, Admiral Kuznetsov, drew Admiral Miles aside after a meeting.

"We have received information," he said, "which we believe to be absolutely reliable, to the effect that there is a serious security leak within the British Embassy at Ankara. Please inform your authorities accordingly."

This information was passed to London by cyphered telegram, but it has not been possible to discover whether it was ever either received or acted upon. We now know that it was about this time that the German agent known by the code-name "Cicero" changed his employment as a valet from the Counsellor of the German Embassy to the First Secretary of the British Embassy in the Turkish capital. Having become valet to the British Ambassador in the autumn of 1943 "Cicero" pursued his espionage activities most successfully until April, 1944, when his employment at the Embassy was terminated. When we consider the intense Russian secretiveness in matters of this kind it is astonishing that they should have brought themselves to give us this warning. The subsequent lack of action by the British Foreign Office is even less easy to understand.

Life in Moscow was no picnic. We worked hard and under siege conditions, but without the variety and excitement of active operations, until, of course, we left the capital for a visit to the northern ports or elsewhere. The Admiral's Secretary, Geoffrey Palmer and Derek Wyburd, my predecessor on the Admiral's staff, had flown in a Russian aircraft in a snowstorm at 300 feet along the railway line from Kuibyshev to Moscow. The aircraft hit a train, which sliced off the undercarriage, crashed in a clearing, one of the few in that area of endless forest, and the fuselage having lost the wings by contact with trees and a telegraph pole, what was left, containing the passengers, slid harmlessly to rest along the snow. Rumour had it that the engine-driver of the train, being junior in rank to the pilot of the aircraft, was subsequently shot, but in fact the only casualty was the U.S. Naval Attaché, who fainted.

But in the capital itself we of the British Mission, well-housed and over-fed, found it difficult to get to terms with our drab surroundings and to make any kind of personal contact with the hungry, patient Muscovites all around us. The xenophobic and chronically suspicious representatives of

37

Soviet officialdom pursued a deliberate policy of segregation, made easier by the language barrier, and at the gates of each building occupied by their allies N.K.V.D. guards were stationed permanently, while each of the three heads of Mission had his two uniformed N.K.V.D. "boys" who accompanied him "for his safety" everywhere. Social contacts were restricted to a few caretaker members of the Diplomatic Corps who had been left behind in the evacuated embassies, and to selected go-betweens such as Alexandrov who worked for an organization dealing with foreigners and was given a licence to hold an occasional drink party at his flat, to which some of us would be invited.

In this curious atmosphere of social solitary confinement, however, there was one saving grace—the incomparable Russian theatre, opera and ballet and, without the relaxation which it afforded to us, the lives of many who served with the Mission in Moscow would have been quite intolerable. The theatre and cinema, assuredly, required a greater knowledge of the Russian language than was possessed by more than very few of us. But the opera, and above all the ballet, enabled us for a time to forget our surroundings and to share with Russian audiences the enchantment of *Boris Godunov, Coppelia* and *Swan Lake*.

Half of the Bolshoi Theatre Company had stayed behind in Moscow after the October evacuation, and with the big theatre closed, it was said through bomb-damage, they performed nightly at the Filial, a small satellite theatre on the Pushkinskaya. In this respect the authorities could afford to be generous to their allies, so tickets were plentiful, and we soon knew the Bolshoi Company's limited repertoire by heart, and of course the names of the dancers who gave us such delight. Especially vulnerable from the monastic conditions of our existence in Moscow, we were all of us soon in love with one or more of them. It was not until later that we discovered that the interest, if not the love, was mutual, and that we were under continual examination by the *corps de ballet* through holes in the curtain provided for the purpose. This extraordinary country, Russia, had produced a situation in which a wholly masculine society was provided, as its main relaxation, with a nightly spectacle of predominantly feminine artistry and charm. At the same time, the complete absence of any social machinery to enable personal contact to be made was reinforced by the fear which even to this day accompanies the simplest of ordinary human relationships between Russians and foreigners. Russian fear, British reserve and the language barrier all assisted in the maintenance of an unnatural situation which was wholly in accord with the ideas, and the convenience, of the Communist authorities.

However, in the true traditions of Russia, there were two loopholes which were to assist me and other members of the Mission in successfully breaching this particular Soviet fortress. The first was a convention, dating from Tsarist times, the second a social custom which has evolved under the Soviets. In the first place, ballerinas and members of the *corps de ballet* possess to this day a special degree of freedom and privilege in their relationships with foreigners. It is an echo, perhaps, of a basic Chinese idea associated with the Middle Kingdom. Just as the barbarians have been permitted to express their respect for China by the bringing of tribute, so in the two great cities of Russia, Moscow and Leningrad, foreigners are allowed a certain freedom in showing their respect for Russian culture by establishing social contact with that culture's more attractive exponents.

Secondly, Russia is still a country where preoccupation with the problems of physical existence absorbs a greater proportion of an individual's time and energy than in countries of Western Europe. There is correspondingly less scope for the operation of social machinery in support of the normal process of natural selection between the sexes. Climatic conditions over a great part of the year rule out any kind of regular *paseo* system, the evening stroll along the boulevards in the towns and villages of warmer Latin countries. There remains the opportunity afforded by the theatre, the cinema and the circus. The Russians like long intervals during stage performances, in which they stroll round the foyers or indulge in beer and sandwiches at the buffet. In this atmosphere of social respectability a well-established convention has grown up, by which it is permissible to strike up an acquaintance with a member of the opposite sex. It was in this way that I first met Lydia.

6. LEARNING ABOUT RUSSIANS

SHE was standing by herself, smoking a cigarette and leaning against one of the pillars in the foyer of the Filial, in working clothes and with a woollen shawl round her neck (the theatre was unheated and it was very cold that winter in Moscow), as different from the milling crowd around us as we British were from the uniformed officers of the Red Army. The first impression was that she was "all eyes", and a second look established with certainty that she was in fact a dancer having a day off. Like a greyhound among beagles, she was clearly, and rather disdainfully, conscious of being a member of a race apart. It was a situation requiring action, and I took it. To this day I have not the remotest idea of how I started the conversation, but the upshot of it all was that a week or two later I was permitted to escort Lydia, after the show, back to the block of flats in which she lived, in the *Vorotnikovsky Pereulok*, on the site of the old church of St. Pimen. This was a block of flats set aside primarily for occupation by families in the theatre and artistic world, and Lydia, a widow, was fortunate enough to have a flat to herself with two rooms, a tiny hall, and a bathroom.

Lydia Konstantinovna Manukhina was a comparatively privileged member of the community, not only by virtue of her position in the State Ballet, but also as a consequence of her husband's former job in the People's Commissariat for Foreign Trade, which had taken him to appointments in New York and Berlin. As a result, and perhaps also by reason of her family background, she had an appreciation of the outside world which gave our friendship a special significance. Nevertheless, we remained members of very different worlds, as I found when I rang her up, as it happened while she was in rehearsal, to tell her triumphantly of the signing of the Anglo-Soviet Alliance, for she nearly broke off our personal relations there and then. She understood better than I did the true significance of the announcement, for she remembered, again better than I did, the short-lived Soviet-German honeymoon in Moscow which followed the Molotov-Ribbentrop pact of 1939.

Lydia taught me a very great deal about her country, its language and its people, and enabled me during my time in Russia to "go native" to an extent which I think was not often achieved by Englishmen in wartime Moscow. This experience was paralleled by that of a naval coder rating whom I had brought with me from Canada, which to some extent reflects the special position which the Royal Navy held in the estimation of the Russians at that time. Lydia's lessons were continuous, and sometimes driven home by flashes of temper and an exhilarating down-to-earthness which I believe to be wholly slavonic.

"Anton, you stupid sailor," she once burst out when I had said something unusually naïve, "when will you come to realize that we Russians are just about half-way between you English and the animals!"

Both my dear wife in England and my Admiral in Moscow proved singularly patient over this somewhat unusual state of affairs, and Geoffrey Miles will not easily forget the evening when we dined together at the National Hotel and Lydia performed for us a few steps from the dance of the Polovtsian maidens out of Prince Igor. He was as human as the rest of us, and she could be irresistible.

One evening in the summer of 1942 Lydia and I strayed inadvertently into an all-male banquet which was in its later stages in a room at the Aragvi Caucasian restaurant on the Tverskaya. The sudden appearance of a British officer in uniform had an electrifying effect. Amid mildly inebriated shouts of "The British Admiral" we were dragged in and put each side of the President for the evening, at which point we realized that we were present at a late stage of the celebration of the Russian Football Cup Final, continued even in war, Spartak having beaten Dynamo the very same afternoon. Amid the flashing of the bulbs of Press photographers the "British Admiral" was compelled to make a speech. Even worse, to the thunderous strains of *Charochka** he was required to stand on the table and to drain the Cup at one draught, filled with the most nauseating alcoholic concoction it has ever been my misfortune to encounter. Finally, after more and yet more protestations of personal and allied goodwill, the "British Admiral" was allowed to leave, on his feet still, and with colours flying, although perhaps I should draw a veil over subsequent proceedings.

The next morning, as I took the Admiral his morning signals, I said, "Before you look at the papers, sir, I think I ought to tell you that last night *you* attended the Russian cup final dinner and made a speech—but I can't for the life of me remember what you said." The Admiral, who knew his Russia, took this in excellent part—but I had not finished. "There is just one final point, sir. I think, perhaps, that I ought to warn you that Mrs. Miles was with you!"

It was with Lydia's co-operation that there took place an occasion that was certainly the first of its kind and which has not, I believe, been paralleled since that time. It occured in the early summer of 1942. After much preliminary negotiation the British Mission issued a formal invitation to fifty members of the Ballet to a party, which they accepted. Headed by Gabovitch, their formidable director, a crowd of chattering girls, for all the world like a flock of Russian starlings, flanked by a few of their menfolk, advanced up the staircase at the Yugoslavsky, where General Mason-Macfarlane was waiting to receive them. The form of the entertainment had presented us with a major problem. Hungry wartime Moscow demanded that as a start we should fill up our guests with excellent British rations. In due course, furthermore, hospitality required that we should entertain our Russian guests with ball-room dancing, where lines of communication might be established which could surmount the language difficulty. But what of the hiatus in between? The problem was solved by the General,

* *Charochka*; an old Russian drinking song.

who decided that he would write—and we would dance—a Ballet.

At that time the three sadly overworked favourites of the Bolshoi theatre repertoire were *Swan Lake, Vain Precautions* (*La Fille Mal Gardée* to the uninitiated) and that lovely old Ukrainian folk-ballet, *The Hump-backed Horse.* What more natural, therefore, than that the English Ballet for the evening should be entitled *The Vain Humpbacked Swan,* and centred around a bottle of vodka in the middle of a lake, to an adaptation of music from *Swan Lake* played by one of the subalterns of the Mission's technical staff? The evening was a huge success, and nothing quite like it ever happened again.

The war bore heavily on us at this time. The massacre of convoy PQ 17 had had its effect on our position vis-à-vis the Soviet Naval Staff, whose contribution to the naval effort in the North continued to be derisory. The Wehrmacht's summer offensive was driving steadily deeper into the heart of Russia, and pressure on us to mount a "Second Front" was intense. The "visa war", by which the Russians made it so difficult for us to help them with the right technical personnel, was at its height: and the arrival of Winston Churchill in August revealed the depth of the chasm which separated Russian ideas and interests from our own.

Fear, too, had come between Lydia and myself, for she had rung up in panic to say that she could say nothing except that we must never see one another again. At last the N.K.V.D. had taken a hand in my affairs and, though not unexpected, this turn of fate against a dear friend roused me to a cold fury against the foul instrument of political despotism under which these millions of delightful Russians had to live. At my next meeting with Zaitsev, naval business being concluded, I turned to personal matters. The gist of my remarks was that it was an extremity of barbarism to which we British were not accustomed for an allied nation to terrorize its women for making friends with those who were fighting and giving their blood for the preservation of the Soviet Fatherland. (I had actually given the Red Army a litre of blood a few days previously.)

Zaitsev was taken aback. Our relationship had become one of close understanding, and he knew that I well appreciated the difficulties under which he and the Soviet Navy were working in their genuine wish to co-operate as fully as possible with their allies. But here was a personal situation which impinged upon our official relationship, and I think he realized that he was faced with a test which could not be evaded. While in duty bound to refute my allegations as pure imagination he nevertheless promised to take the matter to higher authority. Zaitsev was as good as his word, and from that day until my departure from Russia and long after, in fact until a full twenty years had elapsed, Lydia was to the best of my knowledge never again put in fear by the Soviet Secret Police.

I was delighted when the Admiral took me with him to the official dinner in the Kremlin on 14th August, 1942, on the occasion of Churchill's first visit to Moscow. The security precautions were an eye-opener, and the Admiral's Russian chauffeur appreciated the honour almost as much as we did. Leaving our caps in the vestibule of the Great Palace of the Kremlin, we passed up the famous granite staircase to the upper floor, where a group of officials was waiting to receive us in a small antechamber. First we were shown the Hall of St. George, a splendid room in white and gold, with hangings in the famous colours of grey and yellow. This is the heart of the old Order of St. George, the highest award for bravery in battle, now to become, with its old colours, the spiritual centre of the newly-formed Guards detachments of the Red Army and Navy. The setting gave me, at least, an over-whelming impression of the continuing greatness of Russia.

We moved on to the Alexander Hall, dedicated to the memory of Alexander Nevsky, the scourge of the Teutonic Knights who, with Suvorov, Kutuzov and Ushakov, had given his name to one of the new Soviet Orders of valour. The British party was already assembled, and there was a stir in the direction from which we had come as the ranks parted to admit a small, grey figure in Marshal's uniform. It was my first sight of Stalin. With him were Voroshilov, Molotov, Shaposhnikov, Beria, Kuznetsov and a number of Russian Generals, with a sprinkling of sailors. About fifty strong, we moved on into the Hall of St. Andrew and sat down to dinner.

Russian banquets are all much alike, but this one, in the Andreevsky Hall of the Great Kremlin Palace, was unforgettable, and odd vignettes remain engraved on my memory. The old familiar waiters from the National Hotel, standing in for the occasion. The towering bulk of a Soviet General of Artillery, Voronov, sweating with fear and embarrassment on being summoned for a toast by Stalin. A picture of the Prime Minister in his siren-suit, nodding agreeably during the translation of Stalin's speech, which was in fact viciously tinctured with references to intelligence and to Churchill's own handling of the Gallipoli campaign, but whose poisonous implications were quite lost in the awful hash of Pavlov's translation.

After dinner the party broke into small groups, and after interpreting for the Admiral and Kuznetsov I was summoned to a corner in which was sitting Air Marshal Tedder, with a Soviet Air General, facing a mild, balding man in spectacles whom I recognized as Lavrenti Pavlovitch Beria, the head of Soviet Secret Police. It was the opportunity of a lifetime, and I must confess to neglect of my duty towards the Air Marshal in monopolizing the conversation with this remarkable Georgian. As a man of some education and culture, a Caucasian and not a Russian, I think he was pleased at the unexpected opportunity for a conversation with a Russian-speaking Englishman. It seemed a pity that out of the whole visiting British party only General Wavell was able to speak the language of his hosts and allies.

Much of my time at this period was taken up with technical signal matters in which I worked closely with Russian experts on such questions as the proposed Anglo-Russian cypher, a simple Anglo-Soviet Visual Tactical Code, and the involved business of inter-ship recognition signals. At all stages of the work we were handicapped by the ingrained Russian secretiveness and suspicion, which often took a noticeably political form. But we made real progress, and there grew up a kind of tacit understanding through which I gradually came to sense

(I can use no other word) the real reason behind a particular official Soviet attitude to a problem. In this my knowledge of the Russian language in all its allusive and oblique applications made me bless the firm grounding which had been given me by my teacher in Bessarabia. We of the Naval Mission certainly, as I have already said, got far closer to the Russians than any of our Army and Air Force colleagues, and the true extent of this was illustrated one morning when Admiral Miles and I went to a meeting with the Chief of the Soviet Naval Staff and his Deputy, Admiral Alafuzov, who had prepared a little speech in English for the occasion.

"Admiral," said Alafuzov, "this morning I have to congratulate you on a victory over our common enemy—the Soviet People's Commissariat for Foreign Affairs."

After the war both he and Admiral Kuznetsov were to suffer severely for having collaborated too closely with their allies.

In due course my time in Moscow came to an end, as the Admiralty had decided that I must at all costs go to sea, if I were ever to have a chance of promotion. I said goodbye to Lydia, survived my farewell dinner with Zaitsev and his deputy Kostrinsky and embarked for Archangel in a naval PE 3 light bomber. But I was still in Russia, so no arrangement of this kind could be quite normal. In the words of the Moscow War Diary: "Commander Courtney was supposed to lie inside the tail, but his bulk precluded this and he was eventually levered with difficulty into the rear-gunner's seat, that unfortunate but slimmer individual being banished into the tail." Luckily, we met no Messerschmidts on the way north! My onward passage, in company with two Russian naval officers joining the Mission in London, was in a destroyer, *H.M.S. Opportune* which, with *H.M.S. Obdurate* and two U.S. destroyers, acted as escort to the U.S. cruiser *Tuscaloosa*.

The first part of our passage was uneventful, but then occurred an incident which has always made me proud of my connection with the Naval Intelligence Division. In fine weather east of Bear Island, unobserved by German aircraft and mercifully unattended by U-boats, we received a signal from the Admiralty which ran somewhat as follows:

46

"*Opportune* and *Obdurate* from Admiralty. Part company with *Tuscaloosa* and proceed south-west for four hours. If you have sighted nothing, rejoin *Tuscaloosa* and proceed in execution of previous orders. There are no British merchant ships in the vicinity."

Within the allotted four hours we had sighted, engaged and sunk a German minelayer, the *Ulm*, steaming all unsuspecting to the North to supply German outposts on Spitzbergen and to lay mines in Soviet waters off Novaya Zemlya. Our Russian guests were immensely impressed with the whole manoeuvre and so—without of course confessing it—was I.

7. INTELLIGENCE DIVISION, NAVAL STAFF

FOR me the rest of the war was spent far from the country in which I believe I had been most useful to the allied cause. Aircraft carriers in the Mediterranean during Operation "Husky", the occupation of Sicily and the subsequent invasion of Italy during 1943 were followed by a spell in South Africa on the staff of the Commander-in-Chief, South Atlantic, in charge of the great W/T network at the Cape. It was at this period that I was able to complete a Royal Air Force fighter course, my South African instructor being one of the best I have ever encountered. It was an odd kind of war, not made any pleasanter by the knowledge that I had, in fact, missed my promotion, but my spirits rose when a signal at last arrived from the Admiralty, early in 1945, ordering me home without delay to join my old Admiral, Harold Burrough, with the 21st Army Group in order that I should be with him when we met the Russians, as planned, on the Elbe. But it was not to be, as the appointment was cancelled before my arrival in London.

After a few weeks' leave with my wife I was sent out to Gibraltar as Signals Officer on the staff of Admiral Sir Victor Crutchley, V.C., where I stayed for the remainder of the war. There I was able to do something to repair our relations with the French at Rabat and Casablanca, through a few old friends from Halifax days. We had somehow to exorcise the atmosphere of dormant enmity left behind from the terrible experience of Mers-el-Kebir, and gradually to re-establish our former friendly relations with the French Navy. My duties, in the anticlimactic atmosphere of a war finally won, now extended to the Secretaryship of the Royal Gibraltar Yacht Club. North Africa was less than an hour away in the ancient Martinet which the R.A.F. obligingly kept at my disposal. Kind friends in Spain, dating from Civil War days, helped to make interesting what seemed to be an increasingly purposeless existence. I had even succeeded in getting a passage for my wife, with Camp Bay Cottage, one of the loveliest spots on the Rock, to live in on her arrival, when once again I was recalled by signal from the Admiralty. In the postwar reorganization of the Naval Intelligence Division a new look and a new importance were to be given to the Russian Section, which was now placed in my charge, with a restoration of my former Acting Rank of Commander.

The new Section 1 of N.I.D. of which I took charge in January, 1946, like Janus, faced two ways. It incorporated in the first place much of the machinery for Anglo-Soviet co-operation which had developed since the arrival in 1941 of the Soviet Naval Mission under Admiral Kharlamov. With the Alliance still in force there were a large number of problems outstanding which should properly be dealt with on a friendly basis as between allies. In particular, the disposal of the German Fleet and of the German naval research and development establishments was clearly going to strain good relations to a considerable extent, if previous experience of Anglo-Soviet naval relationships was anything to go by.

On the other side of the medal it had become clear that, with the elimination of Germany and Japan, plans concerning the "potential enemy" of the future must already be orientated towards Soviet Russia, and this dual situation required a dichotomy of approach which Their Lordships had entrusted primarily to myself, a "passed-over" officer with no money, no prospects, and with seven years to go before he could retire on pension. Nevertheless, it was a happy time, once more reunited with Elisabeth, who was still working at the War Office, in our tiny flat up 59 cold stone stairs in Thackeray Street, Kensington.

The work at the Admiralty was creative and interesting, and successive Directors of Naval Intelligence and their deputies gave me the scope I needed to make the most of it. Best of all, it involved close contact with the Soviet Naval Attaché in London and his staff, and with visiting Soviet officials, who were not yet inhibited to any serious extent by the barriers which came down with the Iron Curtain in 1949. Those were days when the Soviet naval attachés were permitted much social freedom, and were in fact encouraged to continue the many personal contacts which they had made in Mission days during the war. But the rules were strict and clearly-defined, with swift penalties for infringement, and this was brought home to me in 1947 by an incident which gave me a genuine whiff of the Moscow atmosphere.

I had made a good friend of the Naval Air Attaché, Lt. Col. Pavel Andreevitch Meshchaninov, who visited us in our flat and seemed genuinely to like our society. One hot Sunday afternoon, I remember, in that lovely summer, Elisabeth and I happened to walk past his office in Kensington Palace Gardens. We had been away on my end-of-war leave and had only returned the previous day. As we passed the Naval Attaché's office there was a shout from within, and out bounded Pavel Andreevitch, as bored as a schoolboy kept in from the cricket field and delighted to see his friends once again. We spoke for a few minutes and arranged to lunch together the following Thursday, I undertaking to send round the necessary formal invitation on the following morning.

On Wednesday, having heard nothing, I rang up Pavel's office to check up, and was greeted by a strange voice, "Oh yes, Commander," it said, "we received your invitation addressed to Lt. Col. Meshchaninov but we are sorry to have to inform you that the Colonel took advantage of a Soviet aircraft which was in this country to fly back to Moscow for a little leave." His wife followed him two months later and I have never heard from either of them since.

This incident was one of the first signs of a return after the war to the ruthless system of police control which must inevitably obtain in a society such as that of the Soviet Union which is unsure of itself to the point of seeing a political threat in any genuine human contact between its members and the outside world. Other clouds began to appear on the horizon. There was the case of the "Russian wives", women who had married British service men stationed in the Soviet Union during the war and who, one by one, were seeking divorce, committing suicide or just disappearing.

During 1947 I was attached to the Foreign Office for the visit of the Soviet Parliamentary Delegation of that year, headed by Vasili Kuznetsov and Mikhail Suslov.

At about this time a headline appeared in the evening papers concerning one of the "Russian wives", which I and a colleague drew to the attention of the Secretary of the Delegation.

"Why", we said, "do you spoil the really deep feeling which this country has for yours after our great victory by behaving in this inhuman manner?"

His reply took me back six hundred years into the Tartar period of Russian history, to the *Devitche Polye*, the Field of the Maidens,* in the South-western quarter of Moscow.

"Why do you English make so much fuss about a few women", he said, "get twenty more."

To my great delight, among the members of the party was my old friend Michael Gromov, now a Colonel-General of Aviation, a Hero of the Soviet Union, Member of the Supreme Soviet and head of an important department in the Ministry of Defence. I saw a great deal of him, but never alone, and it caused him obvious distress that he could not visit us privately in our home. Invitations from others of his old naval friends, Admiral Burrough and Admiral Denny, were politely declined in the same way.

During this period I spent ten days in Moscow on a visit

* *The Devitche Polye.* Now a public garden. The place where, by tradition, the Muscovite boyars held the annual meeting with their Tartar overlords at which they handed over tribute in the form of prescribed quotas of gold and young Russian women.

to the Naval Attaché, Duncan Hill, in connection with my
work in the Naval Intelligence Division. He was still in our old
flat in the Skatertni Pereulok and a new set of N.K.V.D.
"boys" kept watch outside the door. It seemed that "our
safety" was as great a concern to the Russians in time of peace
as it had been when I left Moscow in 1942. Duncan Hill, an
active naval officer, felt keenly the frustrations of working in
Moscow, and he owed a lot to the charm and patience of his
attractive wife in making the life tolerable. A theatre party
with Lydia as the fourth member of the party was not a
success, and demonstrated the gulf which separates the foreign
diplomatic community from ordinary Russian people.

It was at this time that I first turned my hand to writing
articles on Russian affairs, and it was a great day when the
first of these appeared in *The Spectator* under the pseudonym
"Richard Chancellor"—the English sailor who had opened up
commercial and diplomatic relations with the Russia of Ivan
the Terrible four hundred years previously. Having some
personal knowledge of the Russian scene I was fascinated by the
problem of the succession to the ageing Stalin. In this way I
became one of the first exponents of the art of "Kremlinology",
and to this there was added the very real attraction of eight
guineas a time. Walter Taplin, the Assistant Editor of *The
Spectator*, was friendly and helpful in guiding my first uncertain
footsteps along the paths of journalism, and he was as delighted
as I was when events justified our forecast of the sharp rise of
Malenkov in the Kremlin hierarchy.

Back at the Admiralty our new organization, with its special
emphasis on Russia, was taking shape, and I had with me as a
constant colleague and companion Commander Peter Belin of
the U.S. Navy, who, with his wife Mary, accomplished what I
used to describe in Intelligence jargon as "the greatest
penetration of the Naval Intelligence Division ever made". The
Belins belonged to the limited circle of "Europeanized"
Americans. They spoke both French and German fluently,
knew England well and were a valuable and delightful asset to
the community. The closeness of our liaison with the Americans
necessitated a trip to Washington, where the Navy Department

proved co-operative and very conscious of the value of the British contribution to naval intelligence. The official American attitude towards the Russians, however, already diverged to some extent from our own. While in Washington I paid a courtesy call on the Soviet Naval Attaché, and it was no time at all before a representative of the F.B.I. was questioning our own naval representatives about such an unheard-of action by a visiting "Britisher".

At this time we in N.I.D. had a good deal to do with the Foreign Office, for it was necessary, on the basis of what was presumed to be a full circulation of information available, to brief our Director before meetings of the Joint Intelligence Committee and to draft Joint appreciations for the information of the Chiefs of Staff. The Foreign Office suffered then, and probably suffers still, from a chronic inability to separate Information from Policy-making, or, in military terms, Intelligence from Operations. In addition we already had grave doubts about Foreign Office security, springing from the "Cicero", King and other affairs, and from experience we had been unable to form a high opinion of its departmental efficiency. Above all, we viewed with disquiet the re-assumption in peacetime of power without responsibility by a Department whose work many of us had seen at first-hand without being particularly impressed. Nevertheless, personal relations were usually excellent, and I was able to co-operate with the Foreign Office by giving naval "cover" to nominees of theirs whom they wished to join the special Russian course at Downing College, Cambridge, which had been arranged through the good offices of the Master, Admiral Sir Herbert Richmond. One Foreign Office representative on this course to whom I gave this "cover" and whom I clearly remember was George Blake, one of the most effective traitors who have ever operated against this country in the interests of the Russian Intelligence Service.

Once again, as in 1933 and later in 1936, my naval duties brought me into contact with the Secret Intelligence Service, and my particular interest in Russian affairs caused this connection to be closer than it would otherwise have been.

I had certain ideas involving the use of fast surface craft and submarines in co-operation with the S.I.S., and I felt sure that the Royal Navy had a great deal to offer in this respect. At that time the head of S.I.S., known to the initiated as "C", was General Menzies, whom I knew well enough to call on with some frequency at his office, where "Miss Moneypenny",* his secretary, and her assistant became firm friends. I think "C" welcomed the opportunity of talking to someone who was enthusiastic and reasonably knowledgeable, yet outside the postwar web of secretiveness and intrigue which was woven so closely around him.

It was in pursuance of these ideas of mine that discussions took place about the feasibility of obtaining information from the Black Sea area. Here there was a kind of silken curtain of security which I had some difficulty in penetrating in order to have a meeting with the individual to whom I had been referred. The irony of this meeting was not to become clear for nearly twenty years, when the man concerned, Kim Philby, was finally revealed as a Soviet intelligence agent of many years' standing. Philby received me with courtesy and listened to my proposals with interest, for he had a wide knowledge of Turkish affairs and his support was essential if Naval Intelligence was to make any contribution to the common effort in the Black Sea, where our information was deplorably scanty. But nothing whatsoever emerged from this meeting, a fact to which I gave no sinister significance at the time, as it was typical of our more general experience of S.I.S. and Foreign Office resistance to any practical initiatives for the improvement of our intelligence effort.

8. SWALLOWING THE ANCHOR**

TOWARDS the end of 1948 it was felt that my job was done, and that N.I.D. Section I was a going concern which should be handed over to someone who was still in the running for promotion. My Director, who at that time was Admiral Parry,

* the pseudonym given to this lady by Ian Fleming in his James Bond books.
** a naval expression signifying retirement.

in my opinion one of the best we ever had, did not want me to leave the world of Intelligence, and I was therefore appointed as Chief of Intelligence Staff to the Flag Officer, Germany, then with his headquarters at Hamburg. It was a job after my own heart, with my own separate headquarters at Minden, and Elisabeth and I joyfully packed up our flat and moved into a comfortable but not very elegant house in the Blumenstrasse which, however, boasted a swimming-pool and tennis-court as well as a garden properly supplied with large quantities of soft fruit.

As the solitary sailor a few miles from Rhine Army headquarters at Bad Oeynhausen, and with a battalion of the Rifle Brigade stationed at Minden, we had a wonderful opportunity of getting to know the Army at close quarters, and we greatly enjoyed the experience. The work was extremely interesting, and involved travel all over Germany to out-stations in Kiel, Hamburg and Berlin, with frequent visits to my American opposite number in Frankfurt. Soviet deserters and defectors of naval interest passed through my hands, and periodical trips to London kept me up to date with the Soviet picture as seen from the Naval Intelligence Division. At this time I was doing a great deal of lecturing on Russia to Staff Colleges and other service audiences, and my object as always, on the basis of personal experience, was to present our potential enemy in comprehensible, human terms, without too much emphasis on the communist dialectic or on the theory of World Revolution, both of which frankly bored me stiff. I was far too conscious of what I believe to be the deep motivating forces inside the Soviet Union to think of Communism as anything but a passing phase in the long tragedy of Russian history. It seemed to me then, as it does now, that an increasing under-standing between the United Kingdom and the Soviet Union offered the best hope of avoiding another world conflict. But this was not to be and it was during my time in Germany that the rift widened between East and West with the Berlin Blockade and the founding of the North Atlantic Treaty Organization. My duty as a serving officer was to do all I could to safeguard my country and its allies from the increasing

Soviet military menace, and for the time being all my cherished ambitions had to go by the board.

Once again I found myself working closely with the Secret Intelligence Service, and at last I had the opportunity to put some of my ideas into practice by providing the S.I.S. with direct naval assistance in the Baltic. This work involved a close liaison with the Lürssen brothers of Vegesack, where I was struck by the potential capabilities of stripped-down ex-Kriegsmarine "E" boat hulls, powered by the incomparable twin Mercedes-Benz 518 diesel engines. With my assistants, the Staff Officers (Intelligence) at Hamburg and Kiel I was frequently at Lübeck and Flensburg and other smaller harbours such as Eckernförde and Kappeln, from which we mounted our operations. Little did I know that the penetration of the Foreign Office and the S.I.S. by the Russian Intelligence Service must have not only doomed our efforts from the start, but had involved me personally in sending many a brave man into the jaws of a Soviet trap.

In the Spring of 1951 my wife and I returned to England for my last two years at the Admiralty before compulsory retirement at the age of 45. There had been, it is true, a powerful move to promote me long out of my turn, and re-employ me on Intelligence duties, but my heart was set on a new life outside the Navy, which still commanded my deep affection, even though it had long since decided that it could not promote me to senior rank.

My work once again took me to the Naval Intelligence Division for the last period of my service, but I was no longer directly connected with Russian affairs. Nevertheless my relations with the S.I.S. remained excellent, and "C" 's deputy, General Sinclair, was sufficiently appreciative of my work in Germany on their behalf to suggest that I joined the Secret Service when I left the Navy. This proposition had a certain attraction for an officer on the threshold of retirement, but it was not to be. There were those in the S.I.S. and no doubt in the Foreign Office also who were determined that I should not enter the charmed circle. Though friendly as ever, "Sinbad" never referred to the matter again.

The shock of the defection of Burgess and Maclean had deepened the mistrust which many of us in the Service Intelligence departments felt for the Foreign Office organization, but although it was already surmised that other traitors remained undetected, this feeling on our part had not yet extended to the S.I.S. itself. It was to be another ten years before I realized the full implications of the penetration by the Russian Intelligence Service. Had I known then what I know now I would have realized that from the moment of my retirement from the Royal Navy in 1953 the Russians had a full dossier of all my activities in the world of intelligence, neatly pigeonholed against the day when the K.G.B. might need it in support of an arrest, should this be considered necessary or desirable.

On May 16th, 1953, I "swallowed the anchor" and left the Navy without regrets. I had a small pension and no capital, but I faced the world with three assets, a naval training, a good knowledge of three languages and the best wife a man has ever been blessed with.

It was a difficult period of transition, and poor Elisabeth must have suffered greatly from the kind of mental indigestion which accompanied it. She was never really reconciled to the two immediate objectives which I set myself, but she supported me devotedly in the achievement of both of them. The first concerned politics. I had for some while toyed with the idea of putting my name on the Candidates' list of the Conservative Party, and I had in fact survived a meeting with John Hope at Central Office, having this end in view. One evening in the autumn of 1953 an old friend, Anthony Sumption, rang me up at our home near Chichester. He had recently fought an excellent by-election for the Socialist-held seat of Hayes and Harlington, but he felt he could not go on with this particular constituency, and had said he would do his best for them to find a suitable successor. Was I prepared to "have a go"?

To a question put in this way by a good friend there could be only one answer, and on a wet evening a week or two later I presented myself at Little Dawley in Hayes, an old farm-house which combined the Conservative Club with the offices of the

Hayes and Harlington Conservative Association, to meet the Committee. As I drank beer at the bar I could hear raised voices upstairs, and gossip with Walter the barman proved so interesting that it came as a surprise when I noticed that 45 minutes had elapsed since the time fixed for my appointment. Fortified by the alcohol, I left a somewhat curt message with Walter and stalked out to my car. It seemed unnecessary to hurry, and my wheels were just turning when a flustered Agent darted out of the front door to give me the profuse apologies of the Chairman and a request to come upstairs to meet him, as he had adjourned the meeting specially for the purpose. The initiative had passed to me—and I kept it. My slightly apprehensive audience was informed in reasonably strong naval language that I was not accustomed to being treated with ill-manners such as they had displayed, and that if they wished to find the man they wanted, they should mend their ways. There was a hush of dismay—and then the Chairman rose to his feet.

"Ladies and Gentlemen," he said, "from the remarks we have just heard I put it to you that Commander Courtney is just the man we require as Prospective Candidate for this rather difficult constituency of Hayes and Harlington."

I had started my political career.

Five years in Hayes taught me a lot and made me some life-long friends. We had a Socialist council, and a Communist, Frank Foster, was a regular candidate at Parliamentary Elections. As Lord Woolton once said to me at a party, "If he stood as a Conservative, the Archangel Gabriel himself would never get in at Hayes and Harlington." Nevertheless, we greatly reduced the Socialist majority at the 1955 General Election, and the open-air meetings which I held regularly outside local factories were both effective and enjoyable. Once, outside Fairey Aviation, I found the field in the possession of the Economic League in the person of an attractive red-headed girl speaker. There was a voice from the crowd as I approached —"Look out Miss. Here comes your father!" The girl glanced in my direction, and quick as a flash came her reply—"No Sir, *that's* not my father, I know what my father looks like— do you?"

57

But all this cost money, and my finances were not in such a state that I could afford to neglect my second objective, the re-establishment of my father's commercial connection with what was now Soviet Russia. Kind friends helped enormously to ease my rather clumsy way into the commercial world. For the sum of five shillings I registered myself under the title of "Anglo-Russian Business Consultants", which in course of time evolved into the more sophisticated "Eastern Trading Group Consultancy Services". A friendly accountant took me under his wing, and I learned to extract from Schedule "D" the minimum of disadvantage in tax affairs. An old friend from Admiralty days, Sandy Glen, put me in line with some ship-broking business, and this in turn brought about renewed contact with Russians, this time with the Soviet Trade Delegation at Highgate. Other opportunities presented themselves. Some manufacturers of flour-milling machinery paid me my first small retaining fee, and at a Ward Social in Hayes a senior manager of Electrical and Musical Industries took me aside to see whether I could help him in some business concerning Moscow. Once a week, furthermore, the B.B.C. Russian Service recorded a talk in Russian by myself, usually on a naval subject, which provided welcome grist to my mill.

Then, in 1955, came an opportunity for a more direct entry into the complex world of East-West trade through my appointment as consultant to a group of engineering companies concerned mainly with diesel engines and generating equipment—Associated British Engineering. It was on behalf of this group that I attended the Poznan International Fair of 1955 and made my first acquaintance with postwar Poland. It was a sobering experience to discover at first-hand what a grip the new Communist bureaucracy had obtained on this likeable, gregarious people, and how our smallest action was watched and checked by the ubiquitous U.B., the Polish Secret Police. During these three years I visited many towns in Poland on business for various client firms, Gdynia, Gdansk, Warsaw, Katowice, Krakow and Szczecin, and made many personal friends. It was during the 1956 International Fair, furthermore, that there occurred in Poznan the remarkable uprising which brought about a major change in Poland's political orientation, and which I was able to observe at first-hand. At one point, the Union Jack flying on the bonnet of my car drew tremendous cheers from the marching ranks of demonstrators moving in an ominous mass towards the City Hall, and I am sure this contributed to the unpleasantness which awaited me on my return the following year.

Polish business methods at this time involved a measure of barefaced blackmail in dealing with British exhibitors, who often brought valuable machinery out to Poznan. British businessmen were frequently misled by Polish half-promises made before the Fair into commitments from which they found it difficult to extricate themselves. My own turn came in 1957 when the Jewish Director of the Fair, one Askanas, endeavoured to take possession of a temporary building belonging to Associated British Engineering without paying for it. Persuasion having failed, he started to threaten, and when I refused to give way he proved as good as his word. Within a day or two I had been sent for and questioned by two highly unpleasant members of the U.B., who informed me that I must leave the country within 24 hours, and stamped my passport to that effect. As a demonstration of the arbitrary power of the Communist bureaucracy the affair was a classic of its kind, and having said goodbye to my British and Polish friends I started out the following morning on the long journey home. A U.B. car followed me to the frontier and waited on the hill above the Oder until I had crossed the bridge into East Germany. I must confess that I was glad to get out, and I have not returned to Poland since that day.

My connection with Electrical and Musical Industries soon involved a visit to Moscow, the first which I had made since retiring from the Navy. The Managing Director, the Head of the Record Division and I paid a visit to Mezhkniga, a department of the Soviet Ministry of Foreign Trade, to discuss the possibility of recording Soviet artists and Soviet orchestras for distribution abroad within the E.M.I. organization. Although we reached agreement on a very limited form of co-operation, nothing very concrete emerged from this first interchange of views. I like to think, however, that we laid the foundation for the recordings of Oistrakh, Rostropovitch, Richter and other famous Russian artists which are so popular in the West today.

Naturally my first call in Moscow was to see Lydia, and I found her well and reasonably happy, though sad at having at last retired from active dancing. More presents from Elisabeth were joyfully received, though in the odd Russian fashion she did not even say "thank you" for them. Though temperamental as ever, Lydia seemed genuinely glad to see me, and made no mention of any further difficulties from the authorities. I felt that I had to re-establish myself in Moscow as a businessman who, despite the political difficulties which had estranged our two countries since the end of the war, was still considered to be a friend of this great land and its people.

During the next few years I had more opportunities of visits to Moscow on business for an increasing number of client firms. This in turn involved an ever-widening circle of Soviet business contacts within the Ministry of Foreign Trade in a variety of different departments. There was, in addition, the State Scientific and Technical Committee, which fulfilled a special function in the promotion of Anglo-Soviet Trade, and which sometimes proved very useful. In due course I found myself in contact with other organizations, outside the Foreign Trade Ministry, such as the State Committee for the Chemical Industry, the State Committee for Mutual Co-operation with Foreign Countries, and the Ministries of the Merchant Navy, of River Shipping, of Forestry and of Communications. I also found myself dealing with the Ministry of Culture, the All Union Chamber of Commerce, Intourist, the Kinophoto-institute, the Mosfilm Studios and the Soviet Register of Shipping. I think I can say that everywhere I made friends, and certainly my Russian improved immeasurably as a result of this multiplicity of new contacts.

Visits to Ministries normally followed a prescribed pattern. A meeting would be arranged for a few days ahead by telephone from my hotel, usually definite but sometimes requiring confirmation from the individuals concerned. My own name,

the name of the firm and the proposed subject for discussion
were normally quite sufficient to achieve a meeting, and I have
always found the girl-secretaries who handle these calls both
courteous and helpful. I would present myself at the appointed
time on the day in question and would soon be sitting at a long
baize-covered table, invariably facing the light, with a selection
of granite-faced Muscovites opposite, usually flanked by a girl
interpreter and a secretary taking notes. It was a sort of East/
West confrontation in miniature, and my job consisted in the
first place of using every artifice to find some common ground
with my Soviet opposite numbers. I soon realized that the
rather forbidding expressions which faced me concealed
normal Russians, with all the gregariousness and insatiable
curiosity of their race. Their system dictated a stylized,
formalistic method of commercial communication with me as a
representative of the capitalist world. As a logical corollary of
its rigid socialist dogma, the system feared the development of
any real human contact between Soviet citizens and emissaries
from the non-socialist world. I hoped and believed that they
would see, eventually, that without such human contact in the
dangerous world of today the future for all of us would be
bleak indeed. And meanwhile I did my best to make friends.

My principal weapons were a good knowledge of the
language, a common experience as an ally in wartime and an
appreciation of the irrepressible Russian sense of humour—
which has so much in common with that of the English. I
always felt that the day was won when the faces opposite at last
creased into smiles and the tension relaxed.

In commercial terms this form of approach was a success,
and my business prospered as confidence was gradually
established between the Russians and the British firms which I
represented. There were setbacks, too, as when the Managing
Director of a major firm of British contractors achieved with
my assistance a virtual monopoly position for the supply of
know-how and equipment for an industrial process which the
Russians had been after for years. It was a situation involving
the biggest single deal ever negotiated with the Soviet Union,
a coup which businessmen normally only dream of. But his

Board took fright at the sums of money involved and the business passed—over my head—to their principal competitors. Despite such disappointments, success in business brought with it a deeper satisfaction, the justification of an old belief that in an atmosphere of political and ideological suspicion and hostility the ordinary processes of trade were the soundest remaining basis for the growth of some kind of mutual understanding between my country and Soviet Russia.

9. BUSINESS AND THE HOUSE

IN England my political career, such as it was, had taken a sharp turn for the better thanks to one of those strokes of fortune which are part of the fascination of the political game. Towards the end of 1958 a junior Minister, the Member of Parliament for Harrow East, resigned in particularly unfortunate circumstances, which necessitated a by-election at a critical time for the Conservative Government headed by Harold Macmillan. Harrow East was a marginal seat and in the new circumstances could even be described as "super-marginal". A General Election was probable within the year, and the result at Harrow East would be a test-case for the political fortunes of the two major parties. The choice of a Conservative candidate was therefore of considerable importance.

An air of horrified prudishness pervaded the atmosphere in the constituency, and the Selection Committee appointed by the local Conservative Association felt it to be its duty to choose, from a list of over a hundred applicants, a man who could be relied on absolutely not to let them down as they had been let down by their former Member. My name duly went forward with the others, and to my surprise and delight I found myself among the last four to be short-listed, a number which included the Chairman of the local Conservative Association, Eric Pratt. Together with our wives we appeared before the

Committee on the fateful evening—Elisabeth in considerable trepidation at the prospect of making a speech. I said my piece and answered a few questions, the atmosphere being courteous and friendly. Elisabeth then spoke, shortly and to the point— "I do not know anything about politics," she said, "and I am no good at making speeches, but I want to tell you that if my husband is selected as your Candidate I shall be with him and behind him one hundred per cent in everything that he does." I believe that it was largely due to this little speech and to the charm with which it was delivered that I was finally selected.

In March, 1959, we fought and won the by-election in Harrow East with a majority of over two thousand.

As I made my way to the Clerk's Table in a crowded House of Commons on the following Tuesday afternoon a Socialist called out "Here comes your battleship!", to which Gerald Nabarro promptly responded, "Yes, and with a battleship's majority!" The Government breathed again, and in the General Election the same autumn we increased the majority to six thousand, thus converting the Harrow East seat in the space of six months from "super-marginal" into "safe".

Despite the new calls upon my time, election to the House of Commons not only consolidated, but also improved my business affairs. On the one hand, I had acquired for the benefit of the firms with which I was connected improved personal contact with the Board of Trade and other Ministries which could and did prove valuable. They felt, too, that their dealings with Russia and the Eastern European countries would be given an aura of official Government blessing through the fact that I was now a Member of Parliament. The reaction on my commercial contacts in these countries was striking, for they tended to ascribe much more importance to the fact of being an M.P. than was justified. With the Conservatives in Government, a Conservative M.P. acquired in their eyes much the sort of cachet as is possessed by a member of the Supreme Soviet in the USSR. I think, perhaps, that the Chinese went furthest in this direction, as was delightfully put by the Chinese Commercial Secretary when he drew me aside in the course of a Chinese National Day celebration. "We would like to know your opinion about the British quota system for trading with our country, Commander Courtney, as we know that you are *on the inside*."

The careful use of English or American idioms by my East European friends was a frequent source of amusement, and it was one of the senior officials of the Soviet Trade Delegation who, when I had told him a rather tall story, looked doubtfully at me and said, "Anton Vasilievitch, I think you are pushing my leg."

To the income from my thriving business I had now added a Parliamentary salary and, even more important, the income-tax allowances which went with it and with the necessity for maintaining a flat in London. For the first time in our married life the family fortunes were prospering, and we had bought a small Regency house with a walled garden in the unspoilt Sussex village of Slinfold, where I believe that Elisabeth was as nearly completely happy as it is permitted for anyone to be on this planet. To her duties as County Superintendent for Sussex of the St. John Ambulance Brigade she now added the constituency, which she treated rather like one of her father's parishes—not a bad example to be followed by any conscientious wife of an M.P. The Courtney barometer, political, social and financial, seemed to be at "Set Fair" and I think we were appreciative of our good fortune. But in addition to the ordinary hazards of existence I had, with my eyes open, exposed myself to the uncertainties of dealing with Russians, and these dealings had now extended beyond the commercial into the political field. Hitherto I had been fortunate, but my luck was not to hold.

PART TWO

10. THE NEW SCHOOL

TO enter Parliament at the age of fifty after thirty years' service in the Royal Navy was an experience which demanded considerable mental flexibility, and I was particularly fortunate to come in on a by-election, which gave me six months to settle down before the General Election in the autumn of 1959. It was in some ways curiously like a return to a disciplined Service existence, and this impression was heightened by finding old naval and marine friends among the officers and doorkeepers of the House. The Serjeant-at-Arms in the Commons came from my home village: the Yeoman Usher of the Black Rod in the Lords was an old naval friend from Mediterranean days: while two Chief Yeomen R.N., one Chief P.O. Telegraphist and a Sergeant-Major Royal Marines were "old ships" among the doorkeepers in the Commons.

There were a few ex-regular Naval Officers among the Members, who had mostly come into the House at an earlier age than myself, with a correspondingly shorter naval background to unlearn in the process of becoming politicians. But whatever our length of service I think we were all rather severely handicapped in one respect. The physical conditions of naval service are such that sailors learn to express themselves succinctly, expressively and often forcibly with the use of a minimum number of words. Their life is concerned, furthermore, with facts and specific situations on which action is required, and they are generally unused to the development of abstract ideas and to the slow formulation of opinion by discussion. It is on account of this ship-conditioned way of life that the mental climate of the House of Commons can bear somewhat harshly on ex-naval officers. In particular, the tempo of debate, which allows for the logical development of a case without straining the capacity of the human brain, often seems unbearably leisurely to an active-minded sailor. Some of us never achieved a good House of Commons delivery, and I think most of us realized our shortcomings in debate by comparison with the younger speakers, particularly on our side of the House, who had been brought up in the forcing-house of University debating societies and of the Young Conservative Movement. A realization of this handicap caused me, at least, agonies of self-consciousness whenever I rose to my feet to speak, whether in the Chamber or in Committee upstairs, but the House is kind in its understanding of this sort of thing, and I shall always be grateful for the tolerant and often attentive hearing which it has given me.

For the first few years I think the constituency side was the most interesting and satisfying part of the job. Someone has likened the work of a backbencher in relation to the Executive to an eternal game of chess against an electronic calculating machine, and it is true that the occasional victory in obtaining Mrs. Buggins's arrears of pension in the teeth of departmental resistance gives one an absurd sense of satisfaction. My Association in Harrow East was friendly and helpful to its new member. Eric Pratt, who had put his name forward for the nomination which I had received, had resumed the Chairmanship and had fought two elections on my behalf and achieved two first-class results in a year. Fred Handley-Page, the President, Theo Constantine, the Vice-President and Blackie Cawdron, the Treasurer, were accommodating and indulgent towards the newcomer, and I was blessed with a first-class young agent in Donald Stringer, who acted as a good two-way sounding board between the Association and their Member.

Donald's professional future required that he should gain experience in a country constituency, and within two years he had been succeeded by George McGowan, an intelligent Scot, who was not, however, destined to stay for long. Before he left us he wrote a detailed analysis of the political situation in the constituency as he saw it. His principal criticism concerned the imbalance of influence between the wards, and the unhealthy preponderance of Stanmore North, which itself was controlled by a small, closely-knit clique. He found shortcomings, furthermore, on the financial side. Stanmore, the wealthiest part of the constituency, was not contributing its proper share to the Divisional funds, and he disapproved of a situation in which the Treasurer was accustomed regularly to put his hand in his pocket when the Association was faced with unexpected financial demands.

It was realized and accepted that my business as an Export Consultant dealing with East Europe necessitated quite a lot of travelling, and it began to be appreciated in the constituency that the M.P. for Harrow East possessed certain special knowledge in this field, more particularly of the Soviet Union. It was in May, 1959, that I paid my first visit to Moscow in my new capacity, and it soon became clear that the pattern of these visits would now have to take on a rather different aspect from formerly. It was, of course, always a first duty to pay a call on the British Ambassador, but as an M.P. the relationship with H.E. and his staff changed, subtly but significantly. It was now understood between us that, as an M.P., it would be my duty to speak to Ministers and in the House on matters of which I had had long experience, and there was an uncomfortable awareness of the fact that I held views on certain aspects of Anglo-Soviet affairs which were by no means shared by either the Embassy or the Foreign Office. At the same time, I had developed a small circle of Russian friends, and in the prevailing conditions of Moscow life, which remain practically unchanged today, it was out of the question to bring any of these Russian contacts into the orbit of the Embassy. I knew that, all other things being equal, I should be allowed to continue to keep this Russian circle of acquaintances provided that I observed the tacit rule of keeping the Soviet authorities aware of my movements, telephone conversations and visits.

For this reason I made a point of doing all my telephoning from my bedroom, and of conveying the general course of my activities to the appropriate quarter within the Intourist organization at the hotel. But should I endeavour to use my new position to extend my Russian contacts into Embassy circles, not only should I get nowhere but I should be exposing my Russian friends to a real and unnecessary risk. In any case the subject was academic: for intelligent Russians knew better than to develop any personal contact with foreign embassies in Moscow except by specific official direction.

In the summer of 1959 Lydia had a "niece" staying with her at her Moscow flat, actually the daughter of an old friend who lived in the country. Mourka was gay and attractive, studying to be a mezzo-soprano with the Bolshoi Opera and engaged to a bearded sculptor in Leningrad. Her views and attitudes were really not very different from those of an English girl of the same age except that she conformed strictly to certain conventions, such as not going to church because "it would not be good for my profession". I had also renewed my contact with General Mikhail Gromov, who had married a second time to a charming woman who taught English, and they had a ten-year-old daughter, Sophia, who showed promise of becoming a first-flight pianist. They lived uncomfortably in a vast flat in the ugly "wedding-cake" skyscraper on the *Sadovaya*. While staying on this occasion at the Hotel Ukraina I had also met a pleasant woman on the Intourist staff, Zinaida Grigorievna Volkova, who ran the hotel car service for visiting foreigners. Through the good services of a colleague in the House, my friend Emrys Hughes, I had also made the acquaintance of the poet Samuel Marshak, who lived with his dear friend and house-keeper Rosalia Ivanovna in an old-fashioned flat on the *Ulitsa Chkalova*.

On one occasion I found Marshak at work with a young man who spoke perfect English with a strong American accent, and answered to the name of Bill Pozner. His father Volodya and his French mother, Gerry, have since become two of my best friends in Russia, and we have discovered a curious family connection which spans half a century. Volodya's family lived near St. Petersburg and had a *dacha** on the northern shore of the Gulf of Finland towards Sestroretsk. A friend of his parents was the man called Weinberg who had been my father's partner in the machine-tool venture before and during the First World War. Weinberg was a shrewd, personable and

* *dacha*; country cottage.

competent Jew about whom my father often spoke, and he had a wide acquaintance among the Russian officials whose good offices were essential, then as now, if any business was to be done. Volodya distinctly remembers as a small boy the arrival of a large Englishman within the family circle, and I have no doubt that it was in fact my father in the course of one of his business visits to pre-revolutionary Russia.

11. FRESH ANGLE ON RUSSIA

IT was during my visit to Moscow in June, 1959, that I became aware at first hand of the continuing activities of the Russian Secret Police against members of the British Embassy Staff. With me in the aeroplane there travelled back to England a Service Attaché, wife, family and nurse, whom the Ambassador had found it advisable to evacuate at 24 hours notice. A contributory factor to this distressing case was the condition of squalor in which the family had been required to live, due in part to the parsimony of the Treasury but also to the sheer incompetence of some of the Embassy staff in dealing with the Russians. They seemed to have learnt nothing since our experiences in Moscow in 1941, and I wrote rather bitterly to the Ministers concerned in the sense that I could not understand how the Ambassador, who could be looked upon as "Senior Officer present" could tolerate such deplorable conditions for his staff. I can record with a certain satisfaction that within a matter of months, some forty sink-units, water-heaters and electric cookers were on their way out to Moscow, so my intervention had been worth while. It was this and other incidents which aroused my disquiet over the seeming inability of the Diplomatic Service to cope with the realities of co-existence with Communist Russians and about the intensity of their efforts to hush up embarrassing evidence of the fact that in the Soviet Union the word "diplomacy" in its traditional sense simply did not apply. They seemed resigned to living a comfortable kind of ghetto existence without any real contact with the people of the country to which they were accredited.

This was, incidentally, my first experience of the discreet type of Parliamentary blackmail by which Ministers can be persuaded to take swift action when faced with the alternative of publicity arising from a suitably-phrased Parliamentary Question. The incident did not endear me to the Foreign Office, but the coolness of Ministers and senior officials was amply compensated by the gratitude of the junior members of the Embassy staff in Moscow. The defection of Burgess and Maclean was fresh in my recollection, and I called to mind other disturbing incidents, such as the security warning which had been given by Admiral Kuznetsov to my Chief in the Naval Mission during the war. The Moscow Embassy was not a happy one, and I had the impression then, as I have now, that the Russians have built up a kind of moral ascendancy over the members of our diplomatic mission which is thoroughly unhealthy.

Back in the House of Commons I lost no time in discussing my experience with two Conservative colleagues who seemed as worried as I was about the two problems of Intelligence and Security, particularly where the Russians were concerned. Lynch Maydon,* a former naval officer, was particularly worried by the security side, while Monty Woodhouse** had had considerable wartime experience of intelligence matters and was under no illusions about the efficiency of the Russian Intelligence Service.

We felt it our duty to take the matter higher, and before the House rose for the summer recess we expressed our anxiety through the Chief Whip, Martin Redmayne, to the Prime Minister, Harold Macmillan, who was good enough to meet us and hear what we had to say. The Prime Minister received us with old-time courtesy in his gloomy office in the House of Commons. But he was clearly not interested. His eyelids drooped as we talked. He was accompanied by a single private secretary who did nothing to enliven the proceedings. In the face of this attitude of disinterested weariness, we found some difficulty in putting our point of view, more particularly as

* Lt.-Cdr. S. L. C. Maydon, Conservative M.P. for Wells since 1951.
** Hon. C. M. Woodhouse, Conservative M.P. for Oxford 1959–1966.

Harold Macmillan never looked us in the face and seldom raised his eyes from the typed foolscap sheets of the brief with which he had been provided. He gave me, at least, the impression that he simply did not wish to know about the unpleasant suspicions which so concerned us, and his reply, made with frequent reference to his brief, was that both the Intelligence and Security situations were in hand, and our fears therefore groundless. We left him with his brief, in no way reassured.

On 8th July I made my maiden speech, in a crowded House of Commons, on Anglo-Russian relations. As luck would have it, Selwyn Lloyd led for the Government in a Foreign Affairs debate, and I was called immediately after Aneurin Bevan, who made one of his last major speeches in the House of Commons. Any maiden speech is rather a dreadful ordeal for the Member concerned; and it is evidence of the effect which it had on me that I failed to observe that Winston Churchill walked out of the Chamber in the middle of it. In my speech I expressed the belief that our best hope of progress in improving Anglo-Soviet relations lay in the commercial field, and drew from my experience in making certain suggestions for the future. I was not particularly proud of it, but the speech was well received by the House.

This year saw the formation of the Great Britain-U.S.S.R. Association, of which I became a Council member, and like others I had high hopes of this new Society as a counterblast to the "Front" organizations along similar lines which had for so many years been manipulated by the Russians through fellow-travelling members in key positions. But we underestimated the skill of our Communist antagonists in taking advantage of the institutions of the West, and of the operation of personal vanities and jealousies within a free society. It remains my view that all efforts to make this Society an effective instrument for taking a British initiative in the improvement of Anglo-Soviet relationships have come to very little, but it has none the less become a useful additional vehicle for the one-way traffic of Soviet propaganda in its broadest sense, handsomely subsidized by the British taxpayer.

In the autumn I was asked to join the Conservative Overseas Bureau, in my capacity of a Member having special knowledge of Eastern Europe, but I never felt that I had very much to contribute to the work of this organization, and dropped out after a year or two.

In December I was once again in Moscow on business, and I noticed that (in the oriental meaning of the term) my "face" had improved, this being reflected in a higher level of contact in the Ministries and Departments which I visited. Mourka had left Lydia's flat—it was not clear whether she had returned to her sculptor in Leningrad or not; the Gromovs and Pozners were at home and as hospitable as ever. Before I left I paid a call at the Supreme Soviet offices in the Kremlin on Paletskis, a senior Party and Government official, who greeted me courteously and with whom I had a long talk. It was evidently a new experience for him to be able to discuss international affairs in his own language with a visiting British M.P. He held closely to the Party line in all matters discussed and he was undoubtedly surprised, and perhaps a shade envious at the freedom with which I felt able to express my views.

In February 1960 I spoke in a Foreign Affairs Debate on disarmament, quoting from my experience of the East German rearmament which took place under Soviet guidance during my time as C.O.I.S. at Minden. I went on to my favourite point about the continuing existence of some 500 Soviet submarines, the largest underwater fleet in history.

"In these matters", I warned the House, "it is no use speaking to the Russians with anything but a united front, and . . . from strength". It was the first of many such occasions.

At home my various Soviet connections had expanded. Membership of the Russia Committee of the London Chamber of Commerce brought about social occasions when we entertained important Soviet officials visiting this country. An Anglo-Soviet Parliamentary Group had been formed which, despite a strong left-wing flavour, provided other opportunities for meeting Russians. I was now on the visiting list of the Soviet Embassy, and membership of the Russo-British Chamber of Commerce gave me additional scope for the fulfilment of my ambitions. At the same time I did not neglect the other East European countries and least of all China, which I was hoping to visit when the time was ripe. In April I was again in Moscow and once more at the Hotel Ukraina. Zina Volkova was as helpful as ever with cars, and an invitation to accompany me to the theatre was readily accepted. It was to be the start of a long friendship.

Lydia was temperamental on this occasion. I think she realized that I was making new friends in Moscow, and the knowledge that one of them was a woman did not help matters. She was troubled with arthritis, the world was passing her by, and the new ballerinas were quite unworthy of the Bolshoi and unable to compare with those of her own day. This time I had made contact with the U.S.S.R.–Great Britain Association, the counterpart of the G.B.–U.S.S.R. Society in London, and lunched with the Chairman, Alexander Surkov, an unimpressive member of the Writers' Establishment. I have always thought of Surkov as the Vicar of Bray of the Soviet literary world, and his activities in connection with the trial of the Soviet writers Sinyavsky and Daniel show that he has lost nothing of his expertise.

To discuss literature with Surkov reminded me of a similar conversation with Mikhail Suslov when he visited London in 1947, but on that occasion the subject had been Russian folk-music. I had mentioned several of the songs which I remembered so well from earlier days, to find them ruthlessly pigeon-holed as "O.K." or "petty-bourgeois" as the case might be. I had not until that moment appreciated how utterly lacking in sense of humour it was necessary to be to hold high Party office in the Soviet Union. Surkov was in the worst tradition of Soviet literary sycophants. But Marshak was an exception, with his lively curiosity, his immense zest for living and his ability to retain a comparative independence of thought without ever, it seemed, antagonizing the susceptibilities of the Party on whose grace and favour his livelihood depended. While he lived he was too valuable to jettison, and I think he knew it.

75

12. BACK TO THE FAR EAST

AT the end of 1960 I paid a visit to Peking and Shanghai at the invitation of the Chinese authorities, my first visit to the country since serving on the China Station in 1930, and I returned greatly impressed with the immense potential of the New China. It is also sufficiently unusual to be worthy of record that I was equally impressed with the quality of British representation in both Peking and Shanghai. Before leaving I had occasion to call at the Soviet Embassy, isolated both geographically and psychologically from its Chinese surroundings, and found myself subjected to close questioning verging on the discourteous regarding my activities. The Russians seemed to be intensely interested in the reasons which had brought a Russian-speaking British M.P. to the Chinese capital.

The usual wait for my aircraft at Peking airport in company with friendly Mr. Chen from the China Travel Agency afforded me a revealing glimpse of Communist dealings with peoples still suffering under "colonialist oppression". A tall, good-looking African carrying an Uhuru stick seemed to be in some trouble with his documents and appeared to have no means of communication with a Chinese who was evidently seeing him off. Scenting an interesting situation I approached and asked if I might help. Mr. Ochwada, who hailed from Kenya, replied in cultured English that he was indeed in some difficulty, and that in his extremity he would gratefully accept any assistance which I might be able to give, particularly if I had any influence with the Soviet Consulate-General in Peking. His trouble was as follows. Holding the position of Acting-Secretary-General of the Kenya African National Union, he had been on a sponsored tour of Communist countries, starting with Czechoslovakia and ending with China, for which he had been issued with a separate set of travel documents, which were not referred to in any way in his British-Kenya passport. It was an easy way of circumventing the ban which was in force at that time on Kenyan Africans travelling to Communist countries. Trying not to smile, I agreed that this was a desirable arrangment in view of the current political situation. However, it seemed that the nuances of anti-colonialist solidarity had not penetrated to Peking, where some clumsy Russian had stamped a full page of Mr. Ochwada's passport with a Soviet transit visa. Did I think the page could be removed? Or at least, could this indelicate revelation of his movements be obliterated? We studied the problem with due regard for all its unfortunate implications.

Mr. Chen translated into Chinese the sense of what Mr. Ochwada had said for the benefit of his companion. The latter ruminated for a moment and replied direct to me in good Russian. The problem was one for Mr. Ochwada to settle direct with the Soviet authorities either in Moscow or in Peking—but before he left China. I passed this information to the troubled Mr. Ochwada in English, and it was decided that he would postpone his departure from Peking until the matter could be cleared up.

A few minutes later my plane was "called", and the loud-speakers followed with the cheerful little jingle which I had heard so often at railway-stations between Peking and Shanghai. With his sensitive Chinese courtesy Mr. Chen was reluctant to reveal its title to his guest, the departing Conservative M.P. It was "Socialism is Good". I never learnt what happened to poor Ochwada, but a word to the British Embassy on my journey home through Moscow ensured that he would have to answer some awkward questions when he eventually arrived at London Airport.

I took off from Peking in a Soviet Tu 104 on a lovely cloud-less October morning. The chrysanthemums and dahlias were reflected in the ornamental pools outside the airport buildings, where chauffeurs took it in turns to fish while the others "kept cave". We flew across the stupendous Great Wall of China, over the Gobi desert and up through the clouds massed above the Yablonovoi mountains and Lake Baikal, to arrive in a snow-storm at Irkutsk in the dirty, badly-run airport of an old-fashioned Siberian provincial town. The shock of this rapid transition from the ancient civilization which I had left gave me a new outlook on Sino-Soviet relations. Together with my Chinese companions I resigned myself mentally to a period among the "northern barbarians". The thin veneer of Socialist brotherhood was insufficient to hide the deep psychological cleavage between the Chinese and the Russians. At the same time I had always realized something of the depth of Russian feeling towards yellow men, dating I am sure from the terrible $2\frac{1}{2}$ centuries of Mongol occupation. When the Tartar slides like a snake across the stage in the first act of *The Fountain of Bakhchisarai* something like a shudder of horror passes through a Russian audience. More evidence of this feeling can be found in Russian popular literature of the time of the Russo-Japanese war, and I believe that this deep-rooted antipathy has now attached itself, in Russian thinking, to the Chinese.

The Christmas of 1960 was a memorable one, and my wife and I spent it in the usual way with old friends in Suffolk, as had been our custom for many years previously. Elisabeth had been ill in the autumn and was finding our busy life something of a strain, so that we specially valued our quiet weekends at Slinfold and began to cut down our end-of-week engagements in the constituency. In the autumn I had yielded to Elisabeth's insistence that we should make fresh wills and tidy up our financial affairs "just in case". It was as though she had had some premonition, for on the 1st March, 1961, the news reached me in London that my wife had been found dead that morning on the stairs at home.

She had read the papers, looked at her letters and even turned on her bath, so that death must have been unexpected and quite instantaneous. The cause was coronary heart disease. There are, I know, very many who have experienced the feeling of utter desolation which came over me after my wife's death, a feeling which was made more poignant by the completeness of the happiness which we had found with each other throughout twenty-three years of the ups and downs of married life. The bond was perhaps even closer from the fact that we had had no children, and the disorientation of my life was complete. Friends were kind and thoughtful, and the village wonderfully helpful; while the Deputy Chief Whip, Michael Hughes-Young, who had himself suffered in the same way, sent me on indefinite leave from the House until I had set my affairs in order.

It was a relief to get away to the Anglo-German Conference of that year at Königswinter, and when I returned to England, Dorothy, our friend and daily help, now turned housekeeper, did her utmost to bring my home back to some kind of normality. My friends in Harrow East felt the loss of my wife acutely, as did the members of the St. John Ambulance Brigade with whom Elisabeth had worked so devotedly for so long. I am afraid that my work in the constituency suffered in the months following this event, and it was over a year before I made another major speech in the House of Commons.

13. BUSINESS DEAL IN MOSCOW

IN the course of my business as an Export Consultant specializing in Russian affairs I had been set the problem of interesting the Russians in the digital computers manufactured by the firm of E.M.I. Electronics Limited, which had recently made a lot of progress in this field. In particular, this company had developed a large computer Type 2400 with some support from the National Research Development Council. The machine was entirely transistorized and represented at that time probably the largest second generation computer in existence. The approach to the Russians was made in two ways, first to the Soviet Trade Delegation in Highgate and the second direct, in Russian, to the Chairman of the State Planning Commission in Moscow. In our approaches we laid emphasis on some of the problems which, it seemed to us, must have been created by the reorganization of the Soviet economy into over a hundred autonomous local units, known as

Sovnarkhozy. Knowing the Russian habits, it seemed clear to me that a great increase of administrative work would be necessary, with the provision of facilities for the recording of a vast amount of statistical information in Moscow.

We put it to the Chairman of Gosplan (the State Planning Commission), that whatever precise form it took, this administrative reorganization would be greatly assisted by the installation in Moscow of a Type 2400 computer. This *démarche* produced what by Russian standards can be considered a rapid, though typically indirect response. Mr. Trusevich, a director of the Moscow Narodny Bank enquired about a small type of Emidec computer and Mr. Petrov of the Institute of Mathematical Machines in Moscow asked E.M.I. about analogue computers. The head of the Soviet Trade Delegation, Mr. Kamensky, also paid a visit to E.M.I. accompanied by a Mr. Gordeev, a visitor from the Soviet Ministry of Foreign Trade. The latter was primarily concerned with Soviet exports to this country, but a visit to E.M.I. had been evidently added to his brief shortly before departure. This produced an unwelcome complication in the suggestion of a possible barter or "compensation" deal in which E.M.I. would take an agreed portion of the purchase price for electronic equipment in commodities. Fuel oil, pig iron and fertilizers were mentioned, but we hoped that if we could stimulate a real interest in the 2400 this thoroughly undesirable side-proposal would be dropped. Eventually, to our relief, this proved to be the case. All these preliminaries had taken place before my election to Parliament.

In June, 1959, however, I visited Moscow for preliminary discussions to follow-up the E.M.I. letter, and had a long meeting with K. A. Bednyakov, the adviser on computer devices to the State Scientific and Technical Committee. Discussions were also held with Z. E. Koroleva and V. V. Yashin of Section No. 5 in Technopromimport, a department of the Ministry of Foreign Trade. This section soon afterwards expanded and merged with others to form a new Department concentrating on all kinds of electronic, computer and control equipment and known as Mashpriborintorg. I was to see a lot of Yashin in the years ahead. These talks, though still exploratory, justified E.M.I. in sending out quotations giving approximate prices for the Emidec 1100 and Emidec 2400 computer systems. The Russians again responded quickly, and a series of technical questions were put through the Trade Delegation which involved a number of meetings at Highgate. It was stated by Terentiev, the local Technopromimport representative, that Moscow was definitely interested in the purchase of one or two type 2400 computers, and we felt that we were at last on the road to success.

There ensued one of those baffling periods of frustration well known to anyone who has business dealings with the Russians. On the technical side, occasional questions were received through Terentiev, a ferret-like and unattractive individual with an excellent technical background and a wide knowledge of the British electronic industry. But on the commercial side there was nothing, and all enquiries at the Trade Delegation proved fruitless. In January I was again in Moscow and saw Gvishiani, the head of the State Scientific and Technical Committee, an agreeable and intelligent Georgian with powerful political connections. He assured me that the State Planning Committee had the E.M.I. proposals under study, but that the problem was very complex and was taking some time to resolve. From my experience I had no doubt of the truth of this statement, but it was not always easy to convince my British principals that delays of this kind are endemic in Anglo-Soviet negotiations. In February, however, the silence was broken, and Mashpriborintorg, the new Department, asked us for a detailed quotation for the Emidec 2400 system, which was despatched six weeks later. The value of the enquiry was estimated at £470,000.

In April I was again in Moscow and had a long meeting with L. L. Golubenin of Mashpriborintorg. It was clear that serious negotiations were about to start, and I had the impression that, after the long period of delay, he was being pressed by the intending purchaser to get on with the business. This also, is typical of this type of deal, as was the stated requirement for an absurd delivery time and a proposal for quite unrealistic terms of payment. Doubt was expressed by Golubenin, with considerable charm and anxiety not to hurt my feelings, whether the 2400 was really the latest computer of its type, observing the interval which had elapsed since the original development contract had been placed. I could detect Terentiev's hand in this. The meeting was followed by another long list of detailed questions. We were also asked to withdraw certain parts of the equipment from the quotation.

This is a normal development in the course of Russian negotiations, being part of the technique by which they endeavour to itemize the cost of certain components which they know must be bought in from outside firms. Yashin was again present at this meeting, and I felt confident that he would be put in charge of the purely commercial side of the negotiations. He is a small and rather sad man who gives the impression of suffering from permanent indigestion, a master of detail, seemingly impervious to fatigue and singularly lacking in the robust and cheerful humanity which usually appears sooner or later in the personality of Russian negotiators. The meeting was also attended by two technicians from "Industry", E. A. Gluzberg and F. F. Gulin. I could not discover to what organization they were attached, but they were obviously unused to dealing with a foreigner, and seemed to enjoy the experience. Finally, the Russians asked if, in the event of an order, two or three Soviet engineers could be attached to E.M.I. during the assembly period. It confirmed my impression that, if we handled matters carefully from that time forward, we should get the order.

It was interesting, a few weeks later, to attend a meeting of the Conservative Trade and Industry Committee in the House of Commons which was addressed by the President of the great American I.B.M. Corporation, Mr. Watson. He described a recent visit to Moscow, where he had evidently had a talk with Golubenin and added the interesting information that his firm had refused to sell their latest computer to the Russians. This was good news in one sense, but a trifle awkward in another, for there were U.S. patents in the 2400, and this might complicate our own negotiations.

It was now time to plan a group visit, and in June, 1960, three of us paid a visit to Moscow to continue negotiations, a technician, a commercial man and myself. The Russian team which greeted us consisted of Khryanin, a Director of *Mashpriborintorg*; Yashin, familiar to us from earlier negotiations; and the two engineers from "Industry", Gulin and Gluzberg. There ensued four days of hard bargaining in which Yashin employed every artifice to whittle down the price and to extract the maximum of advantage from the British side. We were forced to accept a delivery period of 18 months, with severe penalty clauses for delay. It was typical of Soviet tactics to insist that the usual *force majeure* clause, while covering flood and earthquake, would not include strike or lockout, and it was equally typical on our side for this difficulty to be met by insuring against the operation of the penalty clause on account of a strike—the extra premium being absorbed quietly in the price of the computer.

Yashin was adept at sums on bits of paper by which he endeavoured to show that the sum total of the price of individual components worked out at far less than the price we were asking for the whole machine. Our reply was that not only were his calculations based on faulty information (we had successfully resisted detailed enquiries) but we were selling an entire system under guarantee and not a set of pieces of machinery which Soviet engineers might, or more probably might not, be able to assemble for themselves. A knowledge of Russian proved useful when one of the Russians let slip in an aside that the computer was intended for the Central Statistical Bureau. Technically, the Russian negotiators were not well-informed, and by "blinding them with computer science" we were able, on occasion, to score purely commercial points which we would not otherwise have gained. It was hard slogging, and we soon realized that we should leave Moscow without an order. But when four days of negotiation had passed without the Russians offering us so much as a cup of tea, I felt certain that we were "home and dry". We were now sure that the end-user had expressed his intention of buying, and that we had only to hang on to achieve the desired result.

By the end of July cabled exchanges had narrowed down our differences to vanishing point. It was to be a fixed-price contract. Payment terms—5% with order, 90% through irrevocable Letter of Credit on shipment and 5% after acceptance test on site. In October, 1960, the order was received, and nearly two years of negotiation had come to a successful conclusion. My own part in this was described in a letter from Robin Addie, who was in charge of the business from the E.M.I. end.

"There was no doubt" he wrote, "that the negotiations were considerably helped by yourself: one detected an undercurrent of friendship, if not complete trust, and I was conscious that the Company representatives had their job made somewhat easier as a result."

In our small way we had, I believe, demonstrated the possibilities of creating good faith in Anglo-Russian relations.

14. THE TRAP IS SPRUNG

DURING the E.M.I. negotiations we saw quite a lot of Zina Volkova, who had become a close friend. A good-looking woman of about forty, she was unmarried and lived with her mother in one room of a single-storey old Russian house on the Tverskaya-Yamskaya, just off Mayakovsky Square. She spoke good English, which was much appreciated by my companions, and had a passion for English books of the Angela Thirkell variety, the general rule being that the more duchesses the better the book. It seemed strange that she, a cultured woman in a responsible position in the Intourist hierarchy and a graduate of the Marxist-Leninist Institute, should continue to live in one room, and for years she has been promised a flat for herself and her mother in one of the new blocks springing up all round the outskirts of Moscow. I don't think she has been given it, even yet.

The Trap is Sprung

In May and early June, 1961, there was held in Moscow the first British Industrial Exhibition since the Revolution of 1917, and it was an occasion which was given considerable political emphasis by the Russians. The preliminary negotiations had owed much to the Russia Committee of the London Chamber of Commerce, of which I had been a member since 1957, and a prominent part in the organization of the Exhibition itself was taken by my old friend of *Cornwall* days, Derek Wyburd, now some years retired from the Royal Navy. In Moscow on this occasion I was given a vast apartment at the National Hotel, containing a grand piano, badly out of tune, a room which I understood had been intended for the Chairman of one of the biggest British industrial groups exhibiting.

The opening took place in true Russian style with the unexpected arrival of several members of the Praesidium, including Khrushchev, Suslov, Mikoyan and Kosygin, and this clear evidence of the Party line enabled the Muscovites to give the British a really warm welcome. As always in Russia, the crowds took their cue from the leadership, and my thoughts went back to that other occasion in May, 1941, when the radio had announced the conclusion of the Anglo-Soviet Alliance. The populace, however, who had been caught that way before, had not begun to react until they saw the news printed in *Pravda* and *Izvestia*. It was pleasant to renew, even for a moment, my previous acquaintance with Suslov, as intense and unsmiling as ever, but the real pleasure came in a talk with Mme. Khrushcheva, who impressed me greatly as a woman who has refused to allow her warm Russian *shirokaya natura** to be affected by the sombre atmosphere which pervades the "commanding heights of the Kremlin".

However, I have never enjoyed Exhibitions of this kind, and Moscow was no exception. The monotony of constant attendance on the fair-ground was relieved to some extent by official functions, meetings and countless amusing incidents, of which the Pipe Band of the Argyll and Sutherland Highlanders provided a high proportion. So popular were they that

* *shirokaya natura*; literally "broad temperament", an expression often used to describe the Russian character.

at the outset the police were quite incapable of holding back the crowds of enthusiastic Muscovites who pressed in on all sides as the "Jocks" marched and countermarched in a steadily decreasing amount of manoeuvring space.

I am told that the unexpected and unscripted squeal from a piper on at least one occasion showed that a final solution had been achieved by adventurous Russian girlhood after much fascinated speculation about the mysteries lurking beneath a Scotsman's kilt.

Nevertheless, time hung heavily. The Gromovs were away from Moscow, and Lydia on holiday in the Crimea. Zina had given up part of her annual holiday from Intourist to take a job with a British merchanting firm at the Exhibition, which she carried out with considerable success. It was on an evening off from these duties that she came to dine with me at the National Hotel. Zina and I had been friends for a long time, and such are the conditions in Russia today that in all this period I had not once been with her except in a public place. Occasional suggestions that I might meet her mother had never come to anything, and I think this was compounded as much of a genuine feeling that she did not wish me to see the conditions under which they lived as it was of the usual Russian desire to keep contacts with foreigners in separate watertight compartments. Since Elisabeth's death her attitude towards me had been noticeably warmer, and she knew full well how desolate life had become, now that there was no wife waiting for me on my return to England. I think she was—and is—a kind and good woman who developed a sincere affection for the visiting Englishman who so genuinely loves her country and its people. But in Russia a woman's feelings have to be subordinated to the requirements of the all-demanding political system which surrounds her. For hours on end, at Khimki, in the parks, at various clubs and across tables in restaurants Zina and I have talked and argued from entrenched positions, so to speak, which have remained sadly and obstinately separated, despite a great deal of common ground.

This evening was no exception, but somewhere in the course of the meal one of the invisible barriers which had kept us apart for so long was drawn aside. I had known Zina for so long, and she made a pretty picture sitting there, with her fair hair and hazel eyes, animated by the rather acid *sukhoi** champagne which she liked so much. She was very proud, I remember, of her new pleated blouse, in pale blue nylon with its buttons up the back. Just how it occurred, I have no idea, except that it was certainly on her initiative, but it is a fact that for the first and last time in our acquaintance Zina came up to my bedroom after dinner and stayed there with me for several hours. Our affair was not a success. It was therefore not altogether surprising that on the next occasion when we met she expressed some distress at having behaved in the way she had, saying that she knew now that it was not really what I had wanted.

Despite some curious reports of incidents from exhibitors it was not until much later that I learnt that an operation on a considerable scale must have been mounted by the Soviet Secret Police, the K.G.B., against selected British visitors during the course of the Exhibition. In particular, one young Englishman whom I knew had been entertained by some Russian acquaintances at the Hotel Moskva to an excellent dinner accompanied by rather too much vodka. When he woke up he was in bed alongside a young man, and at the end of the bed was one of those old-fashioned photographers with a cloth over his head recording the scene. Seven years ago, the employment of sound-recording devices was well-known, but the use of photographic techniques for blackmail and other purposes was not then as well established as it has subsequently become. In any case, in June, 1961, rightly or wrongly, the thought never entered my head that a successful operation of a broadly similar nature might in fact have been mounted by the K.G.B. against myself.

* *sukhoi*: dry.

15. RETURN FROM MOSCOW

IN the course of the British Trade Fair more than 3000 British and Commonwealth nationals were estimated to have been in Moscow, and this led me to reopen, through a letter to *The Times*, the old question of St. Andrew's Church in Moscow which I had been pursuing for nearly 20 years. Since its expropriation by the Bolshevik Government in 1917 St. Andrew's Church and Rectory have been used for various secular purposes ranging from a dormitory for building workers to a gramophone recording studio. Lacking a church, since that date weekly services have been held, with the occasional assistance of a visiting Chaplain, at the British Embassy.

"Meanwhile," I wrote, "the English Church stands derelict, its very existence unknown to a surprising proportion of the British Community. It would seem that British officialdom has found it expedient to ignore such an uncomfortable reminder of its former standards, while unable to avoid the continuing presence of a mute witness which surely testifies to the unreadiness of the Anglican Church to challenge, by its example, the Soviet contention that Communism has found an effective substitute for religion. . . . Few would deny that in the special atmosphere of Moscow there is a need for a spiritual and social nucleus, outside the Embassies, which can serve the Anglican Community."

As might have been expected, both the Foreign Office and successive Ambassadors put forward every reason why no action should be taken to regain the use of St. Andrew's. It could not be otherwise when the moral ascendancy of the Russians is such that I remember an Ambassador intervening personally to restrain a visiting clergyman from taking a photograph of his tiny congregation at a pre-lunch sherry party on the Embassy balcony—looking out over the river Moskva—because there might be complications if it were published, since the Kremlin appeared in the background. Correspondence and meetings with Archbishops and with successive Bishops of

Fulham failed to produce any better result and to this day, as I wrote in a subsequent letter to *The Times*, St. Andrew's, Moscow, "remains as a constant reminder to the repressed churchmen of Russia of the hollowness of any protestations of support which may reach them from the Church of England." The Russians themselves have treated my minor crusade with amused and indulgent interest, the Cultural Attaché at the Soviet Embassy in London even wishing me well and saying on one occasion he was sure his Government would give us back St. Andrew's, if we tried hard enough.

With the Exhibition of 1961 mercifully at an end, Derek Wyburd and I drove homewards by the southern route through Kursk, Kiev, and the Ukraine to the Roumanian frontier. At frequent points on the excellent highway we passed militiamen on patrol, and it was interesting to note in the driving mirror the sequence of wristwatch, pencil and notebook with which each recorded the progress of a Ford car with a British number-plate. Our unheralded stay at Poltava put the imperialist cat firmly among the Soviet pigeons. Having successfully resisted a suggestion that we might change our rooms, presumably to the "observation block", we were delighted to discover a militiaman huddled under the stairs when we made our departure early the following morning. He had clearly been there all night. The frontier presented no difficulties, but as we accelerated from the Soviet side towards the Roumanian guard post we found we had about half a mile of Russian field-telephone wire caught around the radiator of the car. Luckily for us, the wire appeared to have no connection with the mine-fields which back up the ploughed-earth strips, the barbed-wire and the watchtowers which, in brotherly fashion, demarcate the frontiers between the Peoples' Democracies. In any case the Russian sentry—amiability personified—waved us cheerfully on our way.

At a time, seven years later, when the balance of Anglo-Soviet trade has never been more heavily weighted against this country, despite constant verbal and written reassurances by the Soviet Minister of Foreign Trade, Patolichev, that the situation would be remedied, it is hard to look back on the commercial achievements of the Moscow Exhibition of 1961 with any great satisfaction. It has been even harder to justify the expense of another British Exhibition in 1966. But the influx of British businessmen, many of them making their first acquaintance with the Soviet Union, undoubtedly helped in the long haul back to normality in Anglo-Russian relations.

The incomparable Argyll and Sutherland Highlanders produced an impression in 1961 greater than any. It is, I think, astonishing evidence of the lack of any real understanding by our diplomatic mission of the country in which they are situated that the decision to send the Argylls to Moscow was taken by the British Government in the face of strong Embassy advice. The Jocks would, it was assumed, be a first target of the K.G.B., and the possibility that some of the men might defect, in the Ambassador's opinion, outweighed the obvious advantages of introducing Soviet Russia to the bagpipes. In the event, the only sufferers were those Russians who lost their sleep because of the wail of the pipes, well lubricated with Caucasian brandy, sounding in the corridors of their hotel through the small hours of the morning. Without troubling to acquire either a common language or diplomatic privileges of any kind the Argylls had achieved a perfect understanding with their Russian hosts.

16. REMARRIAGE

I HAVE always supposed that it is normal for happily-married couples to discuss in semi-jocular, semi-serious fashion what either should do in the event of the other one "popping off". In any case, Elisabeth and I had talked about these things on a number of occasions. She had always said that in the event of my dying she would be most unlikely to remarry, but in the opposite set of circumstances she held a firm opinion, expressed more than once in the same words,

"The greatest compliment," she would say, "that a man can pay to his first wife is to remarry at a decent interval after she has died."

In the late summer of 1961 an old friend on the staff of the Imperial Defence College had asked me to a party, the object of which was to meet Elizabeth Trefgarne, widow of a recently-created peer who had previously been a Member of Parliament, first in the Liberal and finally in the Socialist interest. My host's wife had been a close friend of the first Elisabeth, and she had clearly engineered this meeting between an old friend and a charming and attractive neighbour, so the auguries seemed favourable. I was, after all, a disorientated widower who had every intention of marrying again. Suffice it to say that, just a year after Elisabeth's death, Lady Trefgarne became the second Mrs. Anthony Courtney at a quiet ceremony in the Crypt Chapel of the House of Commons.

Friends of both of us welcomed the match as being altogether suitable, the only slight point of doubt being the impact on a childless and middle-aged widower of four stepchildren ranging in age from eight to twenty-one. In the constituency my remarriage was greeted with pleasure and, I think, a certain relief, for my wife was quickly accepted by my friends in the Association as an intelligent and charming asset to Harrow East. It was a blessing once again to have moral support in the constituency on both political and social occasions, and the predominantly business community in Stanmore particularly appreciated the fact that my wife, as a Director of the family firm of machine-tool manufacturers, was a businesswoman in her own right, The general feeling was well summed-up by a friend in the constituency who had known and loved my first Elisabeth and who wrote to tell me that by my remarriage I had disproved a theory which he had long cherished (he is a schoolmaster), namely that lightning never strikes twice in the same place.

After a year in the doldrums I certainly felt that purpose had returned to my existence, and this was reflected in increased political and commercial activity. In May I spoke on the Berlin situation in a Foreign Affairs debate, a speech in which I found it necessary to refer to the three negotiated settlements of the Berlin question, each of which had been broken by the Soviet Union as soon as it suited them, and of the danger of concluding a fourth without the most watertight of guarantees. From my commercial experience with East Germany I dwelt on the importance of inter-zonal trade, a matter in which I declared a personal business interest, and expressed the hope, in passing, that my business would not "fold-up" as a result of anything which I might have felt it necessary to say in the debate. It was the first public expression of the misgivings which I was beginning to feel over the divergence of my political duty in the House of Commons, as I saw it, from my personal interests as a businessman dealing with the centralized economies of Communist Eastern Europe.

In June I was again in Moscow on a short visit. My Russian friends were delighted with the change in my domestic fortunes, particularly when they heard that my wife hoped to accompany me on a visit to the Soviet Union later in the year. Lydia received tangible evidence that the flow of small feminine gifts from England which Elisabeth had started would continue under the new régime. And in the airy living-room of the Turgeniev-style dacha out at Borvikha-Zhukovka I ate bowls of *tvorog* covered with *smetana* and honey (curds covered with sour cream), enlarging to the Gromovs between mouthfuls about the luck which had come to me. Mikhail Mikhailovitch was delighted with my news, but as one of the best known airmen in the world his brow furrowed when he heard about one of my latest projects. My eldest stepson, David, had qualified for his Private Pilot's Licence during the 1962 flying season, and this had given me the idea of myself requalifying as a pilot. I had taken my "A" licence in 1934 and qualified to R.A.F. standards as a fighter pilot during the war, so that once I had successfully passed my medical the rest was easy. In no time David and I were part-owners of an Auster Aiglet, G-AMTA, which we exchanged in due course for a Beagle Airedale, G-AROJ, luxuriously equipped with radio up to full Airways standard. Perhaps a little tactlessly I asked Mikhail Mikhailovitch for his help in obtaining permission for my little aeroplane to fly into the Soviet Union. Surely, I said, with my tongue in my cheek, the support of a Colonel-General of Aviation and Hero of the Soviet Union would be irresistible? But my friend was adamant. He had seen too much of aeroplanes to want to encourage any friend of his, directly or indirectly, to break his neck in this particular way. Anyway, this was his story, and we knew each other too well for further discussion to be necessary.

The year 1962 saw the "breaking" of two grave security cases which more than justified the misgivings which I and my two colleagues had expressed to the Prime Minister three years earlier. The Vassall case was a clear illustration of the operation of a "legal" K.G.B. (Committee of State Security), network, working from within the Soviet Embassy in London, in handling a traitor who had been suborned while a member of the staff of the British Embassy in Moscow. The Portland Spy Trial, on the other hand, revealed the success with which an "illegal" network consisting of Gordon Lonsdale and the Krogers had been working for the G.R.U. (Central Intelligence Directorate) over a long period under the noses of our own security organization. In the Debate on the Address in November I spoke out on the Vassall affair, with support from two sailors on our side of the House, John Litchfield and Greville Howard, and from Reggie Paget on the Socialist benches. I said that I could not help feeling that "within the Foreign Office there is a curious lack of reality in considering the harsh facts of modern international politics" and quoted a number of incidents known to me which reflected on the Foreign Office's competence in security matters.

I referred to the day by day harassment of the members of British Missions in Iron Curtain countries, with the object of attacking at the weakest point. I added, with a jocularity that was perhaps a little laboured, that I frequently told inquisitive Russians that I would save them the trouble of finding out my own particular weakness—it was blondes. I emphasized the utter unreality of the word "diplomacy" when applied in an East European context and begged the Government to take the matter seriously. In conclusion I said that it was now clear that the reassurances given to me and my colleagues by the Government three years previously were "both incorrect and misleading". For all its visible effect on the Government benches I might have saved my breath. Once again I wrote to the Prime Minister reiterating my previous fears and once more I was fobbed off. A letter to Peter Thomas, Joint Under-Secretary of State at the Foreign Office, asking for particulars of the reasons why members of British Missions in Communist countries had left their posts prematurely, fared little better. This section of the "electronic calculating machine" had obviously been programmed to give zero replies.

At the end of 1962 I took my wife on an extended visit to Leningrad, Moscow and China. It was one of the pleasantest and most fruitful in my experience and was assisted by the fact that on this occasion I was representing Lloyd's Register of Shipping, with whom both the Russians and Chinese were anxious to establish a working relationship. My Moscow friends were delighted. Volodya and Gerry Pozner were hospitality itself, and their teenage son, Paul, whose general reactions and behaviour were very close to those of my second stepson, quite won my wife's heart. An overenthusiastic invitation for Paul to learn English with us at Chobham, however, fell on stony ground.

"Perhaps," said Volodya, "such things may be possible one of these days."

The Gromovs were delighted to meet an Englishwoman, and Lydia and Zina in their respective ways made the most of their unaccustomed opportunity. Zina took my wife sightseeing while I was busy at the Ministry of Foreign Trade, which they both seemed thoroughly to enjoy.

Peking greeted us in the capacity of "precious guests", and went to the unusual length of producing Chinese wives to balance my own at parties in both Peking and Shanghai. The combination of a politician-cum-businessman who spoke Russian and a wife who could discuss the technicalities of machine-tools had an impact in both Russia and China which enabled us to extract the maximum of enjoyment and of usefulness out of our journey. Even the formidable and

94

fascinating Madam Chen at Shanghai went out of her way to be kind to us, though I was saddened to find that the oldest British resident in the city was in too great fear of the local authorities to renew the acquaintance we had made two years previously. Finally, Courtney Hsien-sen (myself) and Courtney Fu-len (my wife) gave a farewell Chinese-style dinner-party at the Hsin-Chao Hotel. Thanks to our friends the Garveys, we were able to substitute good claret for Chinese wine, which I have never liked, and we gravely assured our Chinese guests, as we offered them whisky, that we had given the name Mac-Mao-Tai in their honour to this Scottish version of the local fire-water. It was during this meal that I discovered the true test by which a foreigner can show his efficiency with chopsticks. If he can lean forward across the table while continuing polite conversation, extract with his chopsticks a peeled plover's egg floating in thin soup from a dish in the centre and place it gently in the bowl of his principal guest sitting opposite —he has qualified. I failed to do so, but I really think the Chinese appreciated the attempt.

17. GROWING MISGIVINGS

ON our way home through Moscow we found the Gromovs freshly installed in a small flat in an old building on the Niznhi Kislovsky behind the "House of Friendship",* off the Arbat. It was much more their style than the dreary skyscraper in which they had lived previously. Mikhail Mikhailovitch had a problem. He is a dog-fancier of some note and owns a fox-terrier bitch called Tami, from which he was hoping to breed. It must be confessed that Tami was longer in the nose and body than would be normally acceptable in England. As far as I could make out, however, there had been no fresh fox-terrier blood introduced into Russia since 1917 and the problem of a

* The former Japanese Embassy. An architectural monstrosity.

suitable dog was crucial. Did I think I could do anything about it? I promised to try. But in England the difficulty was considerable. Yes—it would be possible to bring a bitch over by Aeroflot and marry her off in the quarantine kennels near London Airport. *But*—the English dog would then be required to spend six months in quarantine before returning to its owner. The impasse was complete, but Fortune was evidently intrigued by this rather original exercise in Anglo-Soviet cultural relations.

Many months had passed when one morning a polite voice on the telephone asked me if I would care to be the honoured guest of Pakistan International Airlines on the occasion of their inaugural trip on a new service to Moscow. I promptly accepted—and a thought crossed my mind. Would it be possible for me to take a dog? The polite voice, when reassured that it had not misheard what I had said, expressed its rather puzzled delight at the idea, and my problem was solved.

In due course, in company with Kelly, a pedigree fox-terrier, in a blue collar with a blue lead and blue portable light-weight kennel, we embarked for Moscow, and I have to record the singular fact that at no point in England or in Russia was a question asked or a form required to be filled in regarding the passage of this dog. Customs men and immigration officials looked the other way and appeared to see nothing—I am sure that the truth is that it was all just too difficult. To quote the *Spectator*, whose correspondent was on the flight—"It is not possible, unhappily, to promise every visitor to Moscow that his journey will be rewarded on touchdown with the sight of a large, red-faced Conservative Member of Parliament parading a white fox-terrier up and down the Airport in the bright sunshine of half-past five in the morning."

The Gromov family was in ecstasies of delight, but as I was to learn, there is a penalty to be suffered when an Englishman earns the deep gratitude of a Russian. In this case it consisted of a bear-hug and a kiss on the lips from a Colonel-General of Aviation. However, Kelly and Tami now have a family of seven pups—and the fox-terrier succession in Russia is assured —so it was worthwhile.

In January, 1963, I visited Paris to take part as a Conservative representative in the seventh Round Table Conference on East-West affairs. While nothing very concrete emerged from the discussions, they afforded an excellent opportunity of meeting Russians of the calibre of Ilya Ehrenburg, Georgi Zhukov, Professor Rubinstein and General Talensky, with whom I had many interesting talks. The next Conference, held in Moscow in December of the same year, was even more intriguing, as the Soviet delegation was headed by Alexander Korneichuk and included a reception at the Kremlin by Anastasi Mikoyan at which the usual effusive speeches were made by the predominantly left-wing members of the foreign delegations. In my own speech I reminded Mikoyan that I had first met him in the terrible conditions of 1941 when the British Navy was convoying merchant ships carrying desperately-needed supplies to Russia, and suffering heavily in the process. In his reply Mikoyan responded with unexpected generosity towards his former allies, which introduced a welcome note of realism into the stale ritual of these political occasions. At a lunch given to the British delegation the wartime Ambassador, Ivan Maisky, was produced to give tone to the proceedings. He had, I believe, turned eighty, and on making my congratulatory speech on his powers of both political and physical survival I could not resist mentioning the fact that I had last met him in London before the war in company with Marshal Tukhachevsky and General Putna (who were both shot shortly afterwards in the purge of the Red Army).

In May, 1963, I spoke again in the House on a Security matter; this time in the Debate on the Report of the Vassall Tribunal. In the interval, apart from the Portland Spy Trial, it had been revealed that George Blake, the man whom I had helped the Foreign Office to "cover" as a naval member of the Russian course at Downing College, Cambridge, was a traitor to his country of many years standing. It was a sickening confirmation of what I had long feared, the penetration of our Secret Intelligence organization at a high professional level by the K.G.B.

From a personal point of view it now seemed probable that

many aspects of my own activities in the Intelligence world would have been revealed to the Russians, and I thanked my stars that in the half-world where overt and covert Intelligence activities meet I had always kept on the uniformed and overt side of the line. It was of course a mistake to imagine that the Russians themselves saw any practical difference between Intelligence and Espionage. In fact their own word *Razvyedka* applies to each indiscriminately. But they recognized and utilized this curious western convention by differentiating between "legal" and "illegal" methods of obtaining the information they needed.

My speech, made on a Tuesday, reflected a growing anger against the Government for their blind acceptance of the Foreign Office case in the face of accumulating evidence of rottenness at the core of that archaic Establishment. I did my best to defend the conduct of the Admiralty civil servant, Mr. Pennells, my old friend now dead, who had been named in the search for a scapegoat, and I traced the main fault to the System. and in particular to the refusal of Foreign Office officials in Moscow to take responsibility for the affairs of the Mission personnel placed in their charge. And this in face of the Russian Intelligence Service which, I said, "has forgotten more than we shall ever know about practical, efficient espionage." We had before us a first-hand example of the efficiency of the centralized direction of Soviet affairs.

On the previous Thursday afternoon, when the business for the following week was announced by the Leader of the House, Romanov, the Counsellor at the Soviet Embassy, had left his accustomed seat in the gallery with the knowledge that the Debate on the Report of the Vassall Tribunal would take place on the following Tuesday. The next morning the Soviet Government announced that the trial of Greville Wynne for espionage would take place in Moscow on the same Tuesday, thus ensuring that Vassall and Wynne would be given equal prominence in the world's newspapers on the Wednesday following. This coincidence, to the best of my knowledge, passed unnoticed by the British Press.

In my speech I went on to refer to the "psychological

dominance" which the Russians endeavoured to establish over the members of foreign Missions in Moscow.

"Individuals who are not prepared to accept this", I said, "are usually removed or 'framed', or find it necessary to go. Life is made a little too difficult for them, for in multifarious ways the Russians can bring pressure to bear on the Embassy staff."

I spoke also about the misuse of diplomatic privilege and immunity in London as a counterpart to the harassment of our staff in Moscow. It astonished me that the Report of the Tribunal should express the opinion that the Ambassador in Moscow "could not be expected to give more than a directing attention to questions of security." This seemed a blind acceptance of a Foreign Office doctrine which amounted to ultimate irresponsibility, as was the remarkable later statement that "the general security system observed in the Embassy was sound and well-maintained."

In conclusion I recommended, in conditions such as the present where the basis of good faith and integrity which normally underlay diplomatic usage is manifestly seen not to exist, that we should take steps to limit the members and status of diplomatic representatives from the countries concerned, together with the facilities afforded to them. Niall MacDermot, a wartime specialist in security matters, who followed from the Socialist benches, congratulated me on a "remarkable and courageous" speech and expressed his agreement with "almost every word". But once again the Government passed over our criticisms and misgivings in silence.

18. FIRST SKIRMISH

IN the constituency there was general satisfaction at the activity of the Member, but there were those who felt that they saw too little of him due to his frequent absences abroad, not only on business in East Europe but also on holiday in the

Bahamas, where my wife had property. Theo Constantine, my guide and mentor in local political matters, and the new Association Chairman, Jack Shrimpton, paid little attention to these cross-currents, but always maintained that the more I could be seen in the constituency—the better. This was not as easy as it sounded, and I pointed out that, except when specifically canvassing, a Member found it difficult to "be seen" in Harrow unless he was invited, and it was noticeable that in neither of my two more prosperous wards, Stanmore North and Belmont, was there much of the type of social activity which would normally include an invitation to the M.P. and his wife. The pattern of private entertainment consisted principally of quite small cocktail, dinner and bridge parties.

Donald Stringer having left to go to a County constituency, a new Agent had arrived in the person of Mrs. Jo Burton, who lived in Harrow and knew the constituency very well from the days when she had not only preceded Jack Shrimpton as Chairman of the Young Conservatives, but had worked as assistant to the Agent who, with my predecessor, had won the seat from the Socialists in 1950. I relied heavily on her to keep me in touch with shifts of local opinion and with current gossip within the constituency about their Member.

In the Debate on the Adjournment before the House rose for the Summer Recess of 1963, I raised the specific question of diplomatic representation between the United Kingdom and the countries of Eastern Europe in the light of the series of grave security cases which had occurred over the previous eighteen months, associated with the names of Vassall, Blake, Houghton and Philby. It had seemed to me that, both in the House and in the Press, this important loophole in our security arrangements was being neglected, and that there was something approaching a conspiracy of silence in releasing details of Foreign Office action against Diplomats who were now admitted to be flagrantly misusing the diplomatic immunities given them in accordance with traditional international usage.

From my wartime experience in the Soviet Union I had long since come to the conclusion that the ancient rules governing the exchange of envoys simply did not apply to the Government of a country which habitually ignored civilized conventions in the pursuit of its sinister purposes. I had seen at first hand something of the effects of the steady pressure, amounting to psychological intimidation, imposed on our diplomatic Missions in Communist countries, and directed by the K.G.B. Obvious successes for this policy had been the seduction of Vassall in Moscow and of Houghton in Warsaw. But less obvious and perhaps more important was the fact that since 1949 over 200 British Foreign Service personnel had had to leave their posts in Communist capitals before the expiration of their normal term, and 78 of these had been sent home for reasons of "misconduct or unsuitability". What worried me was the steady resistance of the Foreign Office, as a matter of policy, to any release of information which might reveal the extent and effectiveness of the Communist activities which had produced these figures.

On the other side of the same picture, a question of mine had elicited the information that since 1949 seventeen Soviet and other Communist diplomats had been declared *persona non grata* by H.M. Government. Others had left the country at short notice when it became evident that their undiplomatic activities were "blown". Presumably the foreign Ambassador was informed in each case, with the reasons for the diplomat's expulsion. But why, I asked, could this information not be given to the House of Commons and to the public?

I continued by pointing out the considerable disparity between the numbers of British and Communist diplomats and diplomatic staff stationed in their respective countries. It seemed that Communist régimes were able to evade the principle of reciprocity with impunity. There was the glaring anomaly by which the Soviet Embassy employed Russian chauffeurs in London while insisting successfully that the British Embassy in Moscow also employed Russians for this duty. How could we continue with the pretence that normal diplomatic arrangements existed with these countries? I concluded with a number of specific suggestions for remedying a situation whose dangers must now be apparent to all concerned. They would at least help to relieve the burden on our overworked Security Service. Our present diplomatic relationship with the Soviet Union, I said, called to mind a pair of dancers, a self-satisfied elderly gentleman performing an elegant minuet, oblivious of the fact that his partner was doing the twist.

In his reply, Peter Smithers,* the Under-Secretary of State, admitted the discrepancy in both numbers and treatment of diplomatic missions but saw little advantage to be gained by correcting it. He considered that the question of declaring a diplomat *persona non grata* was not really a security matter but "one of very delicate negotiation and delicate relationships". Publicity might be harmful to these relationships and "the whole question of representation . . . must be handled in confidence." It was a classic exposition of the diplomatic viewpoint of a former age.

19. POINT OF BALANCE

TOWARDS the end of August I was again in Moscow on an important business negotiation, which I have mentioned earlier, involving the sale to the Soviet Government of manufacturing rights and equipment for artificial fibres of a value then estimated at over £50 million. The contracting firm with which I was associated was negotiating from strength, as we had obtained exclusive negotiating rights for the essential heart of the process, and the Russians were in no position to employ their customary commercial techniques of "divide and rule". Our principal negotiating partners were Klentsov the shrewd and ebullient President of Techmashimport, a Department of the Ministry of Foreign Trade, and Kostandov, an outstanding practical chemist and administrator, Deputy Chairman of the State Chemical Committee of the U.S.S.R.

* P. H. Smithers, Conservative M.P. for Winchester 1950–1964. Secretary-General, Council of Europe, 1964.

Such is the peculiarity of the Moscow atmosphere that my personal relations with the Russians over these negotiations proved to be a good deal more satisfactory than those with the British firm for whom I was working, with the notable exception of the Managing-Director who accompanied me to Moscow. Suffice it to say that our initial efforts eventually succeeded, and the biggest Russian order ever placed in Britain was signed shortly afterwards—but with another group of British firms.

In June, the affairs of the Government arrived at a crisis in the debate on what amounted to a vote of censure arising from the resignation of the Secretary of State for War, Jack Profumo. Much publicity had been given to the undiplomatic activities of the Soviet Naval Attaché, Commander Ivanov, and the admission that he was known to be a "Soviet Agent" coupled with the absence of any action by the Foreign Office confirmed all my worst fears about the state of our security. The Prime Minister's defence of his action, or inaction, in the matter was to me lame and unconvincing, added to which there was the fact that twice within the previous four years he had given me his personal assurance that all was well in this particular field. To a loyal Conservative, the moment when the Division bell rang was one of agonizing indecision, but conscience won the day, and in company with 26 of my colleagues I recorded my alarm and dismay by abstaining from the vote.

At the end of the year I raised the Profumo affair afresh, in the Debate on the Denning Report on security. Harold Wilson had referred to the situation as being one in which we were "nonchalant amateurs opposing the ruthless efficiency of our opponents." I asked why, observing that we knew Commander Ivanov to be an intelligence agent, the Soviet Ambassador had never been sent for and told that his naval attaché was engaged in undiplomatic activity. There was no reply. Once again Reggie Paget rose from the Socialist benches in my support, saying that "The Honourable and Gallant Member for Harrow East probably speaks with more knowledge on the question of Security than any other Honourable Member."

In August a Bolshoi Ballet company visited London, and I was delighted to find among them two former dancers whom I had not spoken to since the famous party at the Mission in Moscow in 1942. Valya Peshcherikova and Lyalya Vanke were now no longer dancing, but still working for the Theatre, Lyalya looking truly regal as the Prince's mother in *Swan Lake*. To my surprise and delight they brought a small party down to lunch at my home in Chobham one week-end. It was a lovely day, and the time passed all too quickly. My Russian friends did not conceal their delighted curiosity in this first visit to an English home. When they had fingered the curtains, the cushion covers and the sheets in our bedroom and had walked across the meadows to see the poll Herefords on the farm, it came as something of a shock to us all when they had to leave to pay a duty visit to the grave of Karl Marx at Highgate before returning to their hotel.

These were not the only Russians to be entertained by us at Chobham. Kim Karaulov from the Soviet Embassy and his wife also came down to lunch with us, the latter exciting my wife's curiosity by the expensiveness of her Parisian clothes and the intensity of the scent cloud with which she was surrounded. We both wondered how she would react to the inevitable return to Moscow standards. We had met the Soviet Ambassador and his wife on a number of occasions, but the Soldatovs were never able to accept an invitation to our home, and we observed that we ourselves no longer appeared to be on the Embassy invitation list. We had, however, developed a close acquaintanceship with the Czechoslovak Ambassador and his wife, M. and Mme. Trhlik, who struck us as a new and welcome type of professional Communist diplomat with whom it was possible to talk politics with a freedom hitherto unusual in such circles. The Hungarians and Roumanians also were friendly and hospitable, and the coolness which we began to sense on the Soviet side did not seem to extend to the Missions of their East European colleagues.

In December I was once again in Moscow for a crowded week on behalf of a British-based international company of some importance, for negotiations with a comparatively new department of the Ministry of Foreign Trade entitled Litsenzintorg. My object, as always, was to demonstrate to the

Russians the benefits which they would gain by relaxing the rigidity of their commercial attitudes and by accepting, with all its obvious difficulties, the possibility of participation in the activities of an International company such as that which I was representing.

The extent of my connections now made it possible to introduce this idea at a high level in other departments than the one prescribed specifically as handling this particular type of business, and I found that the confidence which I had built up over the years, despite setbacks, gained me a ready hearing in responsible quarters. I also had a useful entrée to the Ministry of Communications, where the Chief Engineer, discreet and correct in all his dealings with me, had accepted a tacit basis of personal liking and mutual confidence which was of great value to another of my client firms. By the end of 1963, in fact, I felt that I had proved the point made in my maiden speech four years previously, namely that commerce provided the best field by far in which to try to re-establish normality of relationships between ourselves and the Russians.

On the social side, lunch with the Gromovs, supper with the Pozners, tea with Marshak, meals with Lydia and Zina and a wonderful party at Aragvi given by the group of dancers from the Bolshoi ballet whom I had entertained at my home in the summer, demonstrated that human relationships on a normal scale were now becoming possible in the new Russia. Relations with the British Embassy were pleasant and correct, though a shade circumspect on the diplomatic side, and I had much delightful hospitality from successive Ambassadors, Ministers and Commercial Counsellors. Two of the latter, Douglas Stewart and Alan Rothnie, struck me as the best type of new-style British representative in this rather extraordinary environment. Finally, calls on the Kremlin and informal political talks with senior politicians such as Paletskis, Gubin, Spiridonov and Peive, the last named being President of the Soviet of Nationalities, had become a regular feature of my business visits to the Soviet Union.

My increasing Parliamentary activity on the security side had brought me into conflict with the powerful vested interests represented by the K.G.B. and the G.R.U. But I felt none-theless that firmness and complete sincerity in dealing with Russians would keep them convinced that my advantage to the Soviet Union as a friend more than counterbalanced any danger to their interests which I might represent. Liking them as I did, I could not do otherwise than use in the House of Commons the knowledge which I had gained of Russia, of its people and of the seamy side of Soviet politics. It was a curious kind of love-hate relationship symbolized by a tattered piece of paper which I carried in my wallet against the day when it might be worth more to me in terms of personal safety than my British passport. It was a certificate, dated 1942, of the donation of a litre of blood to a soldier of the Red Army.

PART THREE

—

20. A WARNING DISREGARDED

IT was in February, 1964, at a lunch-party in the House of
Commons that I heard the first faint rumblings of the storm
which was to break. I was acting as host to the wife of the
Soviet Ambassador, Mme. Soldatova, a woman for whom I
have both liking and respect, who told me quite unmistakably,
though in the oblique Russian fashion, that, unlike the speech of
welcome which I had just made (in Russian) in honour of the
visiting Soviet astronaut, Valentina Tereshkova, certain of my
utterances in the House were not looked upon with favour by
the Soviet Embassy. The point was made, I believe deliberately,
in the manner of a warning, and at a reception not long
afterwards it was underlined by one of the Secretaries at the
Embassy, Straenikov, whose duties and activities had previously
aroused my curiosity. In May I was again in Moscow. Through
the years in which I have paid visits to the Soviet and other
East European capitals I have developed a mechanism rather
similar to the sensitive antennae which tell Russians that
trouble is brewing where their affairs are concerned. But on this
and succeeding occasions, despite the flickering of an amber
light in London, I had no feeling that anything untoward was
preparing which might affect me adversely. Indeed, in
commercial matters, the atmosphere was improving steadily.

At home, domestic affairs were taking up an increasing
amount of time. Mary, my stepdaughter, was embarking on
her first London season, and it was mainly for this reason that
we had moved into a larger flat in Roebuck House, near
Victoria, which I was now able to combine with my office.
My work in the House, a prospering business, an increasingly
heavy social round, constituency affairs and family commitments had all somehow to be dovetailed into one another. The
two elder boys, now 23 and 20, showed no inclination to leave
home, and this was a considerable added burden on my wife,
who had her business worries, quite separate from my own

affairs. It was perhaps inevitable, in the circumstances, that some domestic friction should have arisen and I blame myself for the kind of thoughtlessness which only too often accompanies an abnormally busy life. I had planned in the summer to fly in the Airedale with my wife to Visby in Gotland, which I had always wanted to visit, as a preliminary to a more ambitious journey to Eastern Europe during the Summer Recess. But my wife did not wish to come, so my sister gratefully occupied the vacant seat.

In the constituency all seemed well. The Association, under Jack Shrimpton's chairmanship, was in good heart, although the imbalance between the wards on which George McGowan had commented in his report was still evident. Of the five branches, Stanmore North ward represented the more prosperous section of the constituency, and its weight both in voting strength and financial support was decisive in maintaining our Conservative majority. Theo Constantine, who on the death of Fred Handley-Page had succeeded the latter as President, was also Area Chairman of the National Union and had recently received a knighthood for his political services. Theo's life was devoted to politics on the organizational side, and he possessed considerable influence in higher Party circles. I never doubted his support and I knew he had a great admiration for my wife.

Theo was the focal point of the political coterie which controlled the Association's affairs. This coterie had acquired something of the nature of a social clique, which had some attractions for elements from Belmont ward, and to a lesser extent from other wards in the constituency. In all this the agent, Mrs. Burton, played a key role, and she had a complex of loyalties to the Party, to the Association and its officers, and to myself which had not yet seemed to become in any way conflicting with each other. Jo Burton was a widow who had lost her husband in sad circumstances right at the end of the war. She lived in Harrow and knew the constituency and its personalities backwards. Although she was not yet fully qualified, it was a stroke of real good fortune for us when we found that she was available to take over when George

McGowan left. In general I could not have wished for better political backing, though the Conservative weakness in Harrow Weald, Queensbury and Stanmore South wards was a source of some anxiety for the future.

In July the Government introduced in the House of Commons a Bill which revealed a disquieting situation in the field of Diplomatic Privilege. It confirmed many of the doubts and suspicions which had developed in my mind over the Foreign Office handling of this problem as it affected national security. The Diplomatic Privileges Bill (1964) was a measure which was required to give effect in English law to the Vienna Convention on Diplomatic Relations which had been initialled in 1961. This Convention was now in force by reason of the fact that it had been ratified by a majority of Governments, hitherto excluding our own. But the text of the Bill and the Minister's Second Reading speech revealed a remarkable situation. For nine years, by private arrangement between Governments, we had been according a complete degree of diplomatic immunity, normally only given to accredited diplomats, to the entire personnel, including wives, families and servants, of four Embassies in London, which turned out on enquiry to be those of Czechoslovakia, Hungary, Bulgaria and—the Soviet Union.

These "private arrangements" had never been made public, nor had they received the sanction of the House of Commons. They had, nevertheless, provided an excellent framework on which the K.G.B. and associated organizations had built and operated the "legal" espionage networks which had caused the country such immense damage over the previous years. I spoke strongly in the Second Reading Debate, pointing out that the Bill would legalize the position, so long kept concealed, by which four countries, certain of which were known to misuse diplomatic privileges for espionage purposes, would be exempted from the provisions of an International Convention which we had all signed, and would continue to enjoy a scale of diplomatic immunity far in excess of that which we give to the Missions of our best friends and allies. In his reply to the Debate Bob Mathew,* the Joint Parliamentary Under-Secretary, revealed

* The late Robert Mathew, Conservative M.P. for Honiton, 1955–1967.

the true reason for the "special arrangements" which I had called in question as being the necessity for protecting our own diplomatic representatives in the countries concerned, and this, he assured the House, necessarily involved the granting of reciprocal immunities in the United Kngdom.

In the Committee Stage, shortly before the House rose, I tabled an amendment to the Bill calling for the cancellation of Clause 7, which covered the special immunities complained of, and concluded, "I believe that it is the policy of certain countries . . . to bring pressure to bear on British diplomatic representatives abroad . . . with the object of obtaining a reciprocity of diplomatic immunities . . . for their representatives over and above what is allowed for internationally by the Convention." On Third Reading I tried to lay the responsibility for this deplorable anomaly squarely on the Foreign Office which I described as a Department still clinging to a nineteenth-century diplomatic structure and "trying to retain its own secret world of Walter Mitty".

I was particularly disturbed at the reluctance of the Foreign Office to give the House diplomatic information touching on problems of national security and I said that the Government could hardly be surprised, after the sad experience of treasonable activity by highly-placed Foreign Office officials over the past fifteen years, that some of us were now questioning the provisions of this Bill. Peter Thomas, the Minister of State, had come to support Bob Mathew to see the Bill through, and once again the Juggernaut of Government rolled remorselessly across the thinly-manned back benches. John Litchfield, Dudley Smith and Edward Gardner had given me staunch support, but our political masters had left the Bill to a Friday in the dog-days of a dying Parliament, and it seemed that few of my colleagues on either side of the House either knew or cared about what was at stake. It seemed to be generally accepted that the Member for Harrow East was a trifle eccentric, to say the least, when speaking on any matters even remotely connected with Russia; and anyway we were all going on summer holidays.

Universal Pictorial Press and Agency

(5) Investiture at Buckingham Palace: 1949

(6a) Entertaining Russian friends: Chobham, 1964

(6b) Poznan—1956. The Polish Prime Minister visits the stand

21. EAST EUROPE BY AIR

IN the summer of 1964, Parliamentary duties temporarily laid aside, I busied myself with preparations for the flight in the Airedale to Eastern Europe. Derek Wyburd, my old friend, accompanied me as navigator, and all the diplomatic preliminaries had proved surprisingly simple. Fuel of a suitable octane rating appeared to be available all along the route. We were equipped with a radio-compass, so that the East European beacon system could be utilized; we had excellent V.H.F. communication equipment; and we both spoke Russian. So on a fine August morning we said goodbye to our wives on the tarmac and took off on the first stage of our journey to Communist Eastern Europe. My intention was to fly in and out of as many of these countries as possible, in order to demonstrate that travel by private aeroplane could be as normal in Eastern as it is in Western Europe. In addition, we had quite a heavy programme of business commitments. For reasons going back to 1956 I had not attempted to get into Poland, and we had had a polite but definite refusal from the Russians . . . "there being no facilities for the operation of private aircraft in the Soviet Union."

Nevertheless, a journey which took in Prague, Budapesth, Arad, Bucharest, Constanza, Sofia and Belgrade was accomplished without difficulty. At Arad, where we were brought down due to bad weather in Bucharest, I was unable to pay for 20 gallons of fuel.

"How can I, a Communist official" said the Airport Commandant, "put in my books that I have refuelled a private capitalist aeroplane. As far as I am concerned you are a phantom. Take the petrol with my compliments!" He seemed genuinely delighted that we had visited his aerodrome.

Poor Derek had unwisely eaten a dish described on the menu as *mushroom farci* on our last night in Bucharest, and was confined for four days to his room in Sofia as a result.

With the honourable exception of Murray, the Ambassador

in Bucharest, our diplomatic representatives in the capitals visited took singularly little interest in the first British light aeroplane to make this trip, but this was of a pattern which Derek and I knew only too well. Equally typical was the cocktail party, about 100 strong, given by the Ambassador at Sofia on the occasion of the departure of his First Secretary, a pleasant social occasion to which he was kind enough to invite us. Apart from Embassy staff there was not, I gathered, a single Bulgarian present. In an atmosphere where the old concept of diplomatic contacts demonstrably failed to apply, I marvelled once again at the success of the Foreign Office in perpetuating the cosy and expensive diplomatic framework of a bygone age. As a businessman I was able to contrast the single Commercial Secretary (who also doubled up as Consul) with the active and competent West German Trade Missions, operating in Bulgaria as well as in other Communist countries which, judging by results, promote their country's export trade a good deal more successfully than we do. And all this despite the lack of official German diplomatic representation in Communist countries which is the legacy of Professor Hallstein and his famous doctrine, now gradually giving way before the logic of events.

As we arrived in our aeroplane at the capitals of these Communist countries we found that the attitude towards us was of a pattern in which there were three quite clearly-marked stages. The first was genuine pleasure at the arrival of two Englishmen to visit them in a small private aircraft; in some cases the first they had seen. The second stage took the form of a lively interest by airport officials and technical personnel which sometimes reached embarrassing proportions. The third was of the nature of a reaction to the second, and consisted of a noticeable tightening of restrictions on our movements and contacts, despite a continuing friendliness by our Communist hosts.

It was something of an anticlimax for me, when we returned to Prague, to leave both the aeroplane and my companion and fly on by Soviet Aeroflot Tu 104 to Moscow, where I had business commitments. I arrived on 24th August, and once more I stayed at the National Hotel, where a letter was waiting from my wife, the first which I had received since leaving England. It had been despatched by Foreign Office bag to the Moscow Embassy, and it could be taken for granted in the circumstances that it had been opened and a photostat copy taken by the K.G.B. as soon as it left British hands. The letter was very much to the point. My wife had decided to leave me, as our marriage had not turned out the success she had hoped: no more specific reason was given. After two days of mental agony which I prefer to forget, I received a telegram from her through the ordinary Russian post which read as follows:—"Three unexpected letters received from you last two days await your call tomorrow evening all love." I duly telephoned my wife at home and managed to persuade her to change her mind. But great damage had been done. The telephone call, which I was forced to make on an open line from my hotel, had undoubtedly let the K.G.B. discover that there was a weak link in the Courtney armour.

On my return home normal family life was resumed, but the shock and utter unexpectedness of the whole incident had left a feeling of insecurity which I had never experienced before.

22. GATHERING CLOUDS

IN the constituency the tempo of activity had quickened, due to the imminence of the 1964 General Election, and political and social occasions kept us busier than ever. The election campaign itself went well, and my wife was a great help and worked very hard throughout. Once again the blue Landrover, in which I did my canvassing, played a major part, and Andrew Burton, my Agent's son, volunteered to drive it for me, full time, for the period of the campaign. His services were invaluable. We had dreamed of increasing the majority, but it was not to be, and the Harrow East result exactly reflected the area trend by cutting the Conservative majority by over 50% in a straight fight with Labour.

My opponent on this occasion was a highly competent woman, Jo Richardson, who was also in a sense a business competitor, as she was closely associated with Ian Mikardo in promoting East-West trade, and our commercial paths had in fact crossed on more than one occasion. During the election the organization in Stanmore North ward had been noticeably weak, particularly in canvassing, and we had had to transfer our superlative ladies' canvassing team from Harrow Weald, where it was badly needed on the home ground, to help in Stanmore North, the main area of Conservative strength in the constituency.

We should not have done even so well as we did had it not been for the magnificent effort put forward by John Galley, a Greater London Councillor and a tower of strength in the district, who virtually took over direction of the election effort in Stanmore a week before the beginning of the campaign. As in every other of his activities, John threw his whole weight into the work, but he was "over-engined for his beam"; and he died not many months afterwards. I was to miss his energy and robust common sense sadly in the troubles which lay ahead.

With the election behind us, and Mary safely launched, it seemed that my wife and I could now relax a little and repair some of the damage caused to our life together by the events of the summer. But my hopes were not fulfilled, for in November a blow was struck at our marriage of which I will say no more than that it was not of my doing, although I felt that I had to accept part of the blame on account of my absorption in political and commercial affairs. For a fortnight my wife and I were parted and then we resumed life together once more.

For a second time I took a deep breath and determined that the marriage *must* succeed, in spite of the shocks to which it had been subjected. We went to the Bahamas for Christmas, and in the peace and sunshine of that lovely spot I think we both felt that we had passed through a bad time which we were not going to allow to recur. But the moving finger had written, and it seemed that a chain of events had been started over which I had no control. For in January and again in March my eldest stepson, Sir Alec Douglas-Home (then Leader of my Party) and I all received anonymous letters, bearing a Harrow postmark, from a source or sources which appeared to be very well-informed about my wife's private life. The object of the correspondence was reasonably clear from the following excerpt which is typical:—

"We think you should resign as our M.P. before there is a further public scandal in the Party."

It seems that M.P.s are frequently exposed to this sort of thing; and I saw the Chief Whip, Willie Whitelaw, who was helpful and sympathetic. Rightly or wrongly, I did not tell him that there was substance in the allegations, and it was a dreadful thing to feel that my family troubles should be known to others who wished me ill. Scotland Yard was called in, but the anonymous letter-writers had covered their tracks successfully, and no clue to their identity has ever been discovered. In March the letters ceased, but I was not allowed to remain in peace of mind for long.

There can be little doubt that this private worry affected my work in the constituency, and I began to feel that the steadfast support of the officers of the Association, which I had come to take for granted, was by no means as solid as I had imagined. There was no evidence of this from within the ward organizations, and nothing tangible from the agent, but the impression was confirmed at a lunch at the Carlton Club in January during which Jack Shrimpton, the Chairman, and Theo Constantine frankly discussed the political situation as they saw it in Harrow East. They were worried by the possible intervention of a Liberal candidate at the next Election, and they considered that support in Stanmore was weaker than it should be, which they said was due primarily to lack of attention on my part. They felt that I must embark on a serious canvassing programme and devote more time to Stanmore.

While accepting their criticisms I pointed out that to be seen more in Stanmore required some measure of co-operation from local Conservatives, who were singularly disinclined ever to come out canvassing; and that in other wards, notably Harrow Weald, we were making real progress in areas which had not previously been favourable to us. I could not help feeling, as a result of this lunchtime conversation, that the tide of support within the Stanmore coterie had begun to turn against me.

But I have a disinclination, common to most naval officers, to believe ill of anyone with whom I am associated until he clearly and demonstrably proves that he deserves it. So it was in this case. The Association's business was its own affair: I might, and did in my heart of hearts, deprecate the concentration of authority in such a very small group within a single ward, but I looked mainly to a correction of my own shortcomings to set matters right. Jack Shrimpton was a good Chairman, and he and his wife were personal friends of ours, but he was relatively inexperienced and his authority with the agent was perhaps not as great as it should have been.

Theo Constantine, the Area Chairman, with his wife, made up a close-knit foursome with the Treasurer, Blackie Cawdron, and his wife, the latter being active on the social side of Stanmore and in constituency goings-on. These people were competent enough, but my concern rested in the fact that they seemed increasingly unrepresentative of the ward as a whole.

23. THE SECOND WARNING

IN the House, though the Socialists were now in Government, my affairs were prospering. I had been critical of many aspects of the Tory Administration, and had come to realize, with many others on the Conservative back benches, that in the later stages of the last Parliament we had taken over the role of a constructive opposition from our Socialist opponents, who had been single-minded in their concentration on Parliamentary electioneering. It had been in some ways an unhappy period politically, and it was a relief to be able to smite a Socialist Government hip and thigh on important national issues.

It was in this spirit that I initiated a debate on variable-geometry aircraft and pursued another matter in which I have always taken a great interest, the application of nuclear power to the propulsion of merchant ships. In an unwise moment a Socialist back-bencher was given encouragement by the Government to introduce an Anchors and Chain Cables Bill, a technical measure of which the sailors on our side of the House were highly critical. We had the whole-hearted support of Harry Pursey from the Socialist benches, and in Committee he, Reggie Bennett, David Webster and I blinded our opponents with nautical science and finally killed the Bill one Friday afternoon on Third Reading. Within a short period I was given the leave of the House to introduce the Anchors and Chain Cables (No. 2) Bill, which, we felt, was a constructive finish to our campaign against Government arrogance in this minor but important matter. It was a useful Parliamentary experience.

In Defence, too, I was active, becoming Vice-Chairman of the Conservative Navy Committee, and in March Sir Alec invited me to wind up from the Despatch Box in the Debate on the Navy Estimates for 1965. Questions of Security continued to worry me, and there was a small but growing volume of support in all parts of the House for this somewhat eccentric, Russian-speaking sailor, whose Cassandra-like forebodings had seemed so often to be justified by the event.

Early in 1965 I was sent a copy of a book, just published in London, to review for the *Evening Standard*. It was the English translation of the wartime memoirs of Admiral Arseni Golovko, the Commander-in-Chief of the Soviet Northern Fleet, whom I had got to know so well during my time at Polyarnoe. The book, entitled *With the Red Fleet*, was a thoroughly nasty piece of anti-British propaganda. It consisted basically of a vicious travesty of the Royal Navy's thankless task for four years in safeguarding the Arctic convoys which carried supplies to Russia. In it the Admiral made numerous allegations of British incompetence and bad faith, while making childishly exaggerated claims on behalf of the Northern Fleet. In two reviews I left the readers of both the *Evening Standard* and *The Navy* in no doubt about the true state of affairs, and in due course there was a Soviet reaction.

In a long article in the official Soviet newspaper *Red Star* I was bitterly attacked for my "stream of wicked libel" and my "gloomy pictures and evil innuendos". The author, one Captain Eremeev, concluded that "it was by worthless methods that I had attempted to shake the faith of foreign readers in the Soviet Union and its peaceful Leninist foreign policy." Nevertheless, *Red Star* took care not to print my original review, and for this reason *The Navy*, though pressed by the Russians, declined to print the Soviet counterblast. It represented a small success for the British way of doing things in a field where the Russians have come to do very much as they please.

In the early part of the year, also, I had become involved in a curious affair concerning the Harrow firm of Kodak Ltd. Two former employees of the firm were acquitted at the Central Criminal Court on a charge of passing on the firm's secrets, for payment, to an East German organization. I was particularly concerned to defend Kodak against the allegation, made in the form of a Parliamentary Question by Maurice Orbach, to the effect that they had entered into a conspiracy to pervert the course of justice. The Attorney-General, fortunately, was of the same opinion as I was, and said in reply that he could not agree that the court proceedings revealed "a conspiracy on the part of Kodak to pervert the course of justice". It was an affair of considerable complexity, and the inter-relation of business and politics was exemplified by the fact that Orbach and I, though opposed on this issue, were both of us employed as consultants on East-West trade matters by a certain important British Industrial Group.

In the defence espionage field there had been two exchanges which had caused me concern. The Americans had exchanged the U2 pilot Gary Powers for Colonel Abel, one of the most competent Russian spies who ever went on *komandirovka**

* *komandirovka*; assignment.

from the Soviet Union. We, in turn, had agreed to the exchange of Greville Wynne for the brilliantly competent head of the "illegal" Portland spy network, Gordon Lonsdale. Two other highly efficient Soviet spies, Mr. and Mrs. Kroger were, however, still in British custody. In March we heard that a University lecturer, Gerald Brooke, had been arrested in Moscow for distributing N.T.S. literature. The N.T.S. is an *émigré* Russian organization working for the liberation of the peoples of the U.S.S.R. from Soviet hegemony.

In addition, a traitor called Bossard had been discovered in the Ministry of Aviation, no doubt controlled as usual by the K.G.B. network within the Soviet Embassy. Ten days before this last affair "broke" as a result of the arrest of Bossard, I wrote in strong terms to a personal friend who had been appointed to the newly-formed Standing Security Commission. (I reproduce my letter in Appendix A.)

I was due to leave at the end of March, 1965, for another business trip to the Soviet capital, and I had written ahead in the normal way to tell my friends that I was coming, my letter to the Gromovs being dated 2nd March. But for the first time in my long Russian connection the possibility had now occurred to me that my personal safety might at last be at risk in my continued dealings with the Soviet Union. My wife was as concerned as I was, and we discussed the matter at length. She, like the wife of Gerald Brooke, would be the natural focus for efforts to secure my release should anything go wrong, and in this event I told her where to turn for support from influential friends and Parliamentary colleagues in bringing pressure to bear on the Government. On the day of my departure I wrote a letter to the Foreign Secretary which was not to be posted by my wife unless untoward circumstances made it necessary. (See Appendix B.)

This Moscow visit was one of the most successful that I ever made, and gave promise of a real step forward in three commercial fields in which I was particularly interested. In one of them we had achieved the acceptance in principle by the Russians of the formation of a mixed Anglo-Soviet Company on a 50/50 basis, organized along the purest capitalist lines.

My object had been to persuade the Russians, against their background of Marxist economics and endemic suspicion of the capitalist world, that it would be in their national interest to co-operate with us by conforming in one particular field to the international business structure of the western world. In this I believed I had the support of far-seeing elements in *Litsenzintorg*, personified by Tomashinsky, one of the Vice-Presidents, and also of Prikhodov, an intelligent Vice-President of the All-Union Chamber of Commerce, and of Smelyakov, the taciturn but brilliant Deputy-Minister of Foreign Trade. In all this, Alan Rothnie, Commercial Counsellor at the Embassy, was helpful with advice and useful suggestions.

It was a busy week, with little time to spare for my friends, but I had lunch as usual with the Gromovs and saw Kelly, now the proud father of seven live pups. Zina came with me to see *Sadko* at the Bolshoi and I had supper one evening with the Pozners. Paul was at home, for once, and it was a delight to find how closely his ideas seemed to conform, without one word of the language, to those of an English youth of his age. Since my previous visit Samuel Marshak had died, to the great sadness of his many friends, so I paid a call of condolence at the flat and left parcels from Emrys Hughes for Rosalia Ivanovna.

But my usual call to Lydia had struck a strange and discordant note. The number which I had dialled for 23 years was D 13433, but two calls produced an irritated response from a strange voice which denied all knowledge of Lydia Konstantinovna Manukhina, or of the flat in which she lived. It is a strange fact that in Moscow it is not easy to get a sight of a telephone directory, but a helpful girl on the end of the phone at *Spravochnoye*, the local equivalent of Directory Enquiries, elicited the information that Lydia's number had been changed. I dialled the new number and the familiar voice replied.

"Lydia, this is Tony."

Silence—and she hung up.

I dialled once more.

Again Lydia's voice replied, but this was to say that she knew no-one of the name of Tony, that it was not Lydia speaking, that she had no knowledge of any of the people concerned and would I stop bothering her.

Refusing to be defeated I went straight off up the Tverskaya to House 7, Vorotnikovsky Pereulok.

My knock on the door of Lydia's flat brought the response "Kto Kam?" (who is there?) in the well-remembered voice, and once again I replied "Vaska"—the traditional response. Here I should explain that in Russia all cats are "Basil or Vasili" just as bears are Michael, or Misha, and "Vaska" is the usual dimunitive. (In 1942 it had seemed as good a private password as any.)

There was a pause, and once again Lydia, for I was certain that it was she, denied all knowledge of me and refused to acknowledge her own identity.

To make absolutely sure, I called on the neighbours next door, who had been kind and helpful on more than one occasion over the years.

Yes—Lydia Konstantinovna was still in her flat, not very well these days, but she had not gone away.

I left the building and walked back to the National Hotel with the funny feeling between my shoulder blades that I had not experienced since entering the upstairs room in Poznan police headquarters for my interview with the U.B., the Polish Secret Police, in 1957.

It was evident that after 23 years of inactivity since the blazing row which I had had with Zaitsev in 1942 the K.G.B. had once again turned its attention on Lydia. Taken in its Soviet context, the incident was important, perhaps vitally so, and Lydia's conduct could be interpreted as conveying an urgent message to me in time-honoured Russian fashion— "Danger—keep right away".

On the day of my departure I lunched with Rothnie and several representatives of the British Press, who have always taken an interest in my activities in Moscow. Two days previously the Government newspaper *Izvestia* had carried a short paragraph referring to my talk with Peive. It was to be seven months before my name was to appear again in its columns—in a very different context.

24. ACTION STATIONS

FOR the first time for many years it was a relief to get back to London. The sense of foreboding aroused by the Lydia incident nagged at me continually, but I was thankful that, so far at least, she had not apparently been harmed. My mind went back to wartime days when the woman-friend of the brilliant *Daily Telegraph* correspondent, A. T. Cholerton, had been arrested three weeks after his departure to England on leave, as a preliminary to a refusal by the Soviet authorities to grant him a re-entry visa. The leopard, it seemed, had not changed its spots.

In London, public interest in security matters had again been aroused by the revelations of the Bossard case, which were just one more dreadful confirmation of all that I had been trying to bring out in Parliament and outside over the past few years. It seemed to be Government policy to release a minimum of information which might touch on the diplomatic side and so involve the Foreign Office, but nevertheless two points in connection with the case were abundantly clear.

First, it was part of the R.I.S. communication system with Bossard, working as usual from its centre within the Soviet Embassy, to use so-called "dead-letter boxes" (DLBs) at widely separated points. Who more suitable for this work than the swollen numbers of Soviet "administrative and service staff", including of course the dozen or so chauffeurs, each of them absolutely safe by reason of the blanket diplomatic immunity accorded them with the "special arrangements" existing between the British and Soviet Governments?

Secondly, though the Government refused to divulge the names of the Russians involved, there had been personal contact between Bossard and his controllers in the Embassy staff.

Once again, efforts at clarification by Question in the House met the customary stonewalling. The "public interest", yet again, was invoked to prevent the House, the Press and the public itself from enquiring too closely into matters touching national security, or even from being given the facts concerning Soviet activities which were obviously already known to our enemies. My letter to the member of the Standing Security Commission had, I was informed a month later, been referred to the Foreign Office!

In June, 1965, I put down two Questions on security for answer by the Prime Minister, Harold Wilson, who particularly asked me to defer them "for good national reasons". Naturally I did so, and arranged to see him on 29th June. At this interview I set out afresh all my fears at the state of our security and of the major weakness which I believe lay in the organization and mentality of the Foreign Office. I added, as an example of the seriousness of the situation, that we had a colleague in the House of Commons who, when a member of the Diplomatic Service, had had to be removed from Moscow at short notice because of a successful compromising operation by the Russians. It was perhaps significant that this Member had never, to my knowledge, opened his mouth on this subject, of which he had had such bitter personal experience. Once again, with all his facile charm, Harold Wilson endeavoured to reassure me that the security situation was in hand, and I left him with the same feeling of near-hopelessness that I had experienced six years earlier after the somewhat similar interview with Harold Macmillan.

On 6th July I asked the Prime Minister on whose authority my letter of the 4th March had been forwarded to the Foreign Office and what action he intended to take on the recommendations put forward in it. Harold Wilson replied to the effect that the subject matter was more the concern of the Foreign Office than that of the Commission, and he held out little hope that my recommendations would prove acceptable.

My mind went back to 1948 when I had been a member of the delegation sent to Germany by the Joint Intelligence Committee of the Chiefs of Staff, whose Chairman was William Hayter, to study the Intelligence organization in Germany and to make recommendations. We duly visited the Service Intelligence departments and the Intelligence Division,

Control Commission for Germany, prior to making our report. But the Foreign Office insisted that their own arrangements for dealing with Intelligence matters should be substantially excluded from this study, and their case was upheld. Since that date four major and a number of minor traitors have been discovered by the Security Service to have been working for years within the Foreign Office.

And now, in July, 1965, the Prime Minister himself had ruled that a criticism of the Foreign Office made to the newly-formed Security Commission on security grounds was "more their concern (the Foreign Office's) than that of the Standing Security Commission!" I gave up the unequal struggle, despite some limited support from Alec Douglas-Home on the Front Bench, but tabled an Early Day Motion on the Order Paper of the same day which read as follows:—

Danger to National Security
"That this House, recognising the seriousness of the damage caused to the nation by repeated security cases over the past fifteen years, and conscious of the handicap at present imposed on the Security Services by the extraordinary degree of diplomatic immunity accorded to certain foreign Embassies which habitually abuse diplomatic privilege for espionage purposes, calls upon Her Majesty's Government to review as a matter of urgency existing bilateral arrangements which confer immunities greater than those allowed for by the Vienna Convention on Diplomatic Relations and to re-establish conditions of mutual diplomatic representation with these countries on a basis of strict reciprocity."

I had some solid support for this Motion, which was signed, among others, by Harry Legge-Bourke, Irene Ward, Tony Lambton, Rolf Dudley-Williams, John Litchfield, Patricia Hornsby-Smith, Morgan Giles, Simon Wingfield-Digby, Tom Iremonger and Ronald Russell.

My last words before the House rose for the Summer Recess were to ask the Prime Minister when the Government were going to stop behaving like a lot of hypnotized rabbits in face of the efficient Soviet espionage organization. Answer came there none.

It was a relief to turn my mind to another Parliamentary activity which I had started in the spring. I had long been concerned with the distressingly low level of Parliamentary debate on Aviation matters, and it seemed to me that the considerable degree of ignorance of the majority of Members in this highly technical field had played some part in the series of disasters to the British aviation industry which culminated in the cancellation of the TSR2, the P1154 and the HS681 aircraft projects.

I therefore took the initiative in forming a Parliamentary Flying Club, and we got off to a good start by enrolling some 70 members from both Houses, only a few of whom, however, expressed their intention of actually learning to fly. My friend Peter Masefield provided us with a Beagle Airedale on excellent terms, and the Parliamentary aircraft soon began to be seen at places as far afield as Hanover and the Canary Islands. With Geoffrey de Freitas as Vice-Chairman, Frank Taylor as Treasurer and Hector Monro and Derek Page as Joint Secretaries, we looked forward to a slow but steady expansion. In view of their very small majority, it was another headache for the Government Whips, but we saw to it that the Conservative aviators were accompanied whenever possible by an equal number of Socialists!

After a visit to the British Aircraft Corporation's principal factory at Weybridge I had been particularly attracted by a project which had been dropped by the Conservative Government after the Defence White Paper of 1957. This was for a revolutionary type of variable-geometry aircraft designed for specific naval use, being ideally suited for operation from aircraft carriers. It was a product of the brain of Dr. Barnes-Wallis, and before the House rose for the Summer Recess of 1964 I initiated an adjournment debate in which I pressed the Government to retrieve some of its mistakes in the field of military aviation by developing this type of "swing-wing mini" as I described it, as a general purpose aircraft suitable for both Naval and R.A.F. use. The debate attracted little attention at the time, and the Government turned a deaf ear, but subsequent events have justified the case which I then put forward.

In Harrow East the programme of canvassing which I had agreed with Jack Shrimpton was going well, particularly in Harrow Weald, where we were regaining a lot of ground from the Socialists through the enthusiastic efforts of the ladies' canvassing team organized by Vera Charter, wife of Douglas Charter. Douglas had taken on the job of canvassing director during the General Election. On 11th June my wife and I gave a cocktail party for about 200 Conservative workers at "The Limes", Stanmore, very kindly lent for the occasion by Anne Manley-Walker, daughter of the late Fred Handley-Page, our former President. It was voted a great success, and I had a private letter of congratulation from the Chairman referring to the good which it had done among our supporters.

In May, Tomashinsky, the very competent Vice-President of *Litsenzintorg*, had paid us a visit, and the project for the formation of our mixed Anglo-Soviet company had made progress. It was agreed in principle that the Board should consist of three British Directors, three Soviet Directors, some or all of whom could be members of the Soviet Trade Delegation in London, with myself as non-voting Chairman. The idea had received something of a setback after Tomashinsky's return to Moscow, and it was found necessary for me to go out again as soon as I could get free of my Parliamentary duties.

But in the last stages of the Session, with a Government majority of three, to get leave out of our Chief Whip, Willie Whitelaw, was like trying to get blood out of a stone. Having already postponed the visit at his request I finally succeeded in getting the necessary permission, and planned to fly to Moscow on Sunday, 25th July. The usual application to Roshchin, the Soviet Consul-General in London, produced the required visa, accommodation was arranged, and I notified both the Foreign Office and my friends in Moscow that I would shortly be on my way.

I had collected the normal list of small presents to take to my friends. They made up rather an odd collection. Gerry Pozner's

Westminster Press Provincial Newspapers

(7) Entertaining the Bolshoi Ballet: 1960

(8) Zina

French soul hankered after Marmite and Worcester Sauce—
both quite unobtainable in Moscow. There was the usual
bottle of whisky for Volodya. I had promised Zina a large
conch shell from the Bahamas and was taking her yet another
novel by Angela Thirkell, complete with duchesses. For Nina
Gromova, studious as always, there was a book on the House
of Commons at Work, and an Education Guide. Mikhail
Mikhailovitch would, I was sure, like the book on Fox Terriers
which I had found at Hatchard's. On this occasion Sophia
would have to be content with English chocolates. As for
Lydia—I tried not to worry, but I wondered whether I should
ever see her again.

With all these preparations completed I went, all unsuspecting, to a weekly meeting of the 1922 Committee on the
evening of Thursday, 22nd July, where Alec Douglas-Home
announced his resignation from the Leadership of the
Conservative Party. It was a great shock to many besides
myself, and it was a little time before I realized that, in view
of the election of a new Leader which was to take place the
following week, it would now be impossible for me to proceed
with my plan to fly to Moscow on the Sunday following. It was
a nuisance, but no more than that, and I had been faced on
previous occasions with last-minute cancellations of Russian
arrangements. I was intensely busy, and felt under no
obligation to inform Moscow of my eleventh-hour change of
plan, except to leave a message for the Englishman who had
been due to meet me there. Both he and the Russians were
quite used to this sort of thing. My colleague would be well able
to handle the immediate business on his own.

The week opened with a three-line Whip on Monday—a
Vote of Censure which the Government survived, while on
Tuesday I voted in the election for the Party Leadership and
joined a thoughtful and, I believe, far-seeing minority in
supporting Enoch Powell against the two principal contestants.

25. THE K.G.B. STRIKES

IT was the first week of August, 1965. I was in my flat seeing a naval friend who has ambitions to enter politics when the telephone rang. It was John Tilney* from the House. Something extremely important had happened, and would I come along at once to have a word with him? Ten minutes later we met in Westminster Hall: his manner was constrained and anxious as he put a buff-coloured envelope into my hand.

"Have a look at that. Several Members have already received them."

I unfolded a large foolscap-sized sheet of rather poor quality glossy paper headed "I'm not a Profumo, but . . . (a story in photographs)." The broadsheet, as I shall hereafter describe it, contained six photographs, five of them being of myself—with appropriate captions. The sixth was of a typed letter on House of Commons writing-paper defaced by an enlarged business visiting-card. Two of the photographs represented me in company with a woman (or women) in circumstances which plainly indicated sexual intimacy. The whole was a viciously clever attack on my moral, commercial and political character, and the broadsheet ended ominously with the phrase "to be continued".

Poor John was in great distress.

"Why," he said, "did they have to send one of these foul things to *me*?"

For a moment, I was in no condition to reply.

I shall not easily forget the scene. The sombre, stone-flagged magnificence of Westminster Hall on a stuffy August afternoon, sightseers wandering around, members and officials hurrying about their business, with two days to go before the Summer Recess. From the first I myself was in no doubt about the origin of the broadsheet, and the impact was numbing. The fear which pervaded that bare room in Poznan and the funny feeling between the shoulder-blades which I had

* J. D. Tilney, Conservative M.P. for Wavertree Division of Liverpool from 1950.

experienced in Moscow in March had been succeeded by this shattering blow against me right at the heart of the British scene, here in the Mother of Parliaments, within the precincts of the Royal Palace of Westminster.

I stayed long enough to discover that the Labour Chief Whip had received copies from one or two Socialist back-benchers and that Willie Whitelaw, our own Chief Whip, had been told, and I then returned to the flat to make two tele-phone calls.

The first was to an old personal friend, the Director-General of the Security Service, Roger Hollis, who was with me within the hour. The second was to my wife, at home in Chobham.

"Darling," I said, "something terribly important has happened, which I must tell you about, and I shall be down as soon as I can possibly get away."

My interview with Roger was not very reassuring, for in fact there was little he could do other than promise all possible assistance in discovering the origin of the broadsheet, which he took away with him. One of his specialist officers would be in touch with me in the morning. As he left me, the afternoon post arrived. It included a typed buff envelope, addressed to my wife. Inside was another copy of the broadsheet.

I drove down to Chobham and prepared my wife as best I could for the shock before showing her the broadsheet.

"It is too soon to say with any certainty," I said, "but I am sure this is Russian work, and I think one woman in the photo-graphs, if they are genuine, is Zina. Perhaps it is her in both."

I had told my wife soon after our marriage about the short-lived affair in 1961 and she had clearly liked her when they met in Moscow eighteen months later. In April she had written to Zina asking her to spend her summer holiday with us in England if she could get a visa, and offering to pay her fare, but we never had a reply to the letter.

There was little sleep for either of us that night, and we both knew that a time of great trouble lay ahead. A Member of Parliament is specially vulnerable to attacks of this kind, and until we knew how widely the broadsheet had been distributed it was impossible to make any plans to counter it.

On the following day I had arranged to fly three of my Parliamentary colleagues who were interested in naval affairs up to Lossiemouth as part of a group visiting the Royal Naval Air Station, where Buccaneer squadrons were under training.

It was a lovely day for flying, my companions were in high spirits, and as we flew north I found it hard to believe that the situation which I had left behind in London was not just a nightmare. I had confided in Lynch Maydon, who made one of the party.

"Don't worry," was his comment. "Your position is strong enough and I'm sure you'll survive. People are far too sensible to take such things seriously these days."

Willie Hamling's* reaction was even more to the point.

"You'll be all right," he said, "what sort of people do they think we are, anyway?"

But I was not reassured. On the same evening, we were being entertained in the wardroom by the naval aviators when I was called to the telephone. It was the Chief Whip.

Willie Whitelaw sounded tired and worried. He told me that at least half-a-dozen copies of the broadsheet were known to have reached M.P.s, and added that one had been received by my Agent in Harrow East who, in the absence of the Chairman, who was on holiday, had passed it straight to the President, Theo Constantine.

"Anthony," he said, "this is pretty serious. What are you going to do about it?"

It was a difficult moment, for I had as yet no clear idea of how I was going to defend myself, and had nothing to go on until the security people had given the broadsheet a proper examination. Also we were on an open telephone line. I replied briefly, to the effect that I had put the whole matter in the hands of the Security Service, that the photographs, which were probably faked, were undoubtedly Russian, and that I would let him know if there were any developments.

It was a blow to have my fears confirmed that the broadsheet had reached the constituency, although I realized it was probably inevitable. Theo Constantine seemed to have acted

* William Hamling, Labour M.P. for Woolwich West since 1964.

quickly, and I was relieved that the thing had come into his more experienced hands rather than those of Jack Shrimpton. It was going to need the greatest delicacy of handling if we were to avoid a catastrophe.

On Saturday I had an engagement in the constituency at a Garden Fête in Harrow Weald. It is an occasion which I usually enjoy, especially if my wife is with me, but today was very different. Although only two of those present knew of the existence of the broadsheet the poison had started to work and I imagined, without any real reason, that subtly and yet distinctly, the whole atmosphere had changed. I was soon able to have a few words with Theo.

"Hullo there!" he said, in his usual style, and as we moved aside he continued

"Well, Anthony, this is a bad business. If this thing gets out and someone starts leaving copies about in the pubs you can never expect to hold the seat."

We agreed to preserve absolute secrecy in the hope that, at least where the constituency was concerned, distribution had been confined to the one copy which had been sent to the Agent.

As we separated, Bob Arajs, the Chairman of Harrow Weald ward, hurried across, agog with curiosity about "some leaflets". My heart sank.

However, a couple of questions revealed that Jo Burton, the Agent, contrary to my instructions, had unwisely asked him to keep his ears open in Harrow Weald concerning the possible distribution of literature. Arajs had at once scented a mystery.

I gave him a bare outline of what had happened, with strict instructions as to secrecy. It was infuriating that a leak should have occured so soon and I at once told the Agent what I thought of her behaviour. However, if a third was to be in the secret it seemed as well that it was Bob Arajs, for a particular reason.

Arajs is of Latvian origin. He came to this country after the war and married an Englishwoman who, incidentally, has been working with the Agent in our Association offices. To the best of my belief Arajs still has relatives living in the Soviet Union, and for this reason he, above all, should understand the full significance of a K.G.B. operation of this kind. Indeed, he appeared to respond both sympathetically and helpfully, and I felt that no great harm had been done.

Back in my flat, information was beginning to come in to show the extent of the operation. It now seemed that at least five M.P.s had received copies of the broadsheet by post, including George Wigg, who was acting as the Prime Minister's adviser on Security, and my Labour opponent at the 1959 election, who had since been returned for another seat. I discovered that George Wigg's copy had not been posted, but delivered by hand at his London address. Two copies had been posted to my wife (to each of our two addresses) and others to the Labour candidate at Harrow East in the 1964 election, to the Chairman of Kodak, to the Secretary of my Association, as already mentioned, and to the News Editor of the *News of the World*. Later on I discovered that there had been a few more, both to M.P.s and to the Press, which had been destroyed on receipt.

26. REACTION

WITHOUT giving it much thought, I have always considered that my nerves are reasonably steady. But I must confess that this nightmarish situation took its toll during the weeks following. I became jumpy and irritable, and although normally a sound sleeper I now spent many hours lying awake—thinking.

Parliament had risen, and M.P.s are inveterate gossip-mongers. I knew that a number of them, and not all of them my friends, would be taking an excitingly salacious story back with them to their homes and their constituencies. I had heard enough before the House rose to realize that some leakage was inevitable. More than one of my colleagues had clapped me on the back with an assurance of sympathy, but accompanied by an odd, self-satisfied look which, I soon came to understand, reflected an inner thankfulness and, no doubt, an inward admission that "there but for the Grace of God go I!".

I began to feel acutely that I was quite alone. My lawyer, Michael Simmons, was a tower of strength, but he could scarcely be expected to spare me much time from his many other concerns. Ann, my secretary for the previous four years, had just left me, and her successor had not yet got to grips with my affairs. At home in Chobham the atmosphere was tense with foreboding. Apart from my wife there was nobody in whom I could confide.

So it was in virtual isolation that I sat down at my desk in the London flat to study the broadsheet in the hope of finding some clue as to its origin.

The envelopes and the typing provided little of interest, but the poor quality of the paper gave the impression of foreign origin. Two of the addresses were a little more helpful. In the first, the name of the News Editor of the *News of the World* had been misspelt in a way which indicated that it had been obtained phonetically, perhaps through an enquiry over the telephone. In the second, the slightly unusual form of address which was used in the case of Harrow East Association showed that it had probably been taken out of the West Middlesex Telephone Directory.

I then sought expert opinion about the photography. This confirmed my impression about foreign origin, and the experts went on to say that the photos included in the broadsheet could in two cases have been "composite", and that they showed some indications of having been faked.

So far—not much to go on, and I turned to the subject matter itself.

The broadsheet was headed:

"I'm not a Profumo, but . . ." (A story in photographs)

and one paragraph followed which conveyed the general sense of the attack which the photographs were designed to support. It ran:

1959
**Why not try to become an M.P.
to combine business with
pleasure and to conduct shady
business while "Defending
public interests"?**

To say the least, this spoke for itself.

There followed three quite innocuous photographs, all of myself. Two seemed to have been taken from election literature, and I identified the third, in naval uniform, as having been taken by an old friend, Boris Ward. Boris is himself half-Russian, speaks the language fluently, and has had many business dealings with the Soviet Union. There was not much help there.

I turned to the three photographs, which showed me in a state of undress and in two cases accompanied by women, one of them lying sideways on a bed. The first showed me by myself, seated and with no clothes on. It was not pretty and it seemed to have been touched up to make it less so, but it was scarcely damaging. But the other two were dynamite. In the first I was portrayed seated on a bed, partially clothed, beside a fully-clothed woman whose blouse I seemed to be buttoning (or unbuttoning) at the back. For a start, the pillow suggested Germany—or countries further east. The woman, who was seen in profile, was difficult to identify with any certainty, but again and again I came back to the conclusion that it was Zina, my Moscow friend of so many years' standing. My wife, who had met Zina on several occasions in 1962, agreed with me.

The third photograph showed a woman in the background, half-clothed and reclining on a bed. She was shown full face, but a rectangular patch had been blacked out across the eyes and this was evidently intended to conceal her identity. The hair-style seemed to be similar in the two photographs, and the supposition was that they were in fact of the same person, though it was impossible to be sure of this. Again, this photograph had been touched up, with a gross implication.

At the bottom left-hand corner of the broadsheet was the reproduction of a typed letter, written on House of Commons writing-paper and evidently from myself. I say "evidently" because the typescript was almost wholly concealed by an enlarged business visiting-card, my own, superimposed and enlarged for the purpose. But "My D . . ." at the beginning and ". . . . rs sincerely,
            Anthony"
at the end were unmistakably my handwriting. The address shown on the card was "Roebuck House", which gave it a date after November 1964, when I had moved in.

Ann had come to the flat to sort out some of my correspondence and, taking a deep breath, I showed her the broadsheet. Bless her—her face never moved a muscle. But her brows knitted in thought.

"We must find that letter," was all she said.

Ann went straight to the Moscow personal file, and rummaged for a few minutes. She was matching the reproduction on the broadsheet to carbon copies of my letters written over the previous year. A silence, and then

"I think I've got it."

She was at her most clinical and matter-of-fact as she showed me the file copy of a letter dated 2nd March, 1965.

The letter was to the wife of General Gromov (Mikhail Mikhailovitch speaks no English) and ran as follows:—

My Dear Nina,

I am hoping to be in Moscow again from the 28th March to the evening of the 2nd April, staying as usual at the National.

I do hope that you and M.M. will be in Moscow, not to speak of Sofia and Kelly. It will be so nice to see you all again and Elizabeth joins with me in sending you our love.

            With kind regards and all good wishes,
                        Yours sincerely,
                        Anthony.

As far as we could judge, because of the difference in size, the small fragments of typescript which were still visible on the reproduction tallied exactly with the carbon copy of the original. We would need expert help to be absolutely certain, but I was sure that we had found what we wanted.

In fact, within a few days I had confirmed this from a photographer friend who, with the help of one of my visiting-cards and a replica of the original letter (typed by Ann from the carbon copy), produced an exact reproduction of this part of the broadsheet.

I felt better than I had for days, and Ann shared my excitement. We now knew that my letter must have been intercepted in Moscow, and reproduced by the K.G.B. in the broadsheet in a way which they might have hoped would prevent us from identifying it. We had scored a point, if only a small one, and I could now say with certainty that this was Russian work.

Roger Hollis had been as good as his word, and at my flat there arrived a quiet, competent individual, an officer of the Security Service whom I shall call "Soames" for the purpose of this story. I blessed the forethought (it had been the idea of my first Elisabeth) which led me to maintain a certain friendly contact with the Security authorities since my retirement from the Navy and the development of my business with the Communist world. It had seemed a useful precaution against the day when I might need their help—and that day had arrived.

Soames was patient and a good listener, so it seemed to be my rôle to do the talking. In any case it was an enormous relief to be able to open my heart to someone who I was sure would be on my side and who by the nature of things knew a great deal more about this side of Russian affairs than I did. He was in fact an expert on the Russian Intelligence Service, though I was slightly shattered when I discovered that he neither spoke Russian nor knew the meaning of the word *Oprichniki*.* But he had a sympathetic manner which was well suited to the overwrought and nervy customer with whom he now had to deal.

* *Oprichniki*; Russia's earliest Secret Police—the creation of Ivan the Terrible in the 16th century.

I told Soames all I knew, and more that I surmised, from the evidence which I had gathered since the publication of the broadsheet. The Gromov letter was a key point. The photograph in naval uniform taken by Boris Ward—with his Russian connections—gave us another possible clue. I spoke of my belief that the woman represented in at least one of the compromising photographs was Zina, and I gave him a full account of our relationship over the years, including the incident at the National Hotel in 1961. I handed him a photograph of Zina which she had given me, for comparison with the broadsheet, of which Soames had already obtained a copy.

There remained one doubt. Knowing the close collaboration between the Communist intelligence services—after all, Greville Wynne had been arrested by the K.G.B. in Hungary—I could not help thinking of the possibility that the broadsheet might be connected in some way with East Germany. I reminded Soames of my part in the Kodak industrial espionage affair, in which the East Germans had been mentioned and in which a constituent of mine was closely involved. It was odd, to say the least, that the Chairman of Kodak Ltd. had been sent a copy of the broadsheet. As I was employed as Consultant by the firm this could, of course, simply have been intended to damage me commercially. On the other hand, to the best of my knowledge no other of my client-firms—all of whom were well known to both Russians and East Germans—had been approached in this way.

Finally, although the compromising photographs might well be composite, or faked, or both, I told Soames that I could not say, with my hand on my heart, that they were without a possible foundation. Four years had passed since the Moscow incident, and all this, I said, created an atmosphere of doubt which exactly served the purpose of my enemies.

Soames listened with close attention, and he asked a number of questions which revealed a certain skill in the techniques of interrogation. His immense discretion made his reaction seem a little colourless, though I felt that he was grateful—and perhaps a little surprised—at the complete frankness with which I had spoken. After all, it would have been far simpler for me to have simply denied everything. He was wholly non-committal, but said he would study the material I had given him and get in touch with me again as soon as he could.

Now that MI5, and therefore the Government, were fully seized of my end of the story I turned my mind to a pressing problem—the appalling possibilities which stemmed from the copy of the broadsheet which had reached the *News of the World*. I must, somehow, stop the story from "breaking" until I had thought out my best line of action, and I had hopes that the Government might be persuaded to come to my defence. The *News of the World* was quick off the mark, and in no time at all my doorbell rang and one of their leading men, Peter Earle, was standing on my doorstep.

Peter Earle is a highly intelligent newspaperman, and he will not be surprised, in the light of the politician's chronic distrust of his kind, if I say that my first impressions of him were far from favourable. Here was a man who, while outwardly urbane and even sympathetic, had it in his power to print a few lines that could bring all Fleet Street round my ears. He scented a story, and was determined to get it. When he handed over the copy of the broadsheet which his Foreign Editor had received I was not surprised to hear that they had prudently taken a photostat copy.

But Peter (we have since become good friends) was unsure of his ground. This was something new in even his very wide range of experience. As he spoke, I began to realize what a great variety of such matters had come his way and how often it was that, for one reason or another, such material could not be used in the columns of his paper. On this occasion he was feeling his way in unfamiliar surroundings, and I was certainly in no mood to help him. Irritable from lack of sleep and resentful of the whole business, I mustered what courtesy I could in parrying every question and ignoring every speculation on the part of my interrogator—for such, in fact, he was.

At the end of an hour we parted, with a certain mutual respect and the beginnings of a friendly understanding which was to develop in the months ahead. I was able to breathe again, for he had failed to penetrate my defences, and he left my flat reasonably confident that the broadsheet was either the work of a personal enemy, or of a "nut-case". He had concluded that both alternatives had deprived the matter of any serious news-value, at least for the time being.

My immediate crisis was over.

27. *COUP DE GRÂCE*

IN July my wife had been in hospital for an operation, and this new worry was hardly calculated to help her convalescence. We were both on edge, and neither of us sleeping well, but I was able to get home to Chobham every evening now that Parliament had risen.

We went over our problem interminably, and discussed every detail of the plan for a counter-attack which was slowly forming in my mind. On 19th August, Soames joined us for lunch at the flat, and we pooled our ideas. It was now reasonably certain that the broadsheet was of Russian origin. It was an instrument of character assassination, intended to break up my marriage, to ruin me commercially and to secure my removal from the House of Commons.

"I can thank God," I said, "that Liz is standing by me. It may be a hell of a battle but I believe that we shall win in the end."

This was an operation of quite a new kind, of direct attack without any attempt to blackmail. I had given a good deal of study to *Their Trade is Treachery*,* which gives many typical examples of this technique, but present circumstances fitted none of them. Perhaps the Russians had made up their minds that I was not a suitable subject for blackmail but, whatever the reason, they had embarked instead on an operation of straight political destruction. All this was now evident, as was the motive. Virtually alone in the House of Commons, I had

* A Government publication, with restricted circulation, concerning espionage.

felt it my duty to campaign against the misuse of diplomatic immunity by the Russians for espionage purposes. People were beginning to listen, and the K.G.B. had decided that my activities had reached a point at which they must be stopped.

My ex-wife makes a charming hostess, and although the circumstances were depressing I think Soames enjoyed his lunch. As he said goodbye, he assured us again that he would do all he could to help, and we both felt better after his visit. A fortnight had passed since the publication of the broadsheet, we now knew as much of the circumstances as we were likely to find out, and it was time for me to take official action. I rang up 10 Downing Street in order to see George Wigg, who made an appointment for a few days ahead.

Liz returned to Chobham and I was left alone in the flat to mull over the problem. In our discussion over lunch everything had seemed to fall nicely into place, and we now knew the enemy, the motive and the broad extent of the actual attack. But doubt nagged at my mind. Was it quite as simple as it seemed? In my long experience of Russia and the Russians I had learned to mistrust anything which gave an appearance of simplicity. Somehow, my knowledge of the K.G.B.'s power and efficiency did not quite tally with the relative feebleness of this operation. The Russians, more than most, know that it is always a mistake to strike softly. Their target, a British M.P., was surely one which justified the greatest caution, because if the operation went awry, and perhaps even if successful, the repercussions for them might be very serious. This, after all, was a deliberate Soviet intervention in British internal affairs, and its importance was such that it could only be entrusted to the K.G.B. "Resident" himself, working within the Soviet Embassy in London. On the face of it we seemed to have a good chance of suppressing the whole affair. How could the Russians tolerate even the possibility that they might fail? My doubts remained.

On 25th August I saw George Wigg, alone, at 10 Downing Street. He was excited, and his eyes sparkled as we talked. Clearly, his work as Security Adviser to the Prime Minister was proving to his taste, and he had been well briefed on my affairs. George Wigg has a deep-seated dislike of Tories, and he possesses few friends on our side of the House. This incident, with its overtones of the Profumo affair in which he had taken a prominent part, obviously interested him, and he seemed genuinely alarmed at what had occurred. While expressing his personal sympathy with me, he gave no indication of either wishing or being able to take any positive action in my defence. It was not a very reassuring interview.

On the following Sunday, 22nd August, my wife and I gave a lunch-party at Chobham to ten of the officers of the Harrow East Association and their wives. It was one of the most successful of such parties, despite the shadow hanging over our affairs. But there was a jarring note when I returned to the house after showing the last of the guests round the farm. My wife had left a short message that she had "gone away to think . . .". The house seemed very empty, and after tea, when she had not returned, I drove up to the London flat. Feeling rather lost, I wrote some letters and turned in early.

Shortly before midnight Liz arrived. She was in a very nervous state and all sorts of wild fancies seemed to have occurred to her in my absence. I felt desperately sorry for her, but it was wonderful to have her back and our troubles seemed suddenly to take on a less menacing shape. If we could stay like this, it would come right in the end.

Monday was the Roumanian National Day and we had been invited to the usual party in the evening. I was determined to go, and to take my wife with me—for the Russians would be present in force and it would be a great chance of "showing the flag" and of letting the K.G.B. see that, at least, the attack on my marriage had failed.

I always enjoy these Roumanian parties, and this was no exception. Enoch and Pam Powell were already there, and we had a few words together. Liz and Pam had been at the same school, so they had plenty to talk about. I spoke to a few Russians, including Edemsky, the Military Attaché; and Rogov, a "Secretary", both of whom I knew quite well. Having made our presence felt we went home, feeling mildly exhilarated by this first physical contact with the enemy.

By Wednesday my spirits had risen perceptibly. After a good deal of thought and discussion Liz and I had decided that we would call the Soviet bluff, and that I would at once apply for a visa and make arrangements to go to Moscow on my postponed business trip at the end of September. Naturally, I consulted Soames, and he gave it as his opinion that if I did this there would be no risk to my personal safety. At this stage of the game it seemed that the situation as regards the broadsheet was being held and that, with firm action on my part, all might yet be well.

On Thursday, 26th August, I went to Birmingham on business, and on my return to the flat in the evening the second blow fell.

It was to prove mortal.

My wife had left me a note, in which she asked me not to return home and she added ". . . by the time you get this I may be abroad."

The shock was stunning.

At that moment the telephone rang. It was Michael Simmons, who had been trying to get me all day.

Yes—it was true. My wife's solicitors had been round to his house to see him, with the information that she had left me and that she intended to file proceedings for divorce.

Long afterwards I was to discover that, immediately after we had been seen together at the Roumanian Embassy, a single additional copy of the broadsheet was posted to my wife at the Chobham address. The Russians may have assumed that I had succeeded in keeping the thing away from her. They were wrong, but their reaction may well have been the straw that finally broke the camel's back.

I remember sitting with my head in my hands for a very long while as I tried to come to grips with this new situation.

Two things seemed certain. Through the break-up of my marriage the difficulties which lay ahead of me were now immeasurably increased. And from now on I should have to fight my battles quite alone.

There followed a distressing anticlimax.

When a man loses both his wife and his home without

warning, the immensity of the calamity, through the dispensation of a merciful Providence, comes on him only gradually. But in the meanwhile there are small complications that can be very irritating. I had been going home to Chobham every night, so that I found myself with few clothes at the flat and practically no shirts or handkerchiefs. Believing that my wife had, as she had said, gone abroad, I drove down on the following day to collect some things. But as I walked in, I met Liz in the hall. Words passed—and there was a scene such as I hope never to experience again.

28. ISOLATION

THE end of August is about the worst time that any man would choose to be in a flat in London and facing the greatest crisis of his life. Many of my friends were on holiday, Parliament had long since risen, and the increasing loneliness and isolation of my position began to tell on my nerves. My new secretary, poor girl, must have suffered severely from my irritability. There were one or two of those infuriating telephone calls, when the caller waits for an instant in silence before replacing the receiver.

I telephoned George Thomas at the Home Office to ask for his help, and in a matter of hours a pleasant and competent Detective Chief Inspector from the Special Branch had called to see me. As a lifelong admirer of John Buchan and his works I could not help comparing my position with that of the "Portland Place murderer" of *The Thirty-Nine Steps*, with overtones of the kind of international conspiracy which I used to read about in *The Power House*. The Inspector exactly fitted into the picture. He was reassuring, and promised to keep an eye on my flat; but I could not help feeling that he saw in me just another lobby-worn *prima donna* of an M.P. whose nerves were in rags and who badly needed a holiday.

After all, how could he or how could anyone, for that matter, living in our comfortable, secure English society, comprehend the malignant reality of the K.G.B. network which had turned its hand against me? I even rescued an old swordstick from a bag of golf-clubs, which gave me certain comfort at weekends, and I kept my .38 service revolver loaded at my bedside.

On Sunday, 29th August, I drove down into Sussex to unburden myself to an old friend and brother-officer, Kenneth Sellar, now a pillar of the City, and I took him and Molly completely into my confidence. It seemed at that moment that to carry out the postponed trip to Moscow was still the best means available of showing the Russians that I was not to be intimidated, despite the breaking of my marriage. But it would be wise to take precautions, and I left with Kenneth a full account of the affair which he was authorized to make use of at his discretion should anything untoward occur during my absence abroad. He agreed to act in this way in conjuction with Theo Constantine, whom I was seeing the following day.

On the Monday following I drove up for the Harrow Show, and called in on Theo on the way.

Theo once more made no bones of the fact that should the matter come out, I would be "fighting for my political life", as he termed it in his melodramatic fashion and he was particularly concerned by the menace implicit in the words "to be continued" at the end of the broadsheet. Once again he conjured up horrid visions of copies being left about in the local pubs, and he expressed concern about the demoralizing effect it would have. It would upset the constituency workers. Nevertheless, he took the second copy of my account of the affair and promised to act on it with Kenneth Sellar should action be required. Despite all his doubts and fears, I still felt that Theo was a friend on whom I could rely.

The petition for divorce, if it became a fact, would be bound to be damaging, but I felt that there was one man at the heart of affairs in Harrow East, Theo Constantine, who had a full knowledge of the facts, including my previous domestic difficulties, and who would speak out in my support.

Isolation

On 31st August the Diplomatic Correspondent of *The Times* wrote an article on diplomatic immunities which expressed exactly the casual indifference to the realities of the situation which seemed to me to permeate Foreign Office thinking, and against which I had been fighting for so long. The article might have been written on a different planet from that of the broadsheet which lay beside it on my desk. I could imagine it as a subject for discussion over dry martinis, perhaps at Lancaster House, between the author of the article, the head of the Northern Department of the Foreign Office and the Soviet diplomat concerned in the K.G.B. operation, perhaps even the "Resident" himself. To read the article a second time gave me a feeling almost of nausea, and without hesitation I rang the News Editor of *The Times*.

I had some rather important information touching on the subject of diplomatic immunities, I told him, and I was particularly anxious to have a letter in the correspondence column the following morning. If he would agree to accept this letter I would gladly place my information at his disposal.

The News Editor was courtesy itself. He would be glad to accept my letter in the special circumstances as I had explained them, and one of his news reporters would be with me within half-an-hour. The reporter, a friendly and intelligent young man, duly appeared, and I proceeded to tell him the entire story, omitting no detail and including a sight of the broadsheet itself, together with the evidence which I had produced to support my conviction that it was of Soviet origin. Once again I had a feeling of helplessness in attempting to convey, in its utter foulness, an actual example of the activities of the K.G.B. to a nice young Englishman whose mental horizon in such matters seemed bounded by the River at Henley.

He was polite, sincere and painstakingly anxious to avoid the slightest inaccuracy in his voluminous notes. We agreed to meet again for a further discussion with a view to publication of an article covering the whole affair and he took away with him my letter, which duly appeared in *The Times*, of the following morning. It read as follows:—

147

Sir,

Your Diplomatic Correspondent's cosy and informative article on diplomatic privilege surely begs certain rather important questions where relations with Communist countries are concerned. For example, how does he justify his view that the special agreement with Soviet Russia, supplementary to the provisions of the Vienna Convention ". . . gives British Chancery Guards and British servants . . ." what may be called "grade one" immunity, when it is only a matter of months since a fully-accredited "grade one" British diplomat was forcibly detained, searched and deprived of his papers in Khabarovsk? The Foreign Secretary has confirmed in the House of Commons that the incident is not an isolated one. What sort of a guarantee is this to the poor typist in the "bugged" Moscow flat that she will not, when occasion requires, be subjected to forcible entry, arrest or blackmail?

In the excellent official booklet *Their Trade is Treachery*, which the Government still, apparently, do not dare to publish, there are set out factual examples of the mediaeval beastliness practised by the Russian Intelligence Service in pursuit of its objectives. The Bossard investigation, furthermore, has illustrated the most recent success of Soviet espionage, working under "legal" diplomatic cover in London. In these circumstances, is it not ingenuous in the extreme for your Correspondent to state, without any particular comment, that the special agreement with Russia required that ". . . in return, the British Government *have had*" (my italics) to concede similar immunity to the Soviet Mission in London? How long must we wait before our diplomats (and your Correspondent) wake up to the fact that the Russians have forgotten more than we are likely ever to know about the business of blackmail and espionage, including the provision of the necessary operational background?

Sir, some day the great Russian people, for whom I have nothing but affection and respect, will realize that the sinister barbarities institutionalized by Ivan the Terrible's

Oprichniki four centuries ago are no longer tolerable in a civilized Europe which dearly wants them back in the European community on equal terms. Meanwhile, it seems that we in Britain must continue to live with this evil thing operating in our midst—by special diplomatic arrangement between the Governments concerned.

Yours &c.,

This letter expressed as much as anything I have written before or since my frustration at the attitude of blind irresponsibility which seems to govern official British attitude towards the Russians.

On 25th August I had written to Ted Heath, now Leader of the Conservative Party, to ask if I could come and see him to discuss a personal matter of some importance. I knew that the Chief Whip had already informed him in general terms of what had occurred. Heath had been away, and was too tied up on his return to see me immediately, which was a little unfortunate, as I should have liked to have told him the whole story before I saw George Wigg for the first time. Before I was able to do this, however, I had a second meeting with Ministers, again at 10 Downing Street, on 6th September, with the Prime Minister and George Wigg.

Once again I was received with personal sympathy, together with an assurance from Harold Wilson that the affair would not be used against me in a Party political sense, but it was fairly clear that no action was contemplated where the Russians were concerned.

I walked back with George Wigg to his office. He was excited and voluble, though he had kept as quiet as any mouse during the meeting with Harold Wilson.

"What I want to know is—who are they getting at?", he almost shouted, "they are cracking the whip at someone and I want to know who that someone is. This may be just the tip of an iceberg."

This was interesting, but I was far more concerned with my own situation, and I was relieved when he continued.

"The Government has been trying to think of some way in

which to show its confidence in you," he said, and went on to ask me what I would say if they put my name up as one of the candidates for Speaker.*

I told him that I could hardly imagine anyone less likely than myself to make a success of such an arduous job, but the idea was appreciated and I told him that I was grateful. Perhaps after all, I thought, the Government may feel compelled to intervene in some way in my support. But it seemed extraordinary that my fate should lie to such an extent in the hands of this man, George Wigg, for whom I had no liking at all; and whose reputation in Security matters rested principally on his activity in connection with the Profumo affair, I could only expect his decision would be influenced by this experience, a decision which my friends in the Security Service would be powerless to influence.

Two days later I went along to Albany to see Ted Heath. I had asked Theo Constantine to accompany me. Not only had Theo seen a copy of the broadsheet, but he was also President of my Association and Area Chairman of the National Union. He knew all about my previous domestic difficulties and I considered him to be a friend. Ted Heath was waiting for us in his flat, with Willie Whitelaw.

Five weeks had elapsed since I had spoken to Willie on the telephone, and it was only since my discussions with Soames that I had been able to piece the story together and to come to some reasonably firm conclusions. I told Heath of my meetings with Ministers and explained that the compromising photographs in the broadsheet, although they might well be faked, could have been based on an actual incident which took place in 1961. I should have liked to have seen him earlier to tell him this, but he had not been available. The reactions of my hearers were wholly unsympathetic, which is as much as need be recorded of the subsequent discussion.

Two shadows hung over the meeting, those of Jack Profumo and of the General Election which all of us knew could not be long delayed. In regard to this meeting with the Leader of

* Sir Harry Hylton-Foster had just died, and negotiations were proceeding regarding his successor.

my Party I feel it is only right to record my impression of a complete absence of that human quality of personal involvement which to me at any rate is the mark of true leadership towards a colleague in trouble. In heading their broadsheet "I'm not a Profumo, but . . ." the Russian psychology had calculated exactly.

I was ushered coldly from the flat, while Theo remained behind with the Chief Whip.

29. THE PUZZLE

ON the same afternoon as my meeting with Heath, Soames dropped in for a talk. We had developed a friendly personal relationship and I had taken the trouble to make a long tape-recording of my experiences with the Russians which I knew he valued for record purposes. He was personally distressed at the break-up of my marriage, because he realized the damage which it was bound to do me politically, whether or not the matter of the broadsheet came into the light of day. It was, after all, only a fortnight since the three of us had lunch together at the flat. Before he left, Soames made a remark of some significance. He was leaning on the piano as he said it and it made such an impression that I can remember his exact words.

"By the way," he said, "the last time I saw you I gave it as my opinion that there would be no risk to your personal safety if you continue with your intention to visit Moscow. I am afraid I must withdraw what I said then, as I could not give the same advice today."

On the next morning I was summoned to 10 Downing Street, where George Wigg wished to see me for the third time in a fortnight. The principal object of the interview soon became evident, when he asked me directly whether I was still going to carry out my expressed intention of paying the postponed visit to Moscow. I had had some time to think since my talk with Soames, and I had already decided to give up the idea, at least for the time being. I told him so, and George Wigg was greatly relieved.

"Our strong advice to you," he said, "is not to go to Moscow in present circumstances."

This was explicit, but a cowardly way of giving what amounted to an order to the citizen of a free country from a member of the Government. Had he been honest, George Wigg might have said:—

"We are not going to stop you from going to Moscow, because if we did we would have to explain why, and then there would be revelations which at the very least might harm Anglo-Soviet relations. But if you do go, and anything happens to you, we shall consider that, having disregarded this warning, you will have forfeited any claim to our further protection."

I walked back in the September sunlight across the Park to my flat. There was certainly much to think about.

In the space of twenty-four hours I had been given clear notice of the fact that neither the Leadership of my Party nor the Socialist Government were prepared to lift a finger in my support. In the first case I had to assume that, politically speaking, my only further use to the Conservatives would be from a position six feet underground. While, as far as the Socialist Government was concerned, George Wigg and Harold Wilson had washed their hands of me.

Oddly enough, this depressing conviction took second place to a resurgence of the doubts which had assailed me over the whole course of the Russian operation. I felt that I was on to something, but I could not yet say what it was. Some inconsistency—some experience from my Russian past—whatever it was, some instinct told me that something vitally important was bubbling up from the depths of my sub-conscious.

Lunch seemed an irrelevancy, so I poured myself a stiff gin and sat down to think it out.

And then I had it. In one instant all my meandering thoughts crystallized along the clearest lines.

Exactly one week had elapsed between the date of my

intended arrival in Moscow and the posting of the broadsheet in London. For reasons of their own, the Government and the Security Service preferred to pass over this fact as a coincidence. But from my knowledge of Russians I was now absolutely sure in my own mind that it was not.

The K.G.B. is efficient. But it is arrogant from success and it suffers from the rigidity which accompanies its own security and from the chronic inability of Russians to act on their own initiative in unexpected situations. This made it perfectly possible, in my reasoning, for the fact of my non-arrival in Moscow on 25th July *to be unknown to the K.G.B. "Resident" in the London Embassy a week later.*

Things happen like that in Russia. I just did not believe that there was not a direct and planned connection between the posting of the broadsheet and my supposed arrival in Moscow a week earlier.

Dr. Samuel Johnson made a wise remark when he said that ". . . when a man knows he is to be hanged in a fortnight it concentrates his mind wonderfully."

I now knew that I was worse than alone in fighting my battle, for I had become an embarrassment both to my Party and to the Government. The Russians had won the first two engagements. They had broken my marriage and destroyed my business. But I was bothered if they were going to get me out of Harrow East.

My thoughts had slid easily into their new gear, and my mind turned to Gerald Brooke, to Greville Wynne, to Gordon Lonsdale—to the Krogers.

What had been the real scope of "Operation Courtney"?

I came to one firm assumption. This was simply that my physical presence in Moscow was an essential part of the K.G.B.'s plan.

There were then two possible alternatives. First, they may have intended to try blackmail. In accordance with well-established precedent, a suave gentleman, who might well be an acquaintance, would have asked me out to dinner or called on me at my hotel. At a suitable point he would have shown me a copy of the broadsheet. When the effect had sunk in sufficiently, he would have informed me that it was intended to circulate it widely by post in precisely a week from that date—unless of course I were prepared to co-operate with them on lines to be specified later. While I was making up my mind, he might have added, it would be "inconvenient" for me to try and get in touch with the British Embassy. Should I try to do so, the broadsheets would be posted at once.

I have always been half-consciously prepared for a situation of this kind, though no man can say with any certainty just how he would react to it. The Russians knew that I had for years accepted the risk that my business might be brought to a standstill overnight, should I incur their displeasure—and this had now taken place. They have studied me closely over the years, and my guess is that they would calculate that my answer to this type of proposal would be an uncompromising refusal.

On balance I felt sure that the blackmail possibility could be discarded. In any case, why, for this purpose, was it necessary for me to be in Moscow? A simple operation of that kind could quite as easily be mounted in England.

I was left with a second alternative, which was surely the only one which could be made to fit the facts. This was to accept from the outset that it had been intended to arrest me at some time after my arrival in Moscow, as I had planned, on Sunday, 25th July. To support this theory, something had happened, or some information had reached the Security Service which had caused Soames to change the advice which he had given me a week earlier. Then, it had apparently been safe for me to go to Moscow. Now, both he and George Wigg had specifically "advised" me not to go.

The tangle was beginning to unravel, and I tried mentally to put myself in the place of the Second Directorate of the K.G.B. which would be responsible for an affair of this kind.

As constructed in my imagination, "Operation Courtney" had been planned in two Phases, the first to begin on D–Day, 25th July, when I was due to arrive in Moscow.

My journey was on business and I should have been left alone for the first day or two to make my arrangements in the normal way and in particular to make my accustomed call on the British Ambassador. Having done this, the Embassy would not necessarily expect to be in contact with me again before my departure.

On D+3 or D+4, I estimated, they would have arrested me, possibly at my hotel, but more probably on my way to or from a business appointment. I should have been taken to the K.G.B. headquarters on the *Lubyanskaya Ploshchad* and interrogated, using the methods which have become so sickeningly familiar in such cases. There is little doubt that I should have been charged with espionage, for the Russians would have been able to use my background in Naval Intelligence to build up a plausible story. They would have doubtless been helped by Philby and others in recording my contacts with the Secret Intelligence Service. Naturally, I should have been held incommunicado, and denied any contact with the British Embassy.

By the weekend, whether or not my absence had become known, the Russians would have been ready with their story, no doubt of the unmasking of an experienced British agent, operating under the guise of a businessman and claiming the special position customarily accorded by the Russians to British Members of Parliament.

They knew that in England the House was about to rise for the summer recess, so that no co-ordinated action by back-benchers would be likely. They would perhaps calculate that the Labour Government would not be unduly concerned over the fate of a Conservative who had embarrassed them in this and other ways. The Russians have studied us closely enough to be able to forecast the ensuing situation with some accuracy —the demands for immediate consular access—the "strong protest"—followed by the talk of "no smoke without fire" and a general tendency to allow events to take their course while Parliament and people went on holiday.

I have remarked on many occasions upon the curious psychological ascendancy which the Russians have established over the British Foreign Office, and I just do not believe that the fuss and hullabaloo which would have followed my arrest would have stimulated the Government into taking any effective action.

But meanwhile, on or about D + 7, the K.G.B. would have put Phase Two into operation. This was planned to consist of the wide circulation of a defamatory broadsheet with the object of countering as far as possible the reaction in England to Phase One. The weakness of my matrimonial situation had been revealed to the K.G.B. by the events of August 1964, and it is surely significant that in fact no less than three copies of the broadsheet were posted to my wife. In this way they may have reckoned, quite correctly as it turned out, that the main prop and support of my defence would be knocked away.

In my absence, the selective circulation of the broadsheet could have been relied on to do me the maximum political damage, and the Russians had guarded against the possibility of "hushing-up" by sending a copy to the *News of the World*. Human nature and British institutions being what they are, the K.G.B. must have felt that they could hardly miss. The poison of character assassination, *in the absence of the victim*, could surely be relied on to spread quickly within our bourgeois society. In any case, by the time they had finished with me in the *Lubyanka* I should have been in no fit state either physically or mentally to have regained the ground lost. My political liquidation must have been complete.

But Russians are excellent card-players, and they would have appreciated the value of the trump which they held in their hand. Soviet spies, notably the Krogers, were still being held in English jails. Gordon Lonsdale had been successfully traded for the infinitely less significant Greville Wynne. But public opinion had stuck at the exchange of the university lecturer, Gerald Brooke, for other Soviet spies. However, an M.P. with such a record of Intelligence involvement would certainly turn the scale. In this way the Krogers, at least, would join Lonsdale, Abel, Maclean, Philby and the rest as a living testimony to the power of the K.G.B. to look after its own.

This is how my thoughts turned on that September afternoon, and I felt that I had come as close to the truth as was possible on the evidence available.

The actual course of events had been thrown out of gear by my non-arrival in Moscow on 25th July. But despite this hitch in the proceedings, Phase Two had been put into operation on D+7 as originally ordered. Had someone blundered? Whether they had or not, I was determined that the K.G.B. should pay for its mistake.

Two months later an article in *Izvestia*, the official Soviet Government newspaper (see Appendix C) lent support to my theory in one important respect. In denying that they ever contemplated arresting me the article was at pains to point out that I had not been granted a Soviet visa for the July trip, as there was no necessity, from the business point of view, for me to make the journey at all. The Russians are careful in making such statements, and their explicit denial of a fact which can be proved so simply is strong evidence of their sinister intent. The actual visa is reproduced on plate 10.

30. DILEMMA

IN my disillusion over the amount of support to be expected from either the Socialist Government or the Conservative Party leadership I flew to Wolverhampton on 10th September to see Enoch Powell. It was weather in which no normal person would have taken a small aeroplane into the air, but I was past caring, and I welcomed the stimulus of the practical and intellectual exercise involved. I was forced down by low visibility on a disused airfield, miles out of my course, but ascertained my position from a passing motorist and flew on to Wolverhampton in a rainstorm, arriving at Enoch's house just an hour late on schedule. It was a rewarding visit, to escape out of the morass of insincerity and political expediency to a quiet talk with a man of inflexible principle and an intellect and experience which far out-stripped my own.

I had come to visit a Conservative politician whom I

scarcely knew, but greatly respected. After a long talk with Enoch and tea with the family I felt I had left behind a friend whose advice I was prepared to follow, whose sympathy and understanding would help me to face my problems.

The first step was to take counsel's opinion on the broadsheet. What protection could the law give me against the further circulation of this vicious libel? I was very worried about the constituency, as there was an ominous silence from Theo, Jack Shrimpton and the Agent. My lawyers now told me that a fresh copy of the broadsheet had come somehow into my wife's possession, and that she had showed it to various members of her family. I was pretty certain that it would be used as grounds for the divorce proceedings which we knew were in train. On 17th September, accordingly, we had a long session with David Hirst, Q.C. in the Middle Temple.

Counsel was uncompromising in his view of my prospects, and this was gloomy in the extreme. Two of the Russian objectives had been achieved, and it seemed inevitable that the third, my removal from the House of Commons, would be effected by a gradual process of attrition within the constituency. This process was being supported tacitly, but none the less effectively, I had no doubt, by the leadership of my own Party. The hand held by my opponents seemed to be overwhelmingly strong, but I held a few cards which, if played with skill and resolution, might perhaps still save the game.

It seemed astonishing, and quite intolerable, that a Foreign Power should be able to intervene in this way in British internal affairs, apparently with impunity, and destroy a political opponent out of hand, while his own Party and his own Government stood aside and pretended not to see what was happening.

Being only human, I had considered the possibility of bowing to the storm, resigning my seat and disappearing into obscurity. The critical state of my finances indicated that I might be forced to do this anyway. But now reaction had set in, and I felt spitting mad that the K.G.B. should be trying their filthy methods out on ME. For a moment I had wild ideas of shooting Soldatov—of crashing the Parliamentary

Airedale on 13 Kensington Palace Gardens. The second idea fitted in well with another alternative—suicide—which, I must confess, had also occurred to me. There seemed to be no other way to bring the matter home. But then sanity returned. I decided, soberly enough, that it would only be over my dead body that I would let the Russians win.

One of the few cards left in my hand was the judicious use of publicity, which was obviously feared by both the Government and the Party. If I could use the Press to put the truth across to the best advantage there was still a chance that I might weather the political storm and retain my seat in the House of Commons. I had succeeded so far in putting the newshounds off the scent, so I still held the initiative. But on the other hand a leakage which emphasized the more salacious aspect of the broadsheet could do me great harm. The material was there for my enemies to use if they wished to do so, and my mind turned continually to that sinister little phrase "to be continued" at the foot of the broadsheet.

My isolation was almost complete, and there seemed to be no-one to whom I could turn for advice in the appalling dilemma in which I found myself. Left to myself, my instinct was to "publish and be damned". But I knew in my heart that it was not nearly as simple as that.

I had again seen Willie Whitelaw, who had counselled silence, in my own interests as well as those of the Party. I was to see Willie on many subsequent occasions, and in spite of all that has occurred we have remained friends. His problem was a difficult one, for in his position as Chief Whip he had somehow to reconcile a loyalty to the Shadow Cabinet, to Ted Heath as Leader of the Party, and to me as a backbench member of his flock.

With a General Election in prospect, every political consideration dictated that any publicity concerning a Conservative M.P. which might be even remotely associated with the Profumo scandal must be stifled at all costs. Willie's steady and consistent advice to me, therefore, was not to publish. In this he maintained that my personal interest coincided with that of the Party, and although I now think that he was wrong, I am glad to give him the benefit of any doubt concerning the sincerity of his opinion as expressed to me. Certainly, it was Willie's advice that stopped me from giving the Press a complete account of the affair during September.

By the first week in October a new factor had arisen, and publicity on my own initiative suddenly became impossible.

The new factor was this. My wife had filed her petition for divorce, and the announcement was widely reported in the Press. The grounds which she alleged were adultery with Zina Volkova in Moscow at some date in 1963. It followed that the broadsheet would be used in evidence. As a consequence, the matter was *sub judice*, and my lawyer told me that it was now too late to publish my story without exposing myself to the risk of prosecution for contempt of court. Overnight, I had lost the initiative.

At the same time, there had been a second development. I now had reason to believe that if I were willing to produce other evidence of adultery my wife might consider dropping the Russian case and proceeding on the new evidence alone.

The horns of my dilemma were dismally clear. Should I simply fight the present petition, and win—as I felt sure I would? By doing this I would have to accept the damage arising from the production of the Russian broadsheet in court. Or should I produce new evidence of adultery on which a fresh petition could be based?

Few men can have been faced with such a cruel choice.

31. THE DAM BREAKS

THESE days of the autumn of 1965 were rather dreadful. I had set myself a programme of canvassing in the constituency, concentrating on the wards where we were weakest, and a minute of the Harrow East Executive Council held in July records that "the canvassing which had been taking place with the Member had been highly successful". But despite the friendliness which I met on nearly all doorsteps, the shadow of the Russian broadsheet hung over all, and I was now agonizingly sure that it was only a matter of time before the whole affair "broke" in the national Press.

On 20th September I accepted an invitation to lunch on board the Soviet naval survey vessel *Nikolai Zubov*, lying in the Pool of London. Russian sailors I like and understand, besides which my old Admiral, Geoffrey Miles, and other friends of former days were among the guests. It was quite a memorable occasion, and I wondered how long it would be before I should once again be on normal terms with my Russian hosts.

On 24th September I had had another visit from Peter Earle of the *News of the World*. This time he was accompanied by his News Editor. Their news sense told them that somewhere in my vicinity there was a publishable story, and although the divorce petition had not then been filed I think they knew that my wife had left me. Human sympathy and journalistic persistence were struggling within Peter's breast and I began to feel that here was one pressman, at least, who would be on my side when the time came. But that time was not yet, and they left me little wiser.

"Now I know why the Navy is known as the Silent Service" was the Editor's parting remark.

Social occasions were becoming something of an effort, and the Chinese National Day celebrations on 1st October were not the pleasure to which I had previously been accustomed. The Russians were present in force, as usual, and I felt that those few who knew the state of Operation Courtney were happy to let the inevitable process take its course, and were waiting contentedly for the kill.

I was now becoming aware, too, of movement within the constituency, where Theo Constantine seemed to be playing the leading part. On 6th October I lunched with Jack Shrimpton, whose manner indicated quite clearly that opinion among the constituency officers had hardened against me. He was having his own worries and was genuinely sympathetic with

me in my predicament, but he left no doubt in my mind that
there was already talk of "possible resignation" among the few
who knew the facts about the broadsheet. The divorce petition
had done a lot of damage, and he advised me strongly to supply
other evidence, if there were any available, and suitable, in
the hope that by that means I could get the present petition
withdrawn.

This was to be the substance of much advice from various
people in the weeks to come. There had seemed to be a hope
that the nature of the broadsheet could be kept quiet, but this
conversation with Jack showed me that people were starting
to talk, and to this there could be but one end. Since my
friendly duel with the representatives of the *News of the World*
no word had been heard from Fleet Street.

But on 14th October my cautious optimism was shattered by
a telephone call.

It was Peter Gladstone-Smith of the *Sunday Telegraph*, and
my heart sank.

He asked if he could come and see me. The matter was
somewhat urgent, he said. (It flashed across my mind that it
was Thursday afternoon.)

So this was it. The fat was in the fire. Within a short while
my doorbell rang. It was Gladstone-Smith. He sat down, and
lost little time in coming to the point.

"There is a very strong rumour going around Fleet Street,"
he said, "that the Russians have given some information to
your wife which she is using for the divorce petition which has
been filed against you." He was sure that a story would soon
"break" and he had come to me in fairness to tell me about these
rumours and to check the facts. He implied that he had plenty
to go on for an article in the *Sunday Telegraph*, but as I obviously
knew all about it, could I help?

It was a pistol at my head, and we both knew it, but I had
time to feel glad that this was a responsible Sunday newspaper,
and not an importunate "daily", impatient and jealous of
tomorrow's headlines.

Gladstone-Smith is a tough member of the Press fraternity,
but I was sure from the outset that I could trust him if he felt

it would be in his interests to bargain with me. From my point of view it was vital that the story should come out in the most favourable manner possible. I sensed that he was himself largely in the dark, so some agreement might suit us both.

It was the third time, and it was to be by no means the last, that I had found it necessary to take a journalist into my confidence, and it is pleasant to be able to record that in no instance has this confidence been misplaced.

I told Gladstone-Smith sufficient of the truth for him to see that his story would benefit immeasurably from my co-operation.

"But I must make two conditions," I said. "I want to see your draft before publication. Also, I must have a day's grace. The Tory Conference is on at Brighton, and I have promised the Chief Whip that I would warn him, if I could, before any publicity took place."

If Gladstone-Smith agreed, I proposed that we should meet again on the following evening after I had seen the Chief Whip, and if he would bring along his draft I would do my best to make it as accurate and interesting as possible. I thought I could assure him that, so far, none of his fellow-journalists were on the scent, and this relieved him a lot.

It seemed a fair offer, and it was accepted. We parted on terms of excellent understanding.

There was not much sleep for me that night. Where the Party was concerned, this was the crunch. I could not escape a grudging admiration for the Russian psychology which had headed the broadsheet "I'm not a Profumo but . . ." and ended it "To be continued", just before a General Election. Now there was the certainty of publicity a few days ahead, and my standing with the leadership of the Party must inevitably lose any shreds of sympathy and support which might have remained to my credit. By Sunday morning I should have become a political outcast.

It was with these thoughts in my mind, and I must confess a sinking heart, that I drove down to Brighton after lunch the next day. In and around the Conference Hall I ran into many friends who greeted me warmly, oblivious of the underlying situation which was soon to make me a political untouchable.

Those who buttonholed me for a word on my way down the hall little realized how soon they would prefer to forget that they had ever known me.

I found Willie at the back of the hall. It was a bad moment, for he was listening to the special debate on Rhodesia.

Patrick Wall and Salisbury were to speak. Would Rhodesia split the Party? He turned a gloomy eye on me as I approached, and it took all his fund of affability to pretend that he was pleased to see me.

Willie did his best to listen as I tried to penetrate the din, but it was with only half an ear. His gaze rested lugubriously on the rows of heads which stretched away down the hall in front of us. At intervals, as he listened, he would start, almost audibly, to count—a habit acquired from his long experience as "Pairing Whip".

"Publicity," I managed to utter, at a pause in the general pandemonium.

At the sound of this dreadful word Willie's attention was diverted, for a brief moment, from Rhodesia.

"I'm afraid there is nothing that either you or I can do to stop it," I said, but added encouragingly, "however, I am seeing the man again tomorrow and I will certainly try. I'll do my best."

My companion reverted to his previous mood. The considerable mental effort of switching to my problem was obviously distasteful. As I moved off through the crowd I was glad to get away. This was no longer any place for me.

Back in the flat, Michael Simmons, my lawyer, was waiting, and our gloom deepened as the doorbell rang. It was Gladstone-Smith, perky and business-like—perhaps a shade unsure of his reception.

With whisky-and-soda at our elbow we went through the draft which Gladstone-Smith had produced.

It really wasn't at all bad.

From a few facts and a good deal of rumour he had built up a passably accurate story.

As we finished reading, Michael and I exchanged a glance of understanding and I turned to Gladstone-Smith.

"This is a pretty good effort on your part," I said, "and with my lawyer here to support me, I should like to renew my offer of last night. There are gaps and inaccuracies in your story, and I know I can make it much better. If you will undertake not to publish any more than we can agree, I will improve it for you."

It may have been unorthodox, but this was not a time for beating about the bush, and I was greatly relieved when Gladstone-Smith accepted my offer.

We set to work, and within the hour Gladstone-Smith left the flat. He had got hold of a first-class story. As for ourselves, we had retained the initiative, and the publicity which was now inevitable would, from our point of view, be launched along the right lines.

32. PRESS AND POLITICS

THE main *Sunday Telegraph* article on 17th October, 1965, ran as follows:—

"Information has reached Whitehall that the Russian Intelligence Service, K.G.B., intended to detain Commander Anthony Courtney, Conservative M.P. for Harrow East, on a trumped-up charge in Moscow in July. There is evidence in London that the K.G.B. has watched Cdr. Courtney during visits to Moscow on business as an Export Consultant. Secret devices, including the "bugging" of his hotel room with cameras, have been used. But for the resignation of Sir Alec Douglas-Home as Conservative Shadow Prime Minister in July, Cdr. Courtney would have gone to Moscow and walked into the hands of the K.G.B. It is believed that he would have been held incommunicado while negotiations were made for an exchange with the Krogers, or George Blake, now serving prison sentences for espionage in Britain.

"But instead Cdr. Courtney cancelled the trip for which he had already obtained visas. He stayed in London for a meeting of the 1922 Committee which elected Mr. Heath as Conservative Parliamentary leader. Copies of a scurrilous and defamatory broadsheet prepared by the K.G.B. and concerning Cdr. Courtney have reached London. It is believed in Whitehall that this is a premature leakage and that the Russian security men have made a vital mistake. It is believed that this was phase two of an operation in which phase one was intended to be the detaining of Cdr. Courtney in Moscow. There is strong evidence in London that the origin of these documents is in Moscow. Cdr. Courtney, 57, is a former head of the Russian section of Naval Intelligence. He speaks Russian and served in Moscow and north Russia during the war. On July 8 he tabled a Commons motion attacking the "habitual abuse of diplomatic privilege for espionage purposes" by the Russian and other Iron Curtain country embassies in London. He has campaigned for several years against the granting of full diplomatic immunity by special bilateral arrangement to the entire staffs of Communist embassies in London. He has often quoted the particular instance of the 20 chauffeurs employed by the Soviet, Czechoslovak, Hungarian and Bulgarian missions.

"The K.G.B.'s operation is seen in Whitehall as an attempt to eliminate a serious political opponent. This would be done by trying to discredit Cdr. Courtney in his absence from the country, destroy his career in the Commons, and to deprive him of his business which lies mainly in Russia. Soon after Parliament reassembles next week Cdr. Courtney intends to take Parliamentary action. He has given the full facts of the case to Mr. Wilson and to the Government.

"He has been advised not to visit the Soviet Union for the time being. Cdr. Courtney was due to go to Rumania next month in a delegation of six M.P.s of the Inter-Parliamentary Union invited by the Rumanian Government. On advice he has decided not to go. It will be recalled that Mr. Greville

Wynne was arrested by Russian security men in Budapest in November, 1962. Since he retired from the Royal Navy in 1953, Cdr. Courtney has made frequent business trips to Moscow and two to Peking. In 1962 he protested in Moscow about the holding of Mr. Wynne incommunicado.

"Parliamentary colleagues have found themselves being quizzed in Moscow about Cdr. Courtney's visits to China. For some reason they seemed to arouse some Russian antagonism. Although utterly opposed to Communism, Cdr. Courtney has described the Chinese leaders as "the first strong, settled government for 50 years, directing a purposeful, dedicated society."

"In 1957 he was interrogated by Polish secret police at Poznan, Poland, on suspicion of being a British spy, and released after 2½ hours. Cdr. Courtney makes no secret of his respect and liking for the Russian people. He has many times expressed his conviction that it is only through trade with Communist countries that we can hope to establish normal relations with Eastern Europe. He said to me last night: 'This unexpected action by the Russian secret police is a severe setback to my hopes of contributing towards an improvement in Anglo-Soviet relations. It amply justifies the criticisms I have made about the misuse of diplomatic immunity by the Soviet Embassy in London'."

Sunday morning was surprisingly quiet, and apart from the *Express* there were no telephone calls from the Press. That was to come later. At midday the man from *The Times* came round, and we agreed the text of a fuller article based on the information which I had given him. But there was one snag. His paper, cautious as always, could not accept the evidence of the letter which had been reproduced on the broadsheet as indicating with any certainty that the document was of Soviet origin. Their man referred to my manipulation of the photographic enlargement, but in terms which implied too much doubt for my liking. I told him unless his Editor could accept the point I would not allow him to publish, and the article was for this reason never printed. I still believe that this decision on my part was correct. I had failed to convey to *The Times* representative any real understanding of the ruthlessness and foulness of K.G.B. methods, and in these circumstances it would be better from my point of view for the paper to print nothing.

On the previous day my brother Godfrey had rung up, surprisingly, to tell me that he was in England. He normally lives in Australia but was on business in Beirut, and my wife had summoned him urgently to get his help in resolving our family problems. He came to lunch, and I was able to tell him the whole story. In return he passed on a good deal of information which he had gleaned since his arrival. He told me that Theo had been down to Chobham to see my wife, and that both Theo and Jack Shrimpton had been in touch with her on the telephone. I was also told that there had been a meeting between Heath, Maudling, Du Cann and Theo at which doubts had been expressed about my veracity and good faith in handling the subject matter of the broadsheet.

I was very glad to see my brother, who gave me the full and solid support which I would have expected from him, but who was not able to help very much in the short time which he could spare to remain in this country. After lunch the telephone started to ring, and to avoid a spate of calls from the daily newspapers I drove out of London to see friends in Sussex and to stay with my brother-in-law by my first marriage who had bought my old house in Slinfold. It was a haven of refuge to which I knew I could always escape, and I shall always be grateful to my sister-in-law and her family for the kindness and understanding which they have consistently extended to their turbulent relative.

On Monday I returned to London with fresh heart to face my numerous problems. There was to be a routine meeting of the Harrow East Executive on the Wednesday, and I had discussed with Jack Shrimpton the desirability of making a statement to them, now that the story had at least partially "broken". The same evening I had arranged to canvass in Queensbury ward with Darryl and Betty King, Fred Chandler and my old friend the Chairman of the ward, Eric Pratt. As usual, we met in front of Timothy White's in Queensbury Circle, and moved off together into a group of neighbouring streets. As always in Queensbury, it was a heartening experience to find such a wide measure of political and personal support in a predominantly Socialist ward. I had in my pocket a copy of the statement which I intended to make to the Executive at Wednesday's meeting, and in an interval during canvassing I showed it to Eric, who was himself a member of the Executive and who had not heard that anything special was coming up at the meeting. Indeed, had I not spoken to him he would in all probability not have attended it.

Eric is a highly qualified electronic engineer, with heavy business responsibilities which have given him experience of dealings with Communist Eastern Europe, and he saw at once the importance of the affair. His reaction was forthright and typical.

"You were an ass, Anthony, ever to expose yourself to an operation of this kind," he said, "but what you did cannot seriously be held against you by any decent-minded man or woman. Good God! There are precious few of us who would not want to forget events of this sort in our own lives. What is really important is that the Russians should not be allowed to get away with it. Already there is much too much malicious gossip going round the constituency. How I wish you had told me about this sooner!"

It seemed clear that I was breaking my silence only just in time, as the earlier undertaking between Theo, Jack, Jo Burton and myself that we would not talk to any other members of the Association was now demonstrably out of date. On Tuesday, however, Jack and I had another talk on the telephone. I had still to see the Party leaders about the action which I was contemplating in the new Session of Parliament. There was also the continuing handicap of the divorce petition, which effectively blocked any reference to the substance of the broadsheet attack.

Jack and I therefore decided that, in view of all this, it would be better not to raise the matter at Wednesday's meeting, and although I still feel that this decision was a correct one in the circumstances of the moment, I had foregone yet another opportunity of stating my case personally to the Executive of my Association.

A Minute of this Executive Council meeting reads as follows: "The Chairman referred briefly to the recent Press publicity concerning the Member of Parliament, but did not feel that any advantage would result from discussing the matter at the present time. *He had been advised* (my italics) that the Member should not appear before the Executive Council prior to making his proposed statement to the House of Commons."

I am still not clear where this "advice" was obtained. Jack was being personally friendly and helpful, but I knew that he was being subjected to various outside pressures and that he was unlikely to retain a grip of the situation such as I would have hoped for in normal circumstances.

On the afternoon of the 18th October I had another talk with the Chief Whip: it was not a particularly happy one. Willie was worried at the turn which events had taken, and like Jack Shrimpton he stressed the importance of my supplying other evidence for a divorce if it were available and if by that means it would be possible to get the existing petition withdrawn. His attitude to me was now wholly dominated by what I can only describe as the "Profumo sub-conscious", and it became clear to me that the Party leadership was simply unable to accept my views on any points which conflicted with their conviction that publicity must seriously damage the "image" of the Conservative Party. I told Willie of my talks with Mr. Speaker on the subject, and with the Clerk of the House. I could see that he was in difficulties, for his loyalties to the Party leadership were now coming into conflict with his personal support for me as a backbencher. I think also that there had grown up between us a certain bond of human sympathy which tempered the steel of political ruthlessness which is a Chief Whip's *sine qua non*.

The sequel to this meeting occurred on the following day, when I had an unhappy twenty minutes with Willie and Ted Heath in the latter's room at the House of Commons.

I have mentioned Willie's nervous habit of biting his nails when under stress, and never has it been more noticeable than on this occasion. Ted Heath, it appeared, had seen Harold Wilson about my affairs and had received from the Prime Minister information which appeared to conflict in certain respects with what I was now able to tell him. I felt more than ever that my words and conduct continued to be viewed with misgiving amounting to mistrust by the Leader of my Party; and it began to seem that there was nothing I could say which would convince him of the inherent genuineness of my case. Apart from this he made the mistake of trying to bully me, with a kind of hectoring pomposity which I found particularly offensive.

"If you proceed with your intention of a Parliamentary statement on these lines," he said, "the Government will disown you. How then can you expect me to give you any support?"

He had been late for our appointment, and time was short, as I had to speak in a B.B.C. broadcast about the Hungarian diplomatic defector, Szabo. Our meeting, therefore, came to a premature end on an acrimonious note which, I am glad to say, has not since been repeated. But it had enabled me to give Ted Heath some points of information which were clearly in direct contradiction of what he had received from other sources.

I now felt that I must see Theo Constantine again as soon as possible. Accordingly, the following day we lunched together at the Carlton, and I taxed him with the fact that he had been in contact with my wife, which was highly undesirable if I were to weather the political storm which was gathering over my head. It was scarcely a festive occasion, and it now seems clear that I was misled, for I have a note in my diary that after a frank talk with Theo we had once again "made friends".

As the week drew on, the Sunday newspapers began to draft their follow-up articles, and I had a long session with Peter Earle of the *News of the World*, once again with my lawyer Michael Simmons in attendance. As original recipients of the broadsheet, who had held their hand, Peter Earle and his colleagues were a little sore, perhaps justifiably, at having been "scooped" by the *Sunday Telegraph* in the previous week. However, they had earned my gratitude by their forbearance, and I was able to help them with an article, supported by photographs, which I think was what they wanted and which was certainly well received.

33. CONSTITUENCY CURRENTS

IN the constituency, the *Sunday Telegraph* article had aroused lively interest, and when I went canvassing in Stanmore early in the week the reaction was wholly favourable. The surmise that the Russians had intended to arrest me was generally accepted as likely to be true, for it was known that I had done a great deal in the House to expose the machinations of the K.G.B., and this fact supplied an obvious motive. People were intrigued with the amateur detective work which led to the identification of the Gromov letter, and they were delighted that their M.P. had had what appeared to be such a lucky escape.

At the end of the week I was at a Young Conservative dance at the King's Head. The young were far too well-mannered to say anything to me which would imply curiosity, and the fact that I had for so long been associated in their minds with Russia and Communist countries in general was sufficient to convince them that there was a lot which had not been revealed behind the newspaper reports which they had seen and the rumours which had begun to circulate. The great thing was that I had their sympathy and their trust.

Once again the *Sunday Telegraph* and the *News of the World* printed stories, and even with one's inevitable reservations on the subject of journalistic presentation I felt that the affair had been given valuable publicity of the right kind.

Parliament was to reassemble shortly, and I had made it known in the constituency that I was contemplating

Parliamentary action at the earliest practicable opportunity. The problem was to decide on the method most suitable to tell the story in the manner least damaging to my Parliamentary interests.

The personal statement, which I had considered had been discouraged by my friends as being not wholly applicable in the circumstances. Alternatively, I might raise the matter as a question of Parliamentary privilege, and here I received professional advice which was somewhat conflicting. One senior official held that a breach of privilege could not be claimed against foreigners, who in any case were difficult to identify. Another, an officer of the House, maintained that the issue *could* be considered as one of privilege, but that it would inevitable be referred to the Committee of Privileges, which was by its nature not a very suitable body to report on an affair of this type. Furthermore, the Press would be muzzled during the period in which the matter was *sub judice*, and this might prove a serious disadvantage. The same official suggested an Adjournment Debate as the best Parliamentary vehicle in the circumstances.

Adjournment Debates are the opportunity given to back-benchers to raise matters of special interest in the course of a half-hour debate at the end of the Parliamentary day, and the official whom I consulted gave it as his opinion that Mr. Speaker might well consider the matter to be of sufficient importance to justify selection at an early date. A Minister would have to reply to the debate on behalf of the Government, the record would be in *Hansard*, and the publicity would assuredly be considerable. There were, however, disadvantages. The subject might not be immediately selected, with consequent delay. If the debate occurred late at night, as is frequently the case, it would miss full coverage in the national press the following day. Both considerations were important.

There remained one other possibility—the Debate on the Address. This is the debate on the Humble Address which is presented to Her Majesty in response to the Gracious Speech on the opening of Parliament, and by tradition it gives wide latitude to backbench members to raise matters of individual interest. Mr. Speaker was aware of the circumstances, and I had no doubt that I should have the privilege of catching his eye should I wish to do so. I should be speaking at the earliest practicable moment in the new Session of Parliament and there was a good chance of my being called early in the evening. Here, it seemed, lay my best opportunity of the Parliamentary action which I had promised my constituents to take.

On 26th October I put the point to Willie Whitelaw, who was as approachable, helpful and personally sympathetic as ever. But his dislike of any further publicity was as great as always, although he realized that I had committed myself to Parliamentary action and must go through with it. Willie even suggested that I might go abroad for a few months, in the hope that the whole thing would peter out while I was away. But it was a counsel of despair which I was in no mood to accept, and discussion then turned to the Debate on the Address. In his view the actual content of the speech would be a matter for negotiation if I was to get any support from the Government, and for this purpose it would be necessary for me to let him have a draft of what I wished to say. There was plenty of time, as the debate was a fortnight away, and it was a relief to have come at last to the decision to speak out. Willie had done his best to dissuade me, and I still think that in giving this advice he felt that my personal interests coincided with those of the Party, but I was certain that the action contemplated was the best and perhaps the only means of retaining the initiative.

34. ACTION IN PARLIAMENT?

IT was a relief, after all the comings and goings of the previous three months, to set my mind at last to drafting the speech which I intended to make in the Debate on the Address, assuming always that I could catch Mr. Speaker's eye. The constituency knew that I contemplated Parliamentary action of some sort as early as possible in the new session, but I had told no-one outside my lawyer, counsel and my main political contact, Willie Whitelaw, just what form it was going to take. Willie had, I believe, informed the Government, and I had undertaken to give him a draft of my proposed speech for submission to Ministers.

I sat down to prepare my draft—and at once ran into trouble. My object, as it had been throughout the manoeuvrings of previous months, was to place before the House of Commons and the public the full story of the operation which had been carried out against me by the Russian Intelligence Service, as I believed, for endangering their "legal" espionage organization in this country. But it was one thing to make a case in debate about a question of national security. It was quite another to raise the issue against the background of my special experience and thus make it a matter of personal interest. The problem arose from the fact that the two aspects of the Russian operation were inseparable.

It is wrong in principle, and thoroughly distasteful to the House, for a Member to raise personal issues in the course of general debate, and the substance of the case against the Russians would suffer from this cause. But on the other hand it was impossible to point out the seriousness of the matter unless it was put in terms of actual personal experience, which happened to be mine.

The ideal would have been to have persuaded one of my colleagues to raise the question on my behalf, and I had considered this line of action. But the average backbencher recoils in dismay at any suggestion of personal involvement in the murky intricacies of Soviet espionage. With the best will in the world, furthermore, and with friends who I know would have taken action had I asked them to do so, there was *no-one* other than myself who possessed the background knowledge which alone would carry conviction in the House and in the country.

The Russians had made a perfect psychological calculation in exploiting these difficulties, which arose from the meeting of two worlds, from the intrusion of Russian secret police activities within the British concept of a free society. Secondly, there was still the problem of the divorce petition which, being opposed and defended by me, was unlikely to be heard for many months and continued effectively to muzzle me. I began once again to suffer agonies of frustration and indecision. Nevertheless, I set to work and produced a draft, which I gave to Soames to read when he came again to the flat on 1st November. Discreet as ever, he made no comment, but I sensed that he thought as little of it as I did. On the following day I showed the draft to my counsel, David Hirst, who had now had time to study the personal and political implications of my intended move. He knew that I was committed to take some Parliamentary action, but he did not think much of the line proposed.

Half-told, there would be important gaps in my story which could be filled by ill-wishers to my disadvantage. Speculation was inevitable, and it would be difficult to correct subsequently. The advantageous points had already been aired in the newspapers. *We should leave well alone.* I must say that I was relieved at his opinion, tore up my draft and rang Willie to tell him of my decision.

At the end of the week I had a constituency engagement that I always enjoy, the annual dinner of the Harrow Weald Memorial Club. This is a masculine occasion, usually attended by about 200 members who cram the Memorial Hall to capacity, and it is followed by an excellent entertainment. The party was as enjoyable as always, and it gave me a fine opportunity of testing the feelings of an important section of the constituency towards my misfortunes. I had recently been elected a member of the Club and felt myself to be among friends, so it was specially comforting to meet such a wave of sympathy. I understood that I had their sympathy and support in fighting the efforts of the Russians to do me damage. It was a breath of fresh air by contrast with the dubious currents of gossip which I knew were beginning to circulate in Stanmore.

On 10th November another blow fell, from a quarter which I had hoped would not take a hand in my affairs, but to whom these proved irresistible. *Private Eye*, which I had heard of but never read, published a long article. It was cleverly written, with a brand of salacity which served at least one useful purpose, in that it seized on the essentials of the Russian operation in a manner not wholly unfavourable to myself and commented with brutal frankness on the embarrassment which the affair was causing in political circles. The author was rather disturbingly well-informed, as he was aware that I intended to raise the matter during the Debate on the Address, a point which I had been at pains to conceal. "Terrified of anything which smacks of Profumo", he wrote concerning myself, "Heath and his lieutenant Edward du Cann are doing their damnedest to shut the fellow up." The article concluded with a remark about the utter incompetence of the Russians as scandal-mongers for not sending the broadsheet to their paper in the first place. They had a point there, and only in one respect was their information faulty. I had not exchanged a single word with Edward du Cann since the whole affair started in the previous August.

I think it was the *Private Eye* article, followed not long afterwards by a short piece of cheap nastiness on B.B.C. Television, that did me most harm in the constituency, and it seemed to me that, from 10th November onwards, the position deteriorated rapidly.

Once again I took counsel's opinion, which was that, although the *Private Eye* article was certainly libellous, it would be against my interests to start a civil action against this periodical. With the benefit of hindsight I am now pretty sure that, by precipitating the whole issue in the crudest possible way, *Private Eye* in fact did me a service, though it was one which I certainly failed to recognize at the time.

35. THE OFFICERS MEET

THE most important consequence of the *Private Eye* article was an invitation from Jack Shrimpton to meet the Officers of the Association at his house. Accordingly, on the evening of 17th November, I went to Jack's house as requested. It was over three months since the circulation of the broadsheet, and this meeting with the Officers was the first occasion on which

I had had an opportunity of putting my case personally to any body representative of the Association. Even now I was inhibited by the divorce petition, except in conditions of strict confidence, from telling the full story. With the exception of Jack and his wife, friendly and hospitable as always, and thoroughly unhappy at being the centre of affairs at this particular time, my reception was correct, but scarcely enthusiastic.

All five of the Officers of the Harrow East Association were from Stanmore North ward. Theo Constantine, the President, was supported by Jack, the Chairman; Blackie Cawdron, the Treasurer; and by the two ex-officio Officers, Miss Harker, a middle-aged schoolmistress and Chairman of the Women's Advisory Committee, and Keith Gutteridge, Chairman of the Divisional Young Conservatives. Mrs. Burton, the agent, was in attendance. Theo took charge of the meeting from the outset. The atmosphere developed into one which I can only describe as inquisitorial.

I told my audience that I was glad to have this first opportunity of giving them my version of the events which had received so much publicity in the press, and I proceeded to tell them the story of all that had occurred over the previous five years, culminating in the Russian attack by broadsheet, and including a mention of the Moscow incident of 1961. I gave them my reasons for believing that I should have been arrested in Moscow had I paid my intended visit at the end of July 1965. I went into some detail as regards my matrimonial complications and I explained that Theo Constantine had been kept informed.

I was heard in silence, and there were few questions on points of detail. The reception given to me was not unsympathetic, but it was soon clear that the point of our meeting was a practical one.

It was put by Theo in two sentences, the first of which ran roughly as follows:—"It is our opinion," he said, "that we cannot win an election in Harrow East in present conditions with you as candidate."

After some discussion, in which I pointed out that such a

conclusion must remain a matter of opinion and that I did not necessarily share it, Theo came to his second point.

"We feel," he said, choosing his words with care, "that you should consider making it known that you do not intend to stand at the next election."

My reply to the officers was that I would of course consider their views with care and that, as regards standing down, I had an alternative possibility in mind. In my view, an important question of principle was involved, and it had occurred to me that this might be tested by my applying for the Chiltern Hundreds and standing for re-election at the subsequent by-election. What did they think of that?

This was a point which had not previously occurred to them, and it caused consternation; but there was no specific rejoinder.

It was later suggested that the Officers should be at liberty to discuss the matter fully with the Executive Council of the Association, but to this I objected for two reasons. In the first place I was still inhibited by the divorce proceedings from telling the Executive the full story. Secondly, I had now told the Officers the complete story in confidence, and there were parts of it concerning the defamatory broadsheet which, I was advised, could constitute a criminal libel if passed on or "published" by one of them to a third party. They should realize that the matter was of great seriousness to me personally as well as politically, and that I must retain the right to protect myself.

There was little more to be said. I now knew that I had lost the support of the Officers of my Association, and we parted civilly but in an unhappy atmosphere of radically divergent viewpoints.

Two days later the Divisional Dance took place at the Rest Hotel, Kenton. I went along by myself although it was quite an effort to face the members of the Association, after the meeting which I had just had with their officers. Oddly enough, I think the Officers were more embarrassed than I was. Perhaps they had not expected me to come. I did my best to get round all the tables in the course of the evening, and everywhere I was greeted with a sympathy and friendliness which really warmed my heart. Very few people made any remarks touching on my difficulties, with the exception of one woman, a stalwart friend and supporter from the difficult Stanmore South ward.

"What's all this the Russians have been doing to you?" she said, "They can't do this to our M.P." My friend is a lady of robust views and has a forthright manner of expressing them. I remember that incident with gratitude even though, in a matter of weeks, she had been persuaded into becoming one of my most implacable opponents!

36. THE SITUATION DETERIORATES

UNTIL I paid a visit to my doctor in the middle of November I had not realized how great a toll the events of the previous three months had taken on my health generally, and he was uncompromising in his direction that I should go away for a short holiday if worse were not to befall. Helpful as always, Willie gave me leave for the purpose, but asked me not to go until after the vote in the House on the evening of the 29th. I knew I needed a rest badly. My mind was going round in circles and I was beginning to mistrust my own judgment in dealing with the unexpected situations that were continually arising.

It was in this mood that I drafted a letter to the Prime Minister, setting out the facts of the whole case from the beginning and leading to the conclusions which I had reached after a close examination of all the evidence. I had heard nothing from Harold Wilson since my meeting with him on 6th September, and an attempt to get information and support from the Foreign Secretary on 16th September had resulted simply in an unhelpful reply from Michael Stewart to the effect that "it might be more convenient if you were to continue to deal with him (the Prime Minister) on any further aspect of the matter which you may wish to discuss."

Willie Whitelaw received the draft of my letter to Harold

Wilson without enthusiasm, and others with whom I discussed it doubted whether it would be of the slightest use to send it. I had to agree that, after over three months in which to study the facts with the aid of George Wigg and the Security Service, Government action had been confined to the strong "advice" given to me on 9th September not to undertake my postponed visit to the Soviet Union. It was most unlikely that the Prime Minister would raise a finger in my support.

I had long since given up hope of any help from the leadership of my own Party. In the House, too, I was learning a bitter lesson. It is an instinct of most politicians to "shun the unfortunate". At the election of officers for the reorganized Conservative Defence Committee I was dropped from the list of Deputy-Chairmen, though I had been well fancied by my friends after holding office successively as Secretary and Vice-Chairman of the Navy Committee. My colleagues, though personally as pleasant and sympathetic as ever, were conscious that I was under a cloud; though a few stalwart friends, I am glad to say on both sides of the House, took the trouble to tell me how strongly they felt about in the way in which I was being treated.

My business, of course, had collapsed. Client-firm after client-firm had seen the writing on the wall after the *Sunday Telegraph* article and had released itself as soon as practicable, and sometimes with indecent haste, from its commercial obligations towards me. I had been forced to close the Vienna office in August, and to cut my losses in this venture as best I could.

Whatever slender hopes I had had of continuing my business connection with the satellite countries had vanished within weeks of the publication of the broadsheet. True to type, the Czechoslovaks led the way. I had arranged to entertain my friend Trhlik, the Czech Ambassador, to lunch at the Carlton Club, together with his Commercial Counsellor, for further discussion of a project which I had started for a programme of co-operation between the Czechoslovak Aviation Industry and an important group of British companies working in the same field.

The meeting was cancelled by the Ambassador at short notice for family reasons involving the death of a relative, and subsequent endeavours to transfer the conversation to the offices of the British group concerned failed, in circumstances which indicated unmistakably that it was my personal involvement that constituted the difficulty. I was faced with the prospect that in a matter of months my business income would become precisely nil, while my salary as a Member of Parliament stood at risk. This was not simply from the movement of constituency opinion against me, but also from the threat of Liberal intervention at the forthcoming election in the already marginal constituency of Harrow East.

On 17th November, at a moment which coincided with the nadir of my political fortunes—the private meeting with the officers of the Harrow East Conservative Association—the Russians made a surprising move. Over three months had elapsed since the K.G.B. had attacked me by broadsheet, and they knew already that both my marriage and my business were in ruins. Neither the Government nor the Opposition leaders had publicly lifted a finger in my defence. The article in *Private Eye*, following on those in the *Sunday Telegraph* and the *News of the World*, furthermore, had indicated that the publicity was taking a "Profumo" form which nicely suited their further and principal purpose, which was to eliminate me from politics.

Whatever the motive may have been, however, a long article by Boris Troitsky appeared in *Izvestia*, the official organ of the Soviet Government, the greater part of which consisted of an attack on the United States Central Intelligence Agency for alleged clumsiness in the conduct of espionage operations which had, it was said, gravely embarrassed President Johnson. The heading, in heavy type, can be broadly translated as "Boxing their Ears". Reference was made to an Anglo-American wave of spy-mania emanating from C.I.A. headquarters in Washington. In the second half of the article the author turned on the British, after a description of their "Intelligence Service" as more experienced in intrigue and less noisy than its American counterpart. This part of the article concentrated on "the Courtney affair" in a curious and interesting fashion and contained the denial about the granting of a visa to which reference has already been made. (See Appendix C.)

There are several interesting features about this article. First, the section which refers to my affairs gives the appearance of having been inserted as an afterthought, and may even have been written by a separate hand. The Courtney affair is discussed in this section in a context of "Intelligence", both British and American, although at the time of writing there had been no official British backing whatsoever for my belief, echoed in the Press, that the operation was the work of the K.G.B. Secondly, there are two curious errors of fact, which must be known to be so by the Russians who yet, for some reason, wish to place their misstatements on record, despite the ease with which they can be shown to be false. The article speaks ironically of ". . . this Courtney, and how skilfully he avoided the danger" (of arrest) and goes on to point to the "contradiction" of this first idea by the story of cancellation of the trip due to Sir Alec's resignation. This serves to strengthen the view which I had held for some time, which is that the K.G.B., which can scarcely be expected to believe in "acts of God", was convinced that the existence of "Operation Courtney" had been known for some time to the British Secret Service, which had cleverly engineered circumstances which would bring about the cancellation of my trip at the last moment, and thus place the K.G.B. in an embarrassing position.

Finally, and most important, as I have previously mentioned, it is puzzling in the extreme to find any necessity for the Soviet Government newspaper to record a deliberate falsehood in respect of the visa which they state was not granted to me, the purpose of this statement being to support their denial that they ever intended to arrest me. This document, bearing the stamp of the Consular Section of the Soviet Embassy and dated 23rd July, 1965, is before me as I write, with a note to the effect that my journey is sponsored by *Litsenzintorg*, the department of the Ministry of Foreign Trade.

37. THE GROUND IS PREPARED

BUT despite all these worries I had set my heart on an expedition which I hoped to undertake in the Parliamentary Airedale early in the New Year. My friends, Commander and Mrs. Thompson, had a house in La Palma, the westernmost island of the Canaries, and I had decided to accept an invitation to stay with them during the Recess. I hoped to show that the journey could be made, at the worst time of year from the weather point of view, in a single-engined light aeroplane. The Spanish Air Attaché in London proved friendly and helpful, and a letter to the Civil Aviation authorities in Madrid brought a favourable response, so I made my arrangements to leave England on 6th January, which would get me back by the probable date of the reassembly of Parliament at the end of the month.

It was a relief to turn my mind to the practical problems associated with such a long flight, for life in London was becoming insupportable without some distraction from my deep anxieties. Best of all was the sense of regained freedom when I drove north on the morning of 30th November to spend a blessed fortnight away in the depths of the country with friends in Scotland.

A final evening's canvassing in Harrow Weald had given the impression of a deteriorating situation. Although there was no sign of any change of attitude on the doorsteps of the constituency, I learnt for the first time that there was a movement in Stanmore which was gathering momentum and had as its object nothing less than to force my resignation from the Conservative candidature when the expected election finally came upon us. As far as I could make out, the sponsors of this movement based their case on specific allegations which were being widely canvassed behind closed doors. It was being said that I had tried to threaten the officers with action for libel at our meeting on 17th November and that I had been less than frank in trying to cover up the Russian incident. Rumour had it that I had misled the Party leadership over the affair, and, anyway, a man so lacking in judgment as to allow himself to fall into a Soviet trap was not fit to be an M.P. For good measure, it was now also being said that I had not done my proper job as their Member of Parliament.

As I drove North I had much to think about, but I was in a state of nervous exhaustion, and I knew that I must make proper use of my precious two weeks' grace if I was to be in a fit state to fight the battles ahead. Scotland had problems too, but of a different order. The cattleman being away, I tried my hand at milking Primrose, the house-cow. She found the clumsy stranger not amusing, kicked me hard on the thigh so that I fell over backwards, made a mess all over the milking-stool and jammed me in the stall, from which I had to extricate myself by climbing over the partition. This incident, and the laughter of my hostess which accompanied it, showed me that I was in danger of taking myself and my troubles a bit too seriously.

The last two weeks before the Christmas recess were comparatively uneventful. Canvassing in the constituency, even in Harrow Weald, was at a standstill, with everyone's thoughts concentrated on the holiday. I knew the storm was gathering, as there was an ominous silence from those with whom I was normally in touch, but there seemed to be nothing which I could usefully do on the political side, as I was determined not to acquiesce in the suggestion put by the officers at the meeting of 17th November that I should resign the seat.

There was quite a lot of work involved in planning my flying trip, and preparations were just completed by the time I returned to my friends in Scotland for Christmas. I had had a little time to think, and it now had become clear that there was only one means by which I could stop the process through which I was losing political ground so steadily in the constituency. The divorce petition was on the defended list, and I had filed a complete denial of the charges. It might not ever come to court, but while it stood on the list it was immensely damaging. Until it was withdrawn, my hands were tied as regards publicity. The time had come, therefore, to consider seriously whether it would not be best to give my wife's lawyers new evidence of adultery. Michael Simmons had been advocating this course for some time, and at last I gave way. We informed my wife's lawyers accordingly that new evidence would be provided, and we were hopeful that the Petition would now be withdrawn.

Having made this decision it seemed probable that I should soon be free to take the action in Parliament to which I was committed. The opportunity presented by the Debate on the Address had passed, and so much time had now elapsed that the subject was no longer quite so topical and therefore not so suitable for an Adjournment Debate. Taking my chance, I put my name down for Wednesday, 26th January, when I proposed to seek the leave of the House to bring in a Bill under the Ten Minute Rule. This is a means by which back-bench Members, if the House approves, can introduce legislation in a speech of about ten minutes' duration at the end of the Parliamentary day, normally about 10.0 p.m.

The Bill which I had drafted was entitled the Diplomatic Privileges Bill* and was designed to bring an end to the special arrangements under which certain Communist Embassies, including the Russians, were accorded extraordinary diplomatic privileges and immunities, which they habitually abused for espionage purposes. My Bill, in fact, gave Parliamentary expression to all the ideas for which I had fought for so long and for which I believed I had suffered so severely at the hands of the K.G.B. Even if the Russians were finally to secure my removal from Parliament my Bill, whether or not it became law, would be on record, and could be resurrected when need arose, as I was confident it would. From my rough notes Liddell, of Dyson, Bell and Company, produced an admirable Parliamentary draft of the Bill and was not only most helpful but has to this day failed to send in his firm's account for the work done.

I arrived back in London on 4th January to find a letter awaiting me from the constituency Agent, which ran as follows:—

* Reproduced in Appendix E.

"Dear Anthony,

I understand from Jack that you have not yet replied to the question put to you by the informal meeting of Officers, when you were requested to write a letter to the Chairman stating that you would not be seeking re-election as the Member for Harrow East.

The Executive will be meeting on Wednesday, 12th January and I feel it is my duty to tell you that this matter is certain to be raised and your lack of response to this very important question will be mentioned.

I think you should also know that there will be an item on the Agenda concerning the selection of a Parliamentary candidate.

Yours,
Jo Burton."

It was quite improper, in my opinion, for a letter of this kind to be written by anyone other than the Association Chairman and I immediately rang Jack Shrimpton to tell him so. Jack was apologetic, and explained that he was very busy but that he "knew about" the letter, as he had a copy. It seemed from this that the letter had been written at the instigation of someone other than the Chairman. With regard to the meeting of the Executive Council to which the agent referred, I explained that I was due to leave in two days' time on my flying trip, that I had not been invited to attend and that even if such an invitation were now forthcoming it was too late for me to cancel my arrangements. No "question" requiring an answer, furthermore, had been put to me at the officer's meeting on the 17th November; and I had of course given considerable thought to the suggestion which had been put forward on that occasion, although I had not the least intention of accepting it.

This was confirmation that a manoeuvre was in progress to force my resignation, or to prevent my re-adoption, and I telephoned my old friend Eric Pratt to tell him what was happening. His reaction was immediate, and he undertook to be at the Executive meeting without fail to see what form the move against me was going to take. He had been deeply disappointed that I had not made my personal statement, as had been planned, to the Executive meeting before Christmas, but he was now delighted at the prospect of a fight ahead. For many years Eric had regretted the fact that the affairs of the Association were so heavily weighted in favour of Stanmore North ward, and he resented the control which had been exercised for so long by a few individuals in Stanmore itself.

In all the circumstances I felt it was right for me to proceed with my arrangements and to leave England for the trip to the Canaries on 6th January. I now knew I had to be back in any case on 24th January, as Enoch Powell had accepted an invitation to speak in the constituency, the occasion being a by-election for a vacancy on the Greater London Council which was being contested by Harold Mote, the Mayor of Harrow, an active Borough Councillor and, I thought, a friend.

The meeting of the Executive Council had been arranged for 12th January, and although I had not seen the agenda I had been informed by the Agent that the question of a Parliamentary Candidate was to be discussed. The situation was surely unprecedented. As the sitting Member of Parliament for Harrow East I had been given what amounted to "notice to quit" at the next election, which could not now be long delayed. This notice had been given me by the officers of the Association alone, since at no time had the question of my affairs or of my future been raised at the periodical meetings of the Executive Council.

Furthermore, apart from the single private meeting with the officers held on 17th November I had had no opportunity of giving a personal statement to any representative body of the Association. I was fully aware of the efforts being made by the officers to persuade individual members of the Executive of the rightness of their view that I should go. Wild stories were circulating and, in the opinion of an increasing number o gullible constituents, I could easily be credited with horns and a tail. I knew that malicious gossip of every kind was being aimed at my defenceless head. This gossip had grown to a vicious spate of misrepresentation, and often of sheer invention, which it was quite impossible to counter.

But I clung to one conviction which had been greatly strengthened by all the long hours of canvassing which I had spent in Harrow East. I was convinced that, despite the currents of evil stirred up against me by the Russians, the ordinary decencies of British people would triumph in the end.

I was sure that, when the whole truth were known, there would be a strong reaction in my favour which, I trusted, could yet win the day. But in the meantime it was a relief to get into my small aeroplane and fly away.

* * *

Despite bad weather and trouble with my radio I flew across Europe and down the African coast to the Spanish outpost at Sidi Ifni, thence across on the long sea-passage to Las Palmas and on via Tenerife to my friends on La Palma. It was an eventful and interesting flight. Best of all, there was no time to think of politics or of the troubles which I had left behind in England.

The post and telegraph arrangements on La Palma are, to say the least, unreliable, and it was thanks to this that the London papers were unable to get through to me by telephone. In due course, however, I was able to read a report of the Executive Council meeting. It was much as I had feared. A resolution had been put to the meeting, and passed, in the following terms:—

"In the light of the events occurring over the past year, and considering only the need to win the marginal seat of Harrow East for the Conservative Party, the Executive Council has decided that alternative candidates be considered to fight the seat at the next Election."

From the prominence given to the report, the affair seemed to have aroused considerable public interest, and I was not surprised to learn later that the chair at this critical meeting had been taken, not by the Association Chairman, Jack Shrimpton, who was present, but by Theo Constantine. A representative of Central Office had been present.

Theo, it appeared, had done most of the talking, and had given the Executive an account of the private meeting held between myself and the officers on 17th November. He had also given the substance of my statement made at that meeting. There had been a short discussion, in which, apparently, hardly anyone had spoken in my defence. Theo had then proceeded to put the Motion. This had been previously prepared, but it had not been included in the agenda circulated with the notice convening the meeting. Theo gave as a reason for this course of action the fact that I had ignored the suggestion put to me by the officers that I should consider not standing for re-election. After very little further discussion the motion had been carried by 32 votes to 4.

These were details which I was to learn later. In the meantime, braced and relaxed after my holiday, I flew off on the return journey, making a détour via Toulouse and Bordeaux to avoid bad weather over the Massif Central. But a glance at the Bordeaux weather-map showed me that further progress for a small aeroplane was quite impossible for the time being.

Within a few hours I was flying in a Caravelle via Paris to keep my appointment with Enoch Powell in the constituency.

38. SPLIT IN HARROW EAST

I HAD left England a fortnight previously, knowing that events were reaching a climax, but in an atmosphere that was still outwardly peaceful. I returned to find that political war had been declared on me within my Association. As a result I had become once again a figure of public interest, and the Press lost no time in making contact.

But there was a further and rather disturbing factor. I was

quite sure I was being watched, and that my flat in Westminster was under observation. If there is one thing to be gained from experience of living in Russia it is the ability to detect surveillance, and in this case the operation was sufficiently crudely handled for it to be blatantly obvious. Heavy-handedness of this kind is not a characteristic of the R.I.S., so I ruled out at once any suspicion that the Russians might be interested in my movements—or in those of my friends. My wife's lawyers knew that there was now sufficient evidence available for the divorce, so that there was little possibility that this activity could have anything to do with my matrimonial affairs.

There only seemed to remain politics. Was it possible, I thought, that the forthcoming battle over my right to continue as an M.P. was so important to someone that it was thought necessary to stoop to having me watched in the hope of discovering something to my discredit? An important piece of information which reached me two days later convinced me that this was, in fact, the case.

I had arrived back in London on the evening of Sunday, 23rd January and in a few minutes had received a number of telephone calls from friends in the constituency who were horrified by the decision which had been taken by the Executive in my absence and who offered any help that I might require. The two most important were from Eric Pratt, my old friend the chairman of Queensbury ward, and from Douglas Charter, who with his wife Vera was one of my best friends and staunchest supporters in Harrow Weald. The tenor of both conversations was roughly the same. They were appalled at the line taken and had determined to act within the rules of the Association.

After much discussion it had been decided to write a letter to the constituency Chairman requesting a Special General Meeting, and a draft had been taken round to known Conservatives in Queensbury and Harrow Weald wards, both of which are preponderantly Socialist, which had produced over a hundred signatures in a very short space of time.

Time was so short, however, that in my absence abroad they

had had to assume that I would fight the Executive's decision on my return. Knowing me as well as they did, both Eric and Douglas had had no hesitation in assuring the others that I would do so, and the letter to the Chairman was despatched on 21st January.

It read as follows:—

"Dear Sir,

Commander Anthony Courtney, O.B.E., M.P.

We the undersigned members of the Harrow East Conservative Association deplore the recent resolution of the Executive Council to consider alternative candidates for the next General Election.

We further deplore the fact that a matter of this importance was not debated either by Ward Committees or by a General Meeting of the Association prior to the action of the Executive Council.

We request that a special General Meeting of the Association be called as a matter of urgency within 28 days to consider the resolution of the Executive Council and that no action be taken concerning the selection of alternative candidates to the present Member of Parliament pending the outcome of this Meeting.

Yours faithfully."

It was an immense relief to both of my friends that I had not let them down, and we arranged to meet at the earliest opportunity to discuss tactics. It was a fight after their own hearts, and they had no illusions about the treatment which they would receive should the Executive eventually have its way. With the telephoning finished, I settled down to the mass of correspondence which was awaiting my return home. Most of it had to do with the meeting of the Executive, and a number of letters were from colleagues in the House, including a few from Socialist friends. They were most encouraging, and one from a senior backbencher who is greatly respected on all sides of the House ran as follows:—

(9) Jack Shrimpton and Mrs. Courtney: 1964

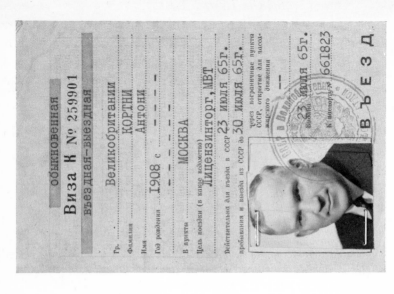

(10b) Entry visa for Soviet Russia, valid
23rd July, 1965

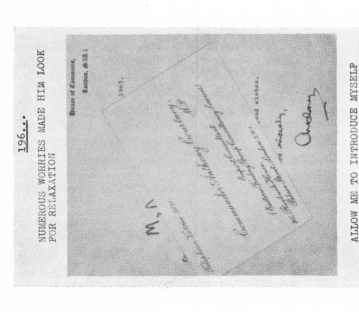

(10a) Extract from the broadsheet. The
Gromov letter

"My dear Anthony,

I feel I must send you a word of encouragement in the
most difficult time you are passing through. I am sure you
have the goodwill of all our colleagues, though they may
be too shy to say so. Whatever happens, you must not be
driven off your perch. If the Association turns you down,
you must declare that you will fight as an Independent
Conservative—and split the vote and lose the seat to
Labour if need be. You will be fighting on behalf of all
Tory M.P.s if you do. Vast pressures will be brought on
you to step down gracefully—but you must resist.

Good luck.

Yours—"

On the following morning Willie Whitelaw rang to tell me
that George Wigg wished to see me the same afternoon. I
had a few words with Willie in his office at the House before we
went along to this meeting and he told me that the officers of the
Association were "absolutely adamant" that I must go. I
replied that there seemed to be a large section of the rank-and-
file who took a different view. It was deplorable that the local
party should be divided in this way, and I believed that only
if they came to their senses while there was still time and
formally re-adopted me as Conservative Candidate at the next
election would we have a hope of retaining the seat.

Willie was non-committal, but I know he felt a certain
personal sympathy for me in my predicament. George Wigg
was waiting for us. He was irritatingly brisk and businesslike.
It was possible, he said, but by no means certain, that action of
some kind would be taken by Her Majesty's Government as
regards the defamatory broadsheet which had been circulated
anonymously six months previously. Would I please verify the
following statements of fact? He proceeded to read a document
at considerable speed, pausing at intervals to obtain my
confirmation of what was contained in it. It was a curious
performance. We left little wiser as to the Government's
intentions, and there was no trace on this occasion of the

relatively sympathetic attitude which had characterized previous meetings with Ministers.

The constituency was my next concern, and here the situation was little short of chaotic. Wild stories were still circulating, and the gossips were having a field-day. Judging from the vote at the meeting on 12th January the Executive had been well and truly won over against me, but my postbag was beginning to show the existence of a large body of Conservatives, not all members of the Association, who were most unhappy at the endeavours of the officers to remove their M.P. I was no longer bound by the previous undertaking not to talk, and hastened to ring up my friends to take soundings.

The response was not encouraging, for the one-sided campaign which had been conducted against me for weeks and perhaps months previously had had its effect, particularly in Stanmore and to a lesser extent in Belmont. Key figures from other wards had been persuaded of the correctness of the officers' view, and in no single case had I been given the opportunity of putting my side of the case and of defending myself against allegations made behind closed doors. To this day I do not know all the fearful things that I was credited with, but the campaign was certainly effective. Every artifice had been used to influence the gullible, and every social blandishment to those, gullible or not, who responded to such things— and they were quite a few.

With her typical sense of fair play my old friend, Mrs. Goldstein, arranged at short notice for a group of ladies from Stanmore to meet at her house and hear what I had to say. It was an odd occasion, made no easier by the desire of one of the group to sit back and take notes. I did my best to answer their questions, and at the end I felt that Mrs. Goldstein had taken an initiative that had been well worth while. Two or three, certainly, had arrived with their minds made up, to my detriment, and nothing would shake them. But there were others, whose thoughtful questions and sympathetic attitude showed that they were not disposed to accept all that had been said about me in my absence.

I also went to see another friend, Rhona Dickson, who had

always shown herself a tower of strength in Belmont ward. As a worker of much experience in Harrow East it had been a serious blow to my prospects when she fell in with the intentions of my political enemies without having referred to me, whom she had known for so long, to hear my side of the story. Now, when I went to visit her at my own request I think she had begun to feel that the political Juggernaut which had been started might not perhaps be quite as all-powerful as she had at first supposed. In the course of a long talk she did her utmost to dissuade me from fighting the Executive's decision and I think she genuinely felt that I would suffer severely if I allowed the affair to continue to a conclusion rather than retire from the fray.

"Anthony," she said, "don't go on with it. They'll crucify you."

I left her in no doubt that as far as I was concerned the fight was on.

On Monday evening Enoch Powell was to speak at a public meeting at the Harrow Weald Memorial Hall, in the heart of the constituency. It was an all-Harrow affair, and I was glad to have supporting me on the platform my two Parliamentary colleagues for the other Harrow constituencies, Jack Page and Anthony Grant, whose sympathy I had.

The occasion was the Greater London by-election, and the meeting had been organized in support of the Conservative candidate, Councillor Harold Mote. But everyone in the crowded hall was conscious of the underlying conflict within the host Association, my own, between the officers and their Member of Parliament. Harold Mote was nominally the central figure, but with Theo Constantine in the chair, Enoch Powell as supporting speaker and myself due to move the vote of thanks, interest in the affairs of the Greater London Council seemed to have moved into second place. The mood of the meeting was difficult to assess, but there was an impression of strong feeling and lively interest which was in no way dampened by a rather discursive speech by Harold Mote and a surprisingly pedestrian performance by Enoch.

But when the Chairman called for questions, a familiar

figure near the back of the hall rose to its feet. It was Sidney Carter, an independent character who has caused a fluttering in established dovecotes in Harrow by forming a Houseowners' Association, with the object of cheapening house purchase by offering certain services, normally provided by Solicitors and Estate Agents, at cut rates. While in no way supporting his movement I have admired his initiative and drive, and on one occasion took the chair at one of his public meetings. Though politically we are totally opposed, there is nevertheless a certain bond between us, and he was once good enough to say that although he would never vote Tory he would always support me personally.

The question Sidney Carter asked was to the point. What did the last speaker (Enoch) think of the Russian plot which had been revealed by the Member for Harrow East, and was it right that the local Conservative Association should take the opportunity to try and get rid of him.

Enoch replied diplomatically and without hesitation. In the first place it was entirely the affair of the Harrow East Association as to how they dealt with their Member of Parliament. Secondly, it was a regrettable fact that people who had dealings with Communist countries must inevitably be at risk, as they were dealing with a system which denies individual rights. When I rose to propose the vote of thanks I was given a cheer of noticeable warmth, but it did not prevent me from making rather a hash of what I had to say.

I was cheered again when I sat down, and I was sure that I could have said my piece in Zulu (if I knew the language) for all that the audience cared. They smelt blood, and I realized for the first time what strong feelings were being aroused in the minds of ordinary people over my affairs. It was some consolation for the sickness at heart which had begun to assail me whenever I visited the constituency.

39. THE DIPLOMATIC PRIVILEGES BILL
(see Appendix E)

THE House reassembled on Tuesday, 25th January, and on Wednesday evening at 10.0 p.m. I was called by Mr. Speaker and made a speech (reproduced in Appendix D) in which I sought the leave of the House to introduce my Diplomatic Privileges Bill under the 10-minute rule.

At the end of my speech the question was put, and the leave of the House granted. I stood in my place and read out the list of sponsors as follows:—

"Bill ordered to be brought in by Commander Courtney, Sir Rolf Dudley-Williams, Mr. Edward Gardner, Mr. Anthony Grant, Dame Patricia Hornsby-Smith, Mr. Iremonger, Viscount Lambton, Sir Harry Legge-Bourke, Sir Godfrey Nicholson, Mr. John Page, Sir George Sinclair and Dr. Wyndham Davies."

The Speaker then called me by name. I advanced from the Bar, making the regulation three bows, and presented my Bill to the Clerk of the House. It had had its First Reading.

My Bill was well received, and a surprising number of Members returned to the Chamber to hear it introduced. I felt encouraged by the fact that the Government, hitherto so faint-hearted in all that touches diplomatic immunities, had allowed it to be introduced, given its First Reading and printed. But I now see that they simply feared the publicity which would have resulted from overt opposition to my Bill, and they knew that they only had to wait a little before gaining their object, which was to kill it.

Sure enough, when my Bill came up for Second Reading on Friday, 11th February, one single voice cried "Object" among the numerous Members in the Chamber. It was that of the Government Whip from the Treasury Bench. My Bill was dead, and the Soviet Embassy observers watching from the Gallery returned contentedly to their duties.

Nevertheless, I had made my Parliamentary gesture, and nothing could wipe my Bill, which had now been printed, off the record. It was there in the record to shame the Socialist Government when the day arrived on which circumstances would force Ministers to take some action along the lines I had proposed. In my speech, I had raised the question of K.G.B. operations in this country by implication and yet I felt had avoided the pitfall of exposing myself to the accusation of using the platform of the House of Commons for personal ends.

For me it was now vital that the Divorce Petition should be withdrawn. The lawyers had been given the new evidence, and I knew that my wife was leaving for Jamaica and the Bahamas at the end of the month. A day or two later I heard with inexpressible relief from Michael Simmons that instructions for the withdrawal of the Petition had been given. This was reported in the National Press on 29th January.

Since the *Sunday Telegraph* disclosures I had had several talks with lobby correspondents in the House of Commons. All of these had been on a "lobby" basis, that remarkable bond of confidence between journalists and politicians which is surely not paralleled anywhere else in the world. In particular, I had discussed my affairs with Gordon Greig and Walter Terry of the *Daily Mail*. They had each had a long-standing interest in my Parliamentary activities in the field of security. Both of them knew full well that while my divorce was *sub judice* there was little they could write, but now all that was behind me, and within two days Walter was sitting in my flat, drinking whisky and taking notes—while I talked.

I have yet to meet a greater cynic than the average experienced lobby correspondent. Walter's interest was purely political, not so much from the international aspect—for it did not really seem to bother him that the Russians were intervening in British Parliamentary affairs—but from the point of view of a backbench M.P. fighting for his political life against slander in his constituency. I soon discovered that he had his own contacts in Harrow and knew at least as much as I did about what was going on within the Association.

From his long experience as a political journalist Walter has developed a natural scepticism and a sense of utter disillusion over human nature as it operates in the political world. He was kind, but he must have found many of my views remarkably naïve.

"Walter," I remarked at one point, "you must remember that I would never describe myself as a politician. I am simply a naval officer who has turned to politics rather late in life." This difference of approach between us, which I attributed entirely to my naval upbringing, led to a difference of opinion over the probable outcome of the political struggle in Harrow East.

As we chatted amicably, contrasting our different points of view, I had a dreadful glimpse of the world of politics as seen day after day with awful monotony by Walter Terry from his pet corner in the Members' Lobby. In the conditions prevailing in this political world it was already blindingly clear to Walter that I had not a hope in hell of retaining the Conservative nomination as Candidate for Harrow East in the forthcoming General Election. He had seen too much of the machine to have the slightest doubt on this score.

He listened patiently while I explained that there was another side of the political world of which, naïve or not, I had already had a great deal more experience than he. This world was entered across the countless front-door-steps of Harrow East, or of any other constituency for that matter, where there lived the ordinary, rather inarticulate men and women who really formed the political backbone of the country. This was the world, I told him, in which I had sensed currents of feeling which could surprise him yet by taking power out of the hands of the professional political manipulators whom he knew so well and despised so utterly. I told Walter that I had an immense confidence in the innate decency of ordinary men and women. If stimulated into activity, I believed that this latent force could achieve surprising results, and I had not lost hope that it might be brought to operate in my support.

"Look at your own Press," I said, "almost without exception, they have been on my side since the start—doesn't it all add up?"

But Walter was not to be persuaded. He shook my hand as we parted, rather in the manner of the condemned cell, but although we had agreed to differ I felt that here was another real friend who could be trusted absolutely to put my case to the best of his not inconsiderable ability.

40. BATTLE JOINED

IN the constituency things were beginning to move, with a slow acceleration that gave promise of a tremendous impact when the forces got to grips. I was reminded for a moment of the superb spectacle of the French cavalry in the film *Henry V*, as they gather momentum in the charge on the English line at Agincourt.

Queensbury and Harrow Weald wards had both held emergency meetings and each had passed resolutions deploring the action of the Executive Council. Queensbury, furthermore, took exception to the fact that a matter of such obvious importance had not been discussed either by ward committees or by a general meeting of the Association prior to the action taken by the Executive. Voting was unanimous, exept for a Borough Councillor, who abstained, though he expressed himself as being fully in sympathy with the general view. But he lives in Stanmore, and despite this assurance he withdrew his support from me later.

The Harrow Weald decision was reversed at a subsequent meeting attended in force by the Association officers, at which it was alleged that I had made untrue statements both to Ted Heath and to the Chief Whip. I am glad to be able to record that Willie Whitelaw, though pressed to do so, refused to support this allegation.

In terms of actionable statements, certain of my bitterer opponents had already overreached themselves, and it had occurred to me that I might now have grounds for legal action.

But I put it out of my mind. This battle could and must be won on its own merits in the political arena and without recourse to the law.

In Belmont ward, at a meeting in support of the Executive, it was remarked that I had been very little seen in the ward. It fell to a staunch friend, Rex Glover-Wright, to remind the meeting that even if this were true it was certainly odd that the matter had never been raised before at a ward meeting. Jack Shrimpton hinted darkly at "further revelations" which might emerge at election time. This was clearly inspired by the words "to be continued" at the foot of the broadsheet, and once again Russian psychology had judged its audience exactly.

The Harrow Press at this time was inundated with letters. Most of these were in protest against the action of the Harrow East Executive. I myself was receiving a heavy mail-bag, from abroad as well as from the United Kingdom, all of the correspondence expressing support for me, with varying degrees of disgust at the manoeuvres of my Association.

After the passing of the Resolution on 12th January the Executive lost no time in setting up a Selection Committee. I was informed about this in a letter which expressed a hope that my name would be among those put forward for selection. The situation seemed, to me at least, to have become almost farcical. My opponents, who were in complete control of the Executive, might at least have had the courage of their intentions. They were being widely accused of mean trickery, but might at least have saved themselves the additional charge of hypocrisy.

Most people were naturally assuming that a candidate other than myself would be selected, and a number of aspirants hastened to send in their applications. They included a former woman M.P. who had lost her seat at the 1964 election, and she was already being strongly fancied. It was being said that a woman candidate would possess distinct advantages. Only in this way, it was reasoned, could Harrow East be saved from further irregularities in the private lives of its Members. All sense of proportion seemed to be going by the board, and feelings were running high and in some cases beginning to verge on the hysterical.

In the meantime my friends, too, had been busy. A faithful few had been round with their letter requesting a Special General Meeting and they had obtained signatures far in excess of the number required by Rule 13 of the Association. There had been promises of support on every side. In due course it was announced that the meeting had been arranged for Monday, 21st February at the Harrow Weald County Grammar School, and I had a letter from the Chairman of the Association inviting me to attend. By the rules, the discussion at this meeting would be limited to the specific question at issue. This had been framed as a Resolution in the following terms:—

"This General Meeting of the Harrow East Conservative Association deplores the action of the Executive Council in the passing of its Resolution of 12th January, 1966, to consider other candidates in addition to the sitting Member, and urges that Commander A. T. Courtney be re-adopted as Prospective Parliamentary Candidate."

It was to be moved by Eric Pratt and seconded by Douglas Charter. The battle was at last out in the open, and it was to be fought out within a matter of weeks on ground of our own choosing.

41. FRIENDS AND CHICKEN-HEARTS

BEFORE Parliament rose for Christmas we had learned of the intended arrival of a Soviet Parliamentary Delegation to this country on 15th February for a stay of about a fortnight. As usual, I put my name in as one of those willing to help as a host. At that time there were only three of us in the House who could speak good Russian. But it froze the marrow of the Foreign Office to think of personal contact between a party of innocent Russian visitors and a British M.P. who was being victimized by the Soviet K.G.B.

Friends and Chicken-Hearts

So on Foreign Office advice I was approached by E. L. Mallalieu,* the Chairman of the British Section of the Inter-Parliamentary Union. Mallalieu's manner was unctuous, and he was unable wholly to conceal his anxiety, for a refusal to co-operate on my part might have led to some unfortunate publicity at his expense. Here was a chance for me to put a breath of fresh air behind the grubby façade of Anglo-Soviet relationships, but I had too many immediate problems on hand to take on any more, and I submitted.

As in the political, so in the commercial world, Soviet psychological dominance was dislodging me one by one from my former points of contact with the Russians. For nine years I had served as an active member of the Russia Committee of the London Chamber of Commerce, probably the most influential body in this country which deals with problems of Anglo-Soviet trade. One morning I had a call from the Secretary, Bill Luxton, who is also an old friend, and I detected a note of embarrassment in his voice. Could he come over for a chat? The purpose of such a visit was already patently obvious.

Bill was soon with me, and over a glass of gin I thought it kinder to forestall him. I knew, I said, that we were on the eve of another "goodwill mission" from the Chamber to the Soviet Union. I quite realized that my colleagues on the Committee, who were themselves still *persona grata* with the Russians, were anxious about the effect my continuing presence might have on their prospects. To save embarrassment, therefore, I asked Bill to tender my resignation as soon as it suited him. He was duly grateful, and there were not a few ambitious commercial figures who breathed a sharp sigh of relief.

But there were compensations. It was warming to be asked to speak at Rudgwick, the next village to my old home at Slinfold, to a crowded and friendly meeting. The occasion was a woman's lunch, but there were several men present, including a very old friend, Admiral Sir Gresham Nicholson, who had been my Term Lieutenant at Dartmouth forty-three years

* E. L. Mallalieu, Labour M.P. for Brigg since 1948.

previously. I was to speak on Russia and the Russians. "Mind you make it juicy!" said a dear old lady to me just before I rose to my feet. I was immensely rewarded by the response at the end of my speech, which included a specially sympathetic reference to my troubles in Harrow East.

Since the meeting of the Executive on 12th January the Press had taken up "the Courtney affair" on an impressive scale. On 2nd February, the *Daily Mail* published the first of a series of three long articles by Walter Terry. The first was headed "The M.P. who fights a smear". Articles nos. one and two dealt in detail with my background of Russian affairs and with the circumstances in which the K.G.B. operation had been mounted. The third and last was entitled "My Advice to Harrow East", and the final paragraph, which was in effect a summing-up of the whole, ran as follows:—

"I am sure that, in the improbable event of myself being a bigwig in the Harrow East Conservative organization, I would give Commander Courtney full support, and reject the nasty, clammy work of the conspirators, whatever their nationality."

I could have wished for nothing better.

Within a few months, Walter Terry planned to visit Moscow with other Press representatives to cover the visit of the Prime Minister, Harold Wilson. By that time he had become Political Editor of his paper, but he had incurred Soviet displeasure in standing up for a fellow-countryman under attack by the Soviet Secret Police.

He was refused an entry visa.

I was getting tired of being labelled the "smear M.P.", but there was nothing to be done about it, and my skin got progressively thicker as time went on.

It was at this point that Independent Television took a hand. I was approached by a forthright, go-ahead and sympathetic producer from Associated Television, Alex Valentine, who seemed to take a real interest in my predicament. Accordingly, at 7.0 on a Friday morning (I was driving North the same day), my flat was invaded by a highly competent team of T.V. technicians, complete with lights, cameras and make-up girl. On 14th February, the usual Bernard Levin interview was displaced by a half-hour programme entitled "The Courtney File". Besides myself, those taking part were Sir William Hayter, a former Ambassador in Moscow, David Floyd, the Communist Affairs expert of the *Daily Telegraph,* Sir Theo Constantine, President of Harrow East, and Eric Pratt, Chairman of Queensbury ward in the same constituency.

The programme, which was both objective and imaginative, had a considerable impact on those who saw it, and not least in Harrow East. It first examined the evidence relating to the Russian campaign against me, and found the case proved. The emphasis then shifted to the effect of the Russian action on my political prospects, and both Theo and Eric were given the opportunity to state their opposing points of view. Discussion then proceeded to take in the wider implications of Soviet techniques of this kind, and I said that I believed that there could be many people, and some in responsible positions, who had exposed themselves in this way and who might well at the present moment be "sweating under the fear of Russian blackmail".

This programme, coupled with Walter Terry's articles, did a great service in arousing wide public interest in "the Courtney Affair".

42. SELECTION COMMITTEE

WITH the main spate of publicity behind me I braced myself for the interview with the Selection Committee on the 16th. There were eight applicants to be interviewed, accompanied in several cases by their wives, and there was a moment of embarrassment when I met two of them, whom I knew personally, in the agent's office, which was in use as a waiting-room.

The oddness of the whole proceeding struck me forcibly as I was bidden to enter the same room in which I had first been selected as Prospective Candidate for the constituency seven years previously, to face another Committee which I knew had already made up its mind. A glance at the twenty or so faces before me was quite sufficient confirmation. Jack was in the chair, fussy and nervous and wishing, I am sure, that he had not had the bad luck to be Association Chairman at this difficult time. The others were well known to me, and several I had counted as my friends. I was glad to see the Central Office Agent sitting beside the Chairman, Cyril Norton, a man in whose integrity and sense of fair play I had complete confidence.

No-one present seemed to have much idea of how to handle such an unusual situation. After all, the stock questions were a little irrelevant in my case. I had not even a wife to divert their attention. As I looked at them, with their notebooks and pencils and smug, would-be judicial air, the black bile of contempt rose in me and I really began to feel rather angry. It was such inmitigated humbug for this committee to try and appear impartial when I was quite convinced that they had long since decided to sack the man who had represented them for so long. I told them in forthright terms what I thought of their behaviour since the publicity had started in October. Many of those present, I said, had taken part in gossip behind closed doors and none of them had had the courage to repeat any of this gossip to my face. I reminded them that, apart from the private meeting with the Officers on 17th November, this was the first occasion on which I had been able to speak in my own defence before a representative body of the Association. Finally I challenged them to make the most of this opportunity and to have the courage to speak up now that they had me for the first time there with them. If they failed to do so I could only assume that they were satisfied with the explanations which I had given to their officers. If there were any other points, now was the time to speak.

At this juncture Jack Shrimpton intervened rather weakly. It seemed that my time had run out and there were several people waiting to be interviewed. It was a typical attempt to evade the issue. But I insisted that my challenge should be taken up. Only three people responded. The first, the Chairman

of the Women's Advisory Committee, a school-teacher, observed
that every word that I had said amply confirmed the opinion
which she held of me previously. I could feel my cloven hoof
positively itching. The second, Bob Arajs, the Chairman of
Harrow Weald, whose English is not of the clearest, put a
rather involved question on the security side. The third, a very
young Young Conservative, asked whether it was true that I
had slept with a woman in Moscow. It was an unimpressive
contribution, and it was noticeable that Blackie Cawdron,
who with his wife had been untiring in his opposition to me,
kept his mouth shut.

By this time the fit of anger had passed, and I began rather
to enjoy myself. I told the Committee that I found it difficult
to take their selection procedure seriously, that I knew I had a
great deal of personal support among Conservatives in the
constituency, that certain of my colleagues in the House had
begged me to stand firm on such an important issue of
principle, and that I therefore felt it only right to inform them
that I intended that my name should appear on the Ballot
Paper at the next Election. With that I left the meeting.

The Press were waiting for me as I came out of the building,
and I repeated my statement about the forthcoming election
with some care. But it was quickly given a different form. One
paper wrote, "Commander Courtney will fight the seat as an
Independent if he is dropped by the local Conservatives".
This was an over-simplification which was to do me harm. In
any event I had made it absolutely clear that I would not "go
quietly" and the responsibility for splitting the Association at
an election, if there was to be a split, would lie with the
Executive Council. For this reason, a refusal to support me
would make nonsense of the phrase "considering only the need
to win the marginal seat of Harrow East for the Conservative
Party" which had been such a prominent feature of the
Executive Resolution of 12th January.

Perhaps influenced by the public interest which was being
taken in my affairs, and possibly shamed by the article in
Izvestia, on 3rd February the Government at last took action.
This consisted of a verbal protest to a member of the Soviet

Embassy summoned to the Foreign Office for the purpose. I was not informed officially that it had been made until I rang the Prime Minister's office on 21st February to find out, and to this day I have not been given the text of the protest itself.

In the constituency I found myself under attack from a rather unexpected quarter. The two senior clergymen of the Harrow Council of Churches took it upon themselves to assail me on moral grounds and issued a statement in which my constituents were asked not to give me their support. One of my critics was Vicar of a Parish within the constituency. This démarche by a small section of the clergy aroused a good deal of criticism, and their attitude was certainly not shared by others of their cloth. Typical of the contrary viewpoint is an excerpt from an article by the Vicar of St. Stephens written subsequently in the St. Albans Parish Magazine. ". . . how wise of the Harrow Tories," he wrote, "to realize that their Commander's little affair in Russia hinders not the effect of his Parliamentary activities."

Passions had been aroused in Harrow East, and there were many who had accepted without question the opinions of the officers of the Association, led by Theo Constantine. Theo was not personally very popular, but he had considerable influence by reason of his long political experience and for his apparently close relationship with the party leaders, and especially with the Party Chairman, Edward du Cann. It seemed to have occurred to few of my opponents that, apart from the single and admitted Moscow incident, there were no allegations to which I had been given any opportunity to reply. The case against me, furthermore, had been substantially weakened by the withdrawal of the divorce petition at the end of January and by a letter which my wife had written to the Chairman of the Association.

Nevertheless there were many who, whatever their inner doubts, were now committed to the official line, and they were confident that in a straight trial of strength the Juggernaut of the Party machine would crush any individual, however misjudged or unfortunate, who had the temerity to challenge it.

(11) "The Courtney File": Associated Television, 14th February, 1966

(a) Sir William Hayter

(b) Eric Pratt

By courtesy of Associated Television

(c) David Floyd

(d) Sir Theo Constantine

(12) We've won! 21st February, 1966

The agent had long since associated herself personally with the view of the Officers, and as the day of the Special General Meeting approached I found myself wholly isolated from social functions to which I would normally have been invited.

My friends, however, continued to keep in touch with me, and my post-bag showed a high level of public interest among all types of people which would, I felt, be reflected to a great extent among the members of my Association. Eric Pratt and Douglas Charter, who were to propose and second the Resolution before the meeting, were constantly on the telephone. I had, in addition, been much heartened by the support of a well-known Stanmore resident, Otto Sputz, who had not hitherto taken much interest in local political affairs. I hoped and believed that he was typical of quite a few intelligent constituents who were unwilling to be stampeded into acceptance of a decision which had begun to appear as little less than a monstrous injustice.

43. THE SPECIAL GENERAL MEETING

IT was with mixed feelings that I drove to Harrow on the evening of Monday, 21st February. The last occasion on which I had spoken in the Harrow Weald County Grammar School was at a poorly-attended public meeting on the occasion of my periodic "Report on Parliament". I remember emphasizing the inevitable results of the Socialist legislation then before the House and forecasting that, on the next occasion when I spoke to them, the consequence of Socialist rule would be such that the hall would be packed.

As I entered, I saw that my prediction had been fulfilled, though scarcely in the way that I had expected. The hall *was* packed, and a deep murmur of conversation lent excitement to an atmosphere which was already tense with expectation. I had found it difficult to park my car, such was the congestion outside, and a crowd of Pressmen thronged the entrance. T.V. cameras were already in position, and I felt myself to be in the grip of a massive but by no means unfriendly movement which had decided that the interest of this meeting extended very far beyond the boundaries of Harrow East.

Jack Shrimpton was to take the chair, and as I entered he passed me a letter, saying that I should have had it earlier but for shortage of time. It was signed by Jack, but had come from a far cleverer debating tactician, for it made two proposals. First, I was to speak for a limit of 15 minutes directly after Eric and Douglas had spoken to the Resolution. In other words I was to have no opportunity to reply to any criticisms or allegations made by opposing speakers. Secondly, it was intended at some point in the proceedings for questions to be invited from the floor. This would expose me to questions, almost literally of the type of "Have you stopped beating your wife?" This proposal, furthermore, was in direct contradiction of Rule 13 of the Association which confined the proceedings strictly to debate on the Resolution before the meeting.

My reaction was swift, and Cyril Norton, the Central Office agent who was there to see fair play, ruled in my favour on both points. It seemed to me that my opponents would take every advantage that they could up to the last moment, and a feeling of resolve swept over me as I moved to the end of the line of chairs on the platform where Eric and Douglas were sitting. The hall seemed full, but people were still streaming in, and I recognized many familiar faces.

Even in my somewhat bemused state I could tell that there was a strong undercurrent of feeling among the audience, which presented a totally different picture from that to which I had become accustomed in ordinary political life. Here at last, and outside election-time, was a British audience which had been roused to an expression of strong opinion on a matter of politics. It was quite impossible to tell what that opinion was, and I felt that the speeches which were to come would be unlikely to sway the outcome, which was already decided, but hidden in the minds behind the sea of faces before me. Some 750 people from my constituency, alert and expectant to an extent which I had not previously seen at a political meeting, were sphinx-like in their determination to conceal the strength —and the direction—of the feelings within them. Beyond that, neither Eric, Douglas nor I had the faintest clue as to what was in their minds.

Jack Shrimpton, nervous as always, opened the meeting, and in a complete hush Eric Pratt rose to propose the Resolution. He spoke well, with forthrightness and complete sincerity to make his main point, that the action of the Executive Council had been unconstitutional, that it was wrong in any case to condemn a man, even a politician, unheard, and that from my record I deserved the continued confidence of the Association. His speech was well received, as was that of Douglas Charter, who introduced his own particular brand of dogged political logic. I could not have wished for two better supporters.

The opposition was led by the Treasurer, Blackie Cawdron, who based his argument on the democratic nature of the local party organization, as a result of which, he said, the decision of the Executive must be truly representative of ward opinion. He, too, was quite well received, and there was as yet no clue as to the feeling of the meeting as a whole. The seconder against the Resolution was the Chairman of the Young Conservatives, who spoke well for the first part of his speech and was listened to in silence until he asked rhetorically how "we" could entrust responsibility for bringing up "our" children to a man of the admitted moral character of Anthony Courtney. At this there was a spontaneous murmur of disgust from the audience, and for the first time I began to feel that matters were going my way.

The main speakers were followed by Theo Constantine, President of the Association, who made a clever speech in which he justified the decision of the Executive on grounds of the shortcomings of the Member in his constituency activities, quite apart from the lack of judgment displayed in the episode which had taken place in Moscow. At this point the Chairman informed the meeting, rather unnecessarily, that the Member of Parliament had declined to answer questions. He added that eight speakers from the floor on each side would now be invited to speak. These speeches were varied and interesting.

It was noticeable that my supporters were mainly active workers who had been out canvassing with me in the more difficult wards. Not one resident of Stanmore rose to his feet in my defence. My opponents included a Vice-Chairman of the Association, whose chairmanship of Belmont ward had not been conspicuously successful and four others who, as far as I know, have done little, if any, active work for the Association and one of whom subsequently proclaimed himself to be a Liberal. But I was saddened to find among them two old friends, a man who had worked nobly in Harrow Weald for many difficult years and, saddest of all, a former Chairman of the Young Conservatives who had been a member of the Selection Committee which chose me after the resignation of my predecessor.

A number of speakers on both sides touched on the Russian issue. One of them, a typical gangly youth and a hard-working Young Conservative, raised a laugh when he declared that I had proved to be a good Member of Parliament, and that, this being so, I might sleep with the entire Bolshoi Ballet as far as he was concerned. But of all of them only Eric Pratt underlined the true significance of the attack by broadsheet.

Finally, I spoke myself. I told my audience of the honour which it had been to represent them in Parliament for the previous seven years, and I explained how the conflict between my personal interests in Eastern Europe and my duty as a Member of Parliament had brought about the situation in which I found myself.

I told them, too, of the Government protest on my behalf, made to Moscow on 3rd February, and of the great difficulties which had developed as a consequence of my re-marriage. I accepted that there might well be room for improvement in any Member's work in his constituency, but that this point, if it had substance, had surely been raised very late in the day. The real question for decision was whether or not a foreign power was to be allowed to dictate to the electors of Harrow East, utilizing all the cross-currents and the weaknesses of our free society for its purposes. It was on this note that I sat down, and the warmth of my reception gave the first real grounds for hope that we had been successful.

Eric Pratt replied to the debate with a temperate and reasonable speech, and during what seemed an interminable interval, the vote was taken. We three remained on the platform throughout, together with the Officers of the Association, who had made it known that they would resign should the vote go against them. Cyril Norton, urbane but nonetheless excited, exuded friendly neutrality. I felt an immense feeling of gratitude towards Eric and Douglas, the two men whose loyalty and energy had enabled them to challenge the authority of the Executive on a matter of principle which affected me so closely.

Outside there milled a crowd of pressmen among the television cameras. Inside, a steady stream of people moved towards the doors after recording their votes: and as the counting agents finally emerged from the back of the hall we all knew that the decision, one way or the other, was likely to be a decisive one, and that Harrow East was going to make political history.

Amid dead silence the Chairman rose to declare the result.

By 454 votes to 277 the Special General Meeting of the Association had overruled its Executive Council, and declared its confidence in myself as their present Member and future Candidate. It was a good moment, but even as the tide of relief flooded over me I found time to wonder how many of those present realized what they had accomplished. By this decision it seemed that we had together ensured that the new technique employed by the Russian Intelligence Service to eliminate a political opponent would not again be used against a British Member of Parliament. In face of a concentrated and skilfully-mounted attack by the Soviet Secret Police the fundamental decencies of our free society, with all its faults, had won a major victory.

PART FOUR

44. DÉNOUEMENT

44. *DÉNOUEMENT*

WE had done it, and the Officers of the Harrow East Association, headed by Theo Constantine, immediately resigned en bloc. They were followed by the Agent, who had identified herself irretrievably with the minority view.

In the House of Commons and outside I basked for a few days in the warmth of a political success which had confounded the prophets, silenced my opponents and delighted my friends. Until that time I had not realized how many back-benchers, Socialist as well as Conservatives, suffer from the pressures applied by local party caucuses, and the strength of their feelings surprised me.

Nevertheless, the cost, in political terms, was heavy, and the General Election of 1966 was almost on us. We had no doubt in our minds about the serious effect which the deep split within the Association must have had on our prospects in the forthcoming struggle.

But the new officers were tried friends: Eric Pratt slipped naturally back into the Chairmanship, with Douglas Charter as his Vice-Chairman, and Otto Sputz as Treasurer. It was hard to contemplate a change of Agent on the eve of an election, and we were relieved when Mrs. Burton withdrew her resignation and stayed. Queensbury ward was solidly for us, and in Harrow Weald we had still our incomparable team of lady canvassers headed by Vera Charter and Betty Painter. But in Stanmore there was an ominous silence, and we knew that a number of our oldest supporters in the ward were simply refusing any longer to give us their help. But thanks to Herculean efforts on the part of my supporters, within three weeks of the Special General Meeting we were launched into a General Election campaign with new officers, a full set of committee rooms and a fully-manned organization. In two of the five committee rooms, however, the workers pointedly omitted the name of their

Candidate from the usual display posters. And in Stanmore North the efforts of a few faithful helpers were neutralized by a dreadful atmosphere of defeatism and a general disinclination to canvass.

A chill breeze to our hopes came in the form of an article in the *Daily Telegraph* from a reporter who had probed into the core of disloyalty which was festering behind the scenes. The headline read "Backing for Courtney Doubtful" and continued "No-one is openly damaging the apparent unity, but it is significant that . . . party stalwarts are not prepared to state publicly their voting intentions." A swift disclaimer from Eric Pratt was published on the 26th March. But we had reckoned without Theo Constantine. On the 30th, the day before the Poll, there appeared a letter over his signature. It was headlined "Harrow East".

"Sir," he wrote, "The implication contained in Mr. Eric E. Pratt's letter (March 26) that as the resigned president of the Harrow East Conservative Association I have promised my support to Cdr. Courtney is not correct. I am clearly on record as opposing his adoption, as were the other officers who resigned at the same time.

Mr. Pratt asked me to meet him to discuss the matter and asked me whether, if requested, I would come back as the president. I told him quite clearly that I would not hold any office in Harrow East so long as Cdr. Courtney was the candidate.

I assured Mr. Pratt that I would take no action to the detriment of the Association, but that as an ordinary member of the Association I was unable to support its present candidate.   Theo Constantine,
Stanmore, Middlesex."

Polling Day dawned, and once again the Tory candidate drove in his blue Landrover round the constituency with Oliver Thorold, the son of two of my oldest friends, at the wheel. With our 1964 majority of 2259 in a straight fight with Labour, we now had the intervention of a new and excellent Liberal candidate, the knowledge of a probable swing towards

the Socialists and the realization that there was treachery in
our midst. After two recounts we lost the seat to Labour by
378 votes, and on the next morning I received a letter from the
politician who commands my greatest respect. "No-one could
have done better," he wrote, "and few would have done so
well. . . ."

There remains little to be told. On 13th June my wife's
second Divorce Petition was heard and she received her
Decree Nisi, having been granted the discretion of the Court in
respect of her own admitted adultery.

Three days later the constituency Annual General Meeting
decide to set up a committee to "review candidates" for the
purpose of choosing a Prospective Conservative Candidate for
Harrow East—not necessarily myself. Three of the five who
had resigned after the Special General Meeting had now
returned to the inner circle. The others were active. Douglas
Charter, my staunchest supporter, had been dropped from the
Vice-Chairmanship, and the writing was on the wall. On 14th
January, 1967, I once again appeared before a Selection
Committee and on 14th March the final meeting was held at
Harrow Weald County Grammar School, the scene of my
former triumph. There were perhaps 300 fewer people in the
hall than on the previous occasion, and it was noticeable that
an unusually large number of Young Conservatives were
present. There were, too, many faces which I do not recollect
having seen before. I noticed with misgiving the absence of the
solid phalanx of middle-aged people who had rallied to my
support just a year previously. The reasons for this were
evident. On the one hand, the quietly constitutional methods
of the old gang, who had learned their lesson, had greatly
reduced the level of public interest. On the other, the back-
stairs campaign of character defamation, which had been
proceeding for many months in continuation of the Russian
attack, was now paying a dividend.

As I looked around the hall I could see that this was a much
smaller assembly than last time, under the control of old
hands at the political game who had had time to prepare their
comeback and were determined to make no more mistakes.

Two others besides myself had been chosen to attend this final selection meeting, both of them being considerably younger men. We made our speeches separately, in accordance with the prescribed ritual, answered questions and retired, with varying degrees of acclamation from those assembled. The proceedings moved to a vote, and once again the wait seemed interminable, but I knew in my heart that the outcome was a foregone conclusion.

The result was declared amid a scene of enthusiasm. A young stockbroker, a member of the Bow Group, aged 27, was selected by a clear majority as Prospective Conservative Candidate for Harrow East. For me the decision was a blow that seemed politically mortal. The process set in train by the K.G.B. in August 1965 had been completed.

EPILOGUE

IT is many years since a wise man declared that there are no experts on Russia—only varying degrees of ignorance. The reader must judge for himself to what extent I am qualified to pass judgment on the affairs of that great country, but he will grant me that my experience has been closer, more varied and longer than most.

There is no need for me to dwell on the contrast between the geographic, climatic and historic factors which have conditioned the physique, character and political institutions of the British and Russian peoples. On the other hand, I believe it to be immensely important that we should understand that in all these things Russians are completely different from ourselves. Similarities in our sense of humour and in appreciation of the arts must not blind us to this fact, nor to the realization that for at least a century and a half successive Russian Governments, both Imperial and Soviet, have made great efforts to persuade us that the differences do not exist, or if they do, that their importance is greatly exaggerated.

In the development of political institutions, for example, our good fortune in being an island is in stark contrast to that of Russia—basically an immense plain with no natural land frontiers. Similarly, our immunity from invasion for 900 years can be contrasted with numerous invasions of the Russian plain and, in particular, with the dreadful two and a half centuries of the "Tartar Yoke", when Russia was dominated by cruel and primitive Mongol overlords. It is arguable that a major aspect of Russian foreign policy since the conquest of Kazan by Ivan the Terrible in the middle of the 16th century has been to play down the effect of this catastrophic period and to pretend that in terms of a civilized society Russia has regained the ground lost and caught up with the rest of Europe.

This is simply not true, and we in Britain must learn to reconcile our admiration for the Russian theatre and ballet, our delight in the virtuosity of Richter and Oistrakh and our respect for the feats of Gagarin and Tereshkova with the continuing existence in Russia of an arbitrary despotism, a political illiteracy and the barbarism of an all-pervading Secret Police.

In the circumstances of the day it was probably inevitable that Ivan the Terrible, faced with the problem of consolidating his Grand-Dukedom of Muscovy round the principality of Rostov-Suzdal, should have found it necessary to create the *Oprichnina*—the forebear of the modern Secret Police. This *Oprichnina*, or "thing apart" was the instrument of autocratic policy created by Ivan for the protection of his person and of the régime. The *Oprichniki*, who also formed the Kremlin Guard, were recruited from the sons of the lesser Russian nobility, and their badge of office was a whip and a dog's head, which signified the ability to sniff out treachery and to extirpate it from the realms of the Tsar.

It became in course of time a State within a State, answerable to the Tsar alone and outside such laws of the land as remained from the earlier Kievan epoch. During the four centuries which have elapsed since the creation of a Secret Police organization in this manner, no autocratic ruler of Russia has found it possible to dispense with it as an instrument of policy. On the contrary, to its internal security functions, which were the principal reason for its creation, there have been added duties involving foreign intelligence, subversion and disintegration, which fit into the new and immensely wide field of contact between Russian and the outside world. Furthermore, and developing sharply since the Revolution of 1917, when the *Okhrana* of the Tsars was transformed almost overnight into the *Cheka* of the Bolshevik Government under Felix Dzerzhinsky, the Secret Police have come to be used as an instrument of foreign policy, both for the gathering of intelligence and for the kind of active operations of which this book furnishes an example.

If it was the political uncertainties of the 16th century which brought the *Oprichnina* into being under Ivan the Terrible, so it is the continuing lack of political stability inside the Soviet Union to which we are indebted for wide and detailed knowledge of the present-day organization and methods of operation of the Russian Secret Police. The very weakness which caused it to come into being continues to supply the West with a steady stream of defectors, from whom it has been possible to build up a reasonably accurate picture of the organizations concerned. Particularly useful defections, both in quantity and quality, have coincided with political crises within the Soviet Union. For example, the Stalin purges of 1936–1938 gave us men of the calibre of Walter Krivitsky, previously head of the Western European network of the 4th Department of the Red Army, which later merged into the G.R.U. or *Glavnoe Razvedivatelnoye Upravlenie,* which may be loosely translated as Central Intelligence Directorate. Similarly, the arrest and execution of Lavrenti Beria a few months after the death of Stalin in 1953 initiated a valuable chain-reaction of defectors, among whom can be numbered Peter Deryabin, Vladimir Petrov and other important functionaries of the K.G.B., the *Komitet Gosudarstvennoi Bezopasnosti,* or Committee of State Security which, interlocking and sometimes overlapping with the G.R.U., makes up the modern Secret Police organization, which is known collectively as the Russian Intelligence Service, or R.I.S. The latest, and one of the most important of this long line of defectors has been Lt. Colonel Evgeny Runge, a senior officer of the First Chief Directorate of the K.G.B., who came over to the Americans in the autumn of 1967.

The stories of these men have painted us a picture of the present R.I.S. Establishment, privileged, well-equipped and numbering perhaps 200,000, as much a State within a State as were their predecessors four centuries earlier. We hear of an internal instability which is perhaps inevitable in an organization with such a long and chequered record as this. But we also obtain a glimpse of another aspect of this picture, of over-organization and excessive secrecy and attention to detail, giving a rigidity to the whole structure which gives rise to surprising errors when operational plans go slightly awry. It is the old story of over-centralized control, enhanced by a modern counterpart of the traditional reluctance of the Russian *Tchinovnik* (minor official) to exercise personal initiative at times of unexpected crisis.

An example from the Portland spy case illustrates this weakness. The British Security authorities, having learnt the details of the R.I.S. communication arrangements, were surprised to receive routine transmissions on the appropriate frequencies from the Moscow clandestine radio transmitter to the Krogers in their Ruislip bungalow—ten days after their arrest had been reported in the world's newspapers.

An organization of this kind which is placed deliberately outside the law of its native country must necessarily develop a ruthlessness which is wholly evil, in that it simply does not consider ordinary human values except in so far as they can be manipulated to serve the needs of the organization itself. It stands to reason that in its international relationships, also, the Russian Intelligence Service will disregard the conventions of the civilized world. A commonplace theme in the stories of all defectors, and brought out with particular force in the Penkovsky papers, is to describe how the Soviet "legal" espionage networks rely for their operation on the diplomatic privileges and immunities accorded by long custom to the embassies of countries which maintain mutual diplomatic relations with the U.S.S.R. We have the testimony of another defector, Alexander Kaznacheev, that over two-thirds of the Soviet Embassy in Rangoon, where he worked, were at the same time members of Soviet Intelligence organizations, responsible direct to headquarters in Moscow. Penkovsky puts the figure for the Soviet Embassy in London at 60%.

In Tsarist times a witty Russian once described the constitution of his country as being "Absolutism, moderated by assassination". The remark would certainly have applied to the Stalin era, of post-revolutionary Russia, and even in the present climate of post-Stalinist thaw the absolute power of Russia's rulers remains concentrated in the hands of the Central Committee of the Communist Party.

The State Security Committee, or K.G.B., is in the true line of descent, not only from the *Cheka* of Felix Dzerzhinsky, but from the original *Oprichnina* of Ivan the Terrible. For it is not a "Ministry", and is therefore quite independent of the Soviet Government. It is described as a "State Committee" and it is responsible direct to the Soviet power nucleus—the Central Committee of the Communist Party. Its present head is Yuri Andropov, a former Secretary of the Central Committee and now a Candidate member of the Politburo.

In historical terms, the rôle of the K.G.B. in Western society today can be likened to that of the Jesuit Order during the Counter-Reformation of the 16th Century, and in some surprising ways its methods are not dissimilar.

It is the Second Chief Directorate of the K.G.B., commanded up to 1965 by Lt. General Gribanov, which chiefly concerns this narrative. This Directorate is responsible for operations against foreigners on Soviet territory, and there can be little doubt that, acting in conjunction with the K.G.B. "Resident" at the Soviet Embassy in London, it was the Second Chief Directorate that mounted "Operation Courtney".

*   *   *

Responsibility for recruiting agents for the purpose of gathering intelligence through the "legal" network in the United Kingdom, based on the Soviet Embassy, is placed on the First Chief Directorate of the K.G.B., headed by Lt. General Sakharovsky. We call to mind the list of names brought out of the Soviet Embassy in Ottawa in 1946 by Gusenko, the cypher-clerk, where the word *Nash* ("ours") is triumphantly noted in the margin as each victim becomes finally entangled in the R.I.S. net.

But the K.G.B.'s interest in British nationals also extends to the activities covered by the Second Chief Direcorate. This interest, by contrast with that of the First Chief Directorate, may be, in Soviet intelligence jargon, either "positive" or "negative".

On the "positive" side can be grouped those individuals who may be useful to the Russians in a fellow-travelling or "front" sense. A "front" organization is the generalized term given to a Society, Group or Association which is ostensibly devoted to the promotion of "Peace" or "Cultural Relations", but which in fact is an instrument of Soviet Communist policy in this country. In the first place there are the "opinion formers",

Members of Parliament, editors of periodicals or officials of organizations such as the Society for Cultural Relations with the U.S.S.R., the Soviet British Friendship Society and the Great Britain–U.S.S.R. Association. Secondly, there are the commercial favourites, the individuals, often high in industrial circles, who can be relied upon to put the Soviet viewpoint favourably to representative gatherings of businessmen, and sometimes in their name to the Board of Trade.

Most important, there are the policy-makers, Foreign Office officials, Civil Servants in other Ministries, Trades Union officials and, of course, members of the Government. Maclean and Philby are classic examples of the last category, and these two men undoubtedly combined pro-Soviet activity within their departments with the collection of intelligence.

Whatever the "positive" interest, whether on the intelligence or the fellow-travelling side, the K.G.B. will endeavour to consolidate the usefulness of the individual concerned once he has become amenable, and will take steps to ensure that there is no going-back after the first slip into treason. It is at this point that the methods employed tie up with those in use for people in this country in whom the Soviet interest is defined as "negative".

There are still, mercifully, a few individuals in Great Britain whose views, attributes or activities are considered by the K.G.B. to stand in the way of Soviet cold-war policies, and these men and women make up this "negative" category. In each case it is from the Soviet point of view necessary to judge whether the effectiveness of an individual's activities justifies action by the K.G.B. with the object of neutralization, or whether, on balance, the disadvantage of publicity is considered to be too great. If the man concerned is a diplomat or a frequent visitor who has developed an undesirably good knowledge of Russia and the Russians, the remedy is simple. He is declared *persona non grata* and refused a re-entry visa when he next tries to enter the Soviet Union.

He may be a businessman who discovers for himself some of the pitfalls of trade with the Soviet Union—and warns his colleagues accordingly. Again, the remedy is a simple one.

Epilogue

The Department of the Ministry of Foreign Trade with which the businessman normally negotiates is instructed to make life difficult for him, and suitable hints are dropped by Soviet officials to his business competitors and colleagues. There are few foreign commercial organizations that have the courage to resist pressures of this kind, and the source of the difficulty from the Soviet point of view is soon and easily eliminated.

There are, however, other and more dangerous opponents who do not lend themselves quite so easily to action of this kind. There are the members of *émigré* organizations, such as the dreaded N.T.S., whose object is nothing less than the liberation of the oppressed masses within Soviet Russia. There are the organizers of disaffection in controlled territories such as East Germany. There are, of course, the representatives of Foreign Secret Services. And there are others who by their words or actions represent a specific threat to Soviet policy in some respect.

All of these must be neutralized, if not eliminated, and we have the testimony of men like Peter Deryabin, Bogdan Stashynsky and Nikolai Khokhlov to support a very grave conclusion. This is that the Russian Intelligence Service will stop at absolutely nothing to gain its ends, even though the methods may vary widely. There are the simple beatings, as administered to Houghton, the traitor of Portland, to make him a compliant tool. There is the age-old use of hostages. There is blackmail in all its forms. There is abduction, as in the case of Generals Miller and Kutepov, and of Germans and Austrians too numerous to mention. Finally there is plain murder, as in the cases of Ignace Reiss, Trotsky, Konovalets, Bandera and of the planned attempt on the life of George Okolovitch.

By the nature of things, the use of the more drastic of the R.I.S. operational techniques, murder and kidnapping, necessarily becomes widely known, and for this reason they are employed sparingly, and only in cases of real political importance. Every incident of this kind damages the image which the Soviet Government is at such pains to present, of Russia as a progressive, peace and freedom-loving democracy. The painstaking work of years in the propaganda fields of culture, athletics and astro-navigation can be ruined overnight by the testimony of a defector such as Khokhlov, who brought with him the devilishly ingenious weapons with which he was instructed to murder a leading member of the N.T.S. on the orders of the 13th Department of the First Chief Directorate of the K.G.B.

Whether or not the victims themselves tell their stories, the use of relatives still living in Eastern Europe as hostages can often be presumed from study of individual records. It is a fact, however, that this method of intimidation is losing much of its force as *émigrés* and their older relatives die off, and as children grow up in a new environment.

But there are many occasions on which the K.G.B. requires to bring pressure to bear or to neutralize a victim, either in the "positive" or "negative" sense, where the cruder methods of abduction or murder obviously cannot be used. The K.G.B. has accordingly developed techniques of blackmail and "character assassination", or defamation, which are well-suited to the more civilized societies of the West.

These new and sophisticated techniques are greatly assisted, in the case of possible potential victims who visit Communist countries, by the deliberate obtaining of damaging evidence which is stored against the day, perhaps years ahead, when it may be required. The evidence may take the form of taped conversations, incriminating documents or damaging photographs, all obtained by clandestine means. If necessary this evidence can, of course, simply be fabricated.

Simple blackmail is employed for the purpose of recruitment in the espionage field, and for this there are many well-documented examples. Attempts, both successful and unsuccessful, have been recorded in this country against an electronic engineer, a civil servant, a War Office clerk, an R.A.F. communications rating, a diplomatic wireless operator and the secretary to a Member of Parliament. In four cases the agent was a Russian or satellite diplomat. The others were a Military Attaché and a known Intelligence Officer working in the Soviet Military Attaché's office in London. All were covered by diplomatic immunity, and they had one thing in common—the charm, thoughtfulness and hospitality which characterized the preliminary contacts before the trap was sprung. Of all famous last words "But he was such a nice chap!" must rank high in the history of operations of this type.

Whether the material used is true or false, the threat is the same—public exposure—geared to the social or professional environment of the victim so as to obtain the maximum degree of effective pressure.

If successful, these methods will produce compliant agents, who can then be operated by either the "legal" or the "illegal" networks within the country concerned, according to convenience. If "legal", the agent will usually be run by the K.G.B. section of the Soviet Embassy, using an elaborate system of cut-outs and dead-letter boxes (D.L.B.s) for the exchange of instructions and information. The "legal" organization's problems are greatly simplified in the United Kingdom by the existence of special arrangements with the British Government by which every member of the Soviet Embassy, including chauffeurs, servants and families, is given diplomatic immunity. It goes without saying that the fruits of "legal" espionage are forwarded to Moscow in the Diplomatic Bag.

If, on the other hand, it is decided to run the agent "illegally", this will be done by an undercover network under the direction of a professional spy of the calibre of Gordon Lonsdale. Here, the means of communication with Moscow are clandestine, based on cypher and microdot techniques, and utilizing high-frequency, low-power radio transmitters of the type discovered in the Kroger's bungalow at Ruislip.

There are, of course, other means of recruiting agents, based on certain types of character weakness. There is the ideological spy, the man who will sell his country for money, and the unbalanced individual with a craving for the exercise of power. But in all these cases the weapons of intimidation or blackmail may become necessary at some stage, if the R.I.S. is to be able to extract the maximum of usefulness from its victims.

There is another field in which the K.G.B. has developed its activities recently in the United Kingdom. This is a general policy aimed at the politico-economic disintegration of non-Communist societies which takes numerous forms, grouped under the general heading of *Desinformatsiya*, which can be translated very roughly as "Disinformation", or even "Deception" in its old war-time sense. Disinformation is the task of Department "D" of the First Chief Directorate of the K.G.B. It relies on mouthpieces within the mass media, radio and Press, the Universities and the so-called "Lilac Establishment" to direct at the British public information and attitudes inspired by the K.G.B. Its object is to build up a British dependance on tainted sources which could eventually become total, as an essential factor in the process by which Communism intends finally to destroy our society.

It also consists of the planting of information designed to mislead. This was in evidence during the Cuba crisis of 1962, and it may well have had quite the reverse effect to that intended when Nasser was persuaded of the build-up of Israeli troops on the Syrian border in the summer of 1967, and responded with an Egyptian advance into Sinai. It is believed that this quite false information came to him from Soviet sources.

The activities of the Russian Intelligence Service have done incalculable damage to Great Britain since the end of the war. For example, the recruitment of the ideological spies Allan Nunn May and Klaus Fuchs, in conjunction with David Greenglass and his collaborators in America, have supplied Moscow with sufficient highly secret information to enable them to manufacture the atomic bomb at least eighteen months before this would otherwise have been possible. In the opinion of the Joint Committee on Atomic Energy expressed in April 1951, Fuchs alone "has influenced the safety of more people and accomplished greater damage than any other spy, not only in the history of the United States but in the history of nations". It seems certain that the great bulk at least of the atomic information betrayed by these four men was passed back through the "legal" networks of Soviet Embassies and through the Diplomatic Bag.

The four highly-placed British Foreign Office officials who turned traitor must also have given valuable information to our enemies quite apart from their considerable usefulness in influencing policy. In particular, our Secret Intelligence organization suffered a crippling blow through the treachery of Blake and Philby. Nothing could have shaken the complacency of successive British governments in facing the malign efficiency of our enemies more greatly than this successful and immensely damaging penetration.

Our rulers should ask themselves whether the lesson has been learnt and the ground which has been lost recovered.

Lesser successes have also been recorded, the whole amounting to a formidable scale of damage to the nation's interests. It is perhaps only natural that a principle target of the R.I.S. has been the Foreign Service, whose members are exposed to every kind of pressure by the latter-day *Oprichniki* of the Second Chief Directorate when serving in Moscow and other East European capitals. Trained as they are in the conventions of civilized diplomacy, our diplomatic representatives, the "cookie-pushers" of American diplomatic slang, are ill-equipped to deal with the secret world of espionage, as is shown with devastating clarity by the report of the Vassall Tribunal.

It is this curious clinging to unrealities which seems to have led the Foreign Office to try to protect our representatives in East Europe by according them a special degree of diplomatic immunity when stationed in Moscow, Prague, Sofia or Budapest. For some unexplained reason these special arrangements have not been considered necessary in the cases of Poland and Roumania. Foreign Office reasoning could, it might be thought, lead to the conclusion that Houghton, of the Portland spy case, might not have been suborned in Warsaw had he been accorded the higher degree of diplomatic immunity enjoyed by his counterpart in Moscow.

But all this is rather like appealing to a policeman in a country where the rule of law does not obtain and, as might be expected, there have been a number of cases in which the extra immunities have proved quite valueless. The drugging and assault on the British Military Attaché at Kishinev in the autumn of 1967 is a case in point.

Convinced as it appears to be by the Foreign Office that this extra immunity is worth while, the Government has had to accept the granting of reciprocal immunities to the entire staff of the Soviet, Czechoslovak, Hungarian and Bulgarian Embassies in London. This represents an added burden on our small and overworked Security Service in its efforts to contain the "legal" espionage efforts, directed mainly from within the Soviet Embassy, of which we now have such abundant proof.

It is not unfair to hold the view that the Foreign Office has been manoeuvred by the Russians into a situation which is causing severe damage to our national security, as the price of a largely illusory measure of protection for its staff in Communist capitals.

Strange as this may seem, it is even stranger that the Anglo-Soviet Consular Convention, signed by the Foreign Secretary in December 1965, should make provision for the opening of Soviet Consulates in places such as Liverpool and Glasgow, each member of the staff in those posts, together with servants and families, to be given the extraordinary degree of diplomatic immunity already enjoyed by their colleagues in London. It seems that such an arrangement is not thought to be inconsistent with the holding of Gerald Brooke incommunicado in a Soviet labour camp. I have heard it argued that the retention of special immunities in Moscow and other capitals is necessary for special reasons and, to put no finer point on it, that "two can play at the espionage game". While the justification for this argument is difficult if not impossible for a layman to judge, it is perhaps worth recalling the quite recent testimony of the K.G.B. defector, Vladimir Petrov.

"In all my 21 years as a professional State Security Officer," he wrote, "I never came across one authentic case of foreign espionage in the Soviet Union in peace time." Since Petrov defected, it is true, there has been the case of Oleg Penkovsky, who himself took the initiative and practically forced his information on the apparently reluctant British.

The Russian Intelligence Service, as an instrument of a Soviet national policy which includes the support of that part of world-communism which is still directed from Moscow, has considerable achievements to its credit, some of the most spectacular having been at British expense. Hitherto, the emphasis has been on espionage, but with the achievement of a nuclear stalemate between Russia and the West, and with the receding possibility of conventional war between the two major Alliances, the relative importance of obtaining intelligence has decreased, except perhaps in the industrial sphere.

It seems probable that more effort is now being concentrated on the exploitation of the weaknesses of key capitalist countries such as our own, by the manipulation of Trades Unions and of unofficial organizations for industrially disruptive purposes. The encouragement of "Peace" organizations and of movements to end the war in Vietnam are similarly being given support.

R.I.S. activity seems to have become more sophisticated through the use of "charm-squads" of freshly-trained Soviet diplomats and trade representatives whose business it is to mix more closely than previously in certain social circles in this country. A good example was Commander Ivanov, the R.I.S. agent who figured prominently in the Profumo affair. The aim would seem to be twofold: to identify potential "front" men and women who can be relied on, after treatment, to further the general line of Soviet policy, and secondly to pick out those more intransigent opponents of Soviet ideas whose activities could prove harmful to them. In both cases the First Chief Directorate of the K.G.B. will not fail, in case of necessity, to use the well-tried weapons of intimidation, blackmail or character assassination to neutralize or eliminate its opponents. Similarly, the first two methods will be used when required to consolidate the K.G.B. hold on their informers or "front" men.

This book has related the course of an actual K.G.B. operation which was carried out with limited success against a British Member of Parliament, namely myself. It has been written in autobiographical form for two reasons. First, to give the reader some idea of the life-long interest which I have taken in Russian affairs and of the knowledge which I have gained in the process. Second, to enable the reader to form his own opinion as to the K.G.B.'s reasons for singling me out for this particular treatment. If it is true that a man is known by his enemies, it has been a compliment indeed.

There remains one seriously disquieting feature of the whole affair. Apart from a half-hearted verbal protest to the Soviet Government, neither the British Government, the Foreign Office or the Conservative Opposition have raised a finger in reaction against this flagrant case of Soviet interference in the internal working of the British political system. On the contrary, every attempt has been made to "sweep it under the carpet".

This raises some important questions. Are we, for example, fully aware of the extent of Soviet blackmail operations against individuals occupying positions of influence in this country? In the words of George Wigg, who are the Russians trying to frighten by showing their teeth in this way? And secondly, can this fear be linked in any way with the attitude of the Foreign Office to the Russians in these and other matters, placatory to the point of subservience?

My own feeling, backed by personal experience extending over some years, is that the rot exposed by the defection of Burgess, Maclean, Blake and Philby has gone deeper than we know and that the taint remains, perhaps at a high level, inside the Foreign Office.

In our society as a whole there are many who are naïve, sentimental and gullible enough to accept Soviet perversion of the truth and unknowingly to lend their support to R.I.S. activities aimed at its destruction. But there are also in our midst K.G.B. agents under control, some of whom may have long since lost their original motivation but have remained shackled by fear of exposure to the Scythian chariot-wheels. The offer to these unfortunate of some form of Amnesty could, I believe, retrieve at one stroke some of the great damage which we have suffered at R.I.S. hands.

If it stimulates a public insistence that all these questions should be properly considered, this book will have justified itself.

APPENDIX A

Letter from Commander Courtney to Admiral of the Fleet Sir Caspar John, G.C.B.

4th March, 1965

Dear Caspar,

I hope that I am right in assuming that the terms of reference of the Standing Security Commission, of which you are a member, include matters such as the following. I refer to the situation in which unreciprocated, and in my view unnecessary, advantage is given by Departments to the Embassies of certain Communist countries in London which are either known to have, or suspected of having, conducted espionage activities under the cover of Diplomatic privilege and immunity.

I refer specifically to the bilateral arrangements existing between H.M.G. and the Soviet, Czechoslovakian, Hungarian and Bulgarian Governments. In accordance with these arrangements the entire staff of the Embassies of these countries in London are accorded a degree of Diplomatic immunity which, as regards those who are not "Diplomatic Agents" within the terms of the Vienna Convention on Diplomatic Relations, have immunities equivalent to those of senior diplomats. It should be noted that we do not accord blanket immunity of this kind to the representatives of other countries, even to our closest friends and allies. As a particular instance, there are twenty chauffeurs on the staffs of the four Embassies referred to who, by virtue of their Diplomatic immunity, are now outside the law of this country when driving, whether on duty or not. The effect of this was shown in a recent case when, in a collision involving a Soviet vehicle, a British subject was killed, and the Soviet Embassy pleaded this immunity as an excuse for not permitting the chauffeur concerned to appear in court. I need hardly add that in the case of chauffeurs there is no reciprocity in the four countries concerned. In London, Soviet, Czechoslovak, Hungarian and Bulgarian Diplomatic officials are driven by chauffeurs of their own nationality. In Moscow, Prague, Budapesth, and Sofia British Diplomatic officials are driven by nationals of the countries to which they are accredited.

If I may set aside for a moment the reasons put forward by the Foreign Office for permitting this anomalous state of affairs to

235

continue, I would submit that it represents a serious danger to security in that it imposes a severe handicap on the Security Service in carrying out its duties. I submit furthermore that it is well known that active political, military and industrial espionage is carried on under the cloak of Diplomatic privilege and immunity by some at least of these four Embassies.

The reasons for the Foreign Office action, as revealed in the course of an Adjournment Debate in July 1964, are principally that the dangers and temptations to which our own Diplomatic representatives in these countries are subjected make it necessary for them to be safeguarded by all means possible. While this is a perfectly laudable viewpoint, the question arises whether any Governmental Agreements with these countries are going to be effective in the manner hoped for, and I need only quote the recent case of the British Assistant Naval Attaché in Moscow, who was forcibly arrested, searched and detained while engaged on his normal duties at Khabarovsk. This is, I believe, the third or fourth such case which has taken place in the Soviet Union over the past three years. In these circumstances I question whether the granting of special immunities to British Diplomatic personnel in these countries is of the slightest real use. At the same time it seems to be an admirable means by which the Secret Services of Communist countries can obtain additional security and facilities when operating in the United Kingtom.

If the situation as I have set it out is anywhere near the truth it would follow that the normal criteria of Diplomatic usage cannot properly be applied when dealing with Communist countries, and I feel I should record my personal opinion that the obvious potential threat to the career structure and privileges of the Diplomatic Service plays a certain part in their acceptance of this wholly unsatisfactory situation.

In conclusion may I say that these views and observations are founded on certain personal experience and study of the countries concerned, particularly Soviet Russia, which I frequently visit on business. Support for my argument is available from the Proceedings of the House of Commons, and from correspondence with Ministers which I shall, of course, be glad to place at your disposal should you so wish. There is, in addition, a wealth of published material arising from the espionage cases of the past fifteen years from which it seems clear that Communist Embassies in London have been closely involved. I shall be grateful, therefore, if you will place this letter before your Committee and, although I shall not expect to be given any special information, I should welcome an assurance in due course that the serious security loophole to which I have drawn attention has been effectively blocked. The Vienna Convention, of which I enclose a copy for ease of reference, contains ample provision, if properly used, for the rectification of the worst of the anomalies concerned."

APPENDIX B

Letter from Commander Courtney to the Foreign Secretary (not posted).

28th March, 1965

Dear Foreign Secretary,

I am writing by way of precaution, as I am leaving today for Moscow on a short business trip, and feel that it is desirable to guard against the possibility, I think a remote one, that I might be detained there by the Soviet authorities. This possibility has arisen in my mind as a result of the latest security incident which is reported so prominently in yesterday's *Daily Telegraph*.

As you know, I have great respect and affection for the Russians, but this does not blind me to the fact that the Soviet Government is completely uncivilized and ruthless to an extreme when it comes to political matters such as those involving espionage and national security. In such matters the use of hostages, agents-provocateurs, "framing" and interrogation under pressure amounting to torture are a commonplace. A simple example, as it has always seemed to me, was the ingenious procedure which led up to the exchange of Lonsdale for Wynne.

As you know, I have recently, in Parliament, drawn attention on a number of occasions to obvious gaps in our security defences such as those represented by the way in which H.M.G. gives a special degree of diplomatic immunity, right outside the provisions of the Vienna Convention, to the entire staff of four Communist Embassies in London, including that of the Soviet Union. I have also underlined the complete disregard of the Russians, when it suits them, for diplomatic conventions, as illustrated recently in Khabarovsk by the forcible arrest, detention and search of our Assistant Naval Attaché, Lieutenant-Commander Laville. As there has been no attempt by your Department to insist on reciprocity in such matters as Service Attachés and diplomatic chauffeurs it does not appear that my representations have had the slightest effect. From the Russian standpoint, however, it might seem that the ineffectiveness of my efforts in these respects implies a degree of disapproval by the "British authorities" which could, in certain circumstances, react to the Soviet advantage, by reducing the force of the official British reaction to a Soviet move. As a businessman who speaks Russian and frequently visits the Soviet Union I am always vulnerable, depending on the degree of importance which the Russians attach to their political requirement of the moment, and the fact that I am a Conservative whose criticisms of British attitudes towards the Soviet Union are not listened to by Governments of either political connection, in my view increases this vulnerability to some extent.

Naturally, if I did not consider myself completely innocent of any hostile intentions, either overt or covert, towards the Russians I would not travel to Moscow in present circumstances. I have the greatest liking for and confidence in them as a people, but I want you to know at the same time that I realise to the full that there is an element of risk, however slight, in paying my visit at this particular moment. My wife holds a copy of this letter, which I have asked her to communicate to the Press at her discretion.

Yours sincerely,
Anthony Courtney.

APPENDIX C

Extract from an article in "Izvestia" (*the National Soviet Government Daily Newspaper*) *of 17th November, 1965.*

The Sunday newspaper *News of the World* has for more than 100 years poisoned the minds of millions of English readers with all kinds of gossip, rumour, criminal sensation, sexual scandal, etc. The latest "sensation" which has been recorded is to the particular taste of this newspaper. As has been revealed by the *News of the World* of the 24th October, a certain Member of Parliament, a Conservative by political conviction and a business man by profession, Commander Anthony Courtney has been leading, to put it mildly, an unseemly way of life. In the course of this, by contrast with other more modest libertines, Courtney has been accustomed to be photographed in company with his casual women friends.

Someone from among Courtney's political or commercial opponents has obtained some of the negatives and, according to the English newspaper *Sunday Telegraph*, passed copies of the photographs to his colleagues in Parliament. The profligate was exposed. Here, surely, should have been an end of the story. But Courtney is not a man humbly to acknowledge his guilt. As he himself has said, he was a friend of the writer, Ian Fleming, the author of a series of books about the famous agent No. 007 of the "Intelligence Service". Recalling the literary style of his deceased friend, Courtney, without much reflection, declared, "I am the victim of a plot by the Russian Secret Police". Courtney's logic is simple to the point of naïveté—to be a debauchee is disgraceful, but to be the victim of the Russian Intelligence Service is in certain English circles considered positively respectable. This is the way in which a petticoat-hunter can appear as a hero even though only in the pages of the *News of the World*.

This unmasked debauchee would not deserve attention if the attitude adopted by him had not been typical. Not long ago, when England was shaken by the scandal of Minister Profumo, who had the same weakness as Mr. Courtney, some of the less squeamish organs of the Western Press were also looking for a plot by "the Russian Secret Police", not without a tip-off from specialist services. One more point, and we shall have finished with Courtney. In an attempt to inflate his own importance and to give some authority to the story of his persecution by the K.G.B. he declared that he had cancelled a trip to Moscow in July of this year because it had been intended to "detain" him there. What a discerning man is this Courtney and how skilfully he avoids the danger! In actual fact the circumstances are much more prosaic. The newspaper *News of the World* contradicts Courtney's version by writing that "The Commander found it necessary to cancel his visit to Moscow" as a result of the resignation of the leader of the Conservative Party, the former Prime Minister, Sir Alec Douglas-Home—so Courtney's discernment scarcely comes into question. Apart from this, as we have been informed by the competent Soviet authorities, the question of a visa for Courtney was decided in a negative sense in view of the fact that the Ministry of Foreign Trade had no questions which it wished to discuss with him. Where is the logic in all this? If there had actually been any "sinister" plans in connection with Courtney by the Soviet organs involved, then why did he not receive a visa? There is only one answer. The respected Member of Parliament is simply lying.

APPENDIX D

Extract from Hansard *of Wednesday, 26th January, 1966.*

Commander Anthony Courtney (Harrow East): My Bill would amend the law relating to the diplomatic immunities and privileges granted to representatives of foreign States here in London. The House will recollect that I have on a number of occasions in the past drawn the attention of hon. Members to the abuse of diplomatic immunity and privilege, a continuing and calculated abuse, which is carried out by the representatives of a small minority of foreign embassies in London. In particular, in the debate on the Diplomatic Privileges Bill, in July, 1964, I endeavoured unsuccessfully, with the co-operation of some of my hon. Friends, to bring to an end certain special arrangements existing between Her Majesty's Government and four particular Governments in respect of diplomatic immunity.

There have been certain developments since then which, I submit, strengthen the arguments which I put forward on that occasion. First, in company with about 100 other nations, the United Kingdom has ratified the Vienna convention on Diplomatic Relations. This, as the House knows, gives a generally accepted and almost universally well-received framework for the conduct of diplomatic exchanges. In addition to Her Majesty's Government, the Government of the four countries to whom I have previously drawn attention have also ratified the Vienna Convention.

Secondly, we owe a debt to the Americans for the recent publication of the Penkovsky papers, which give evidence from internal Soviet sources of the activities of two powerful intelligence organisations operating from within the Soviet Embassy in London. I refer to the K.G.B. and the G.R.U. K.G.B. can be loosely translated as the Committee of State Security and G.R.U. can again be loosely referred to as a Central Intelligence Directorate. We have, in Penkovsky's own words, the story of the continuing activities of these two organisations from within the Soviet Embassy in London.

Appendix D

Thirdly, there is the now well-known technique which is applied by the K.G.B. here in this country against individuals whom it considers to stand in its way. I refer to the methods by which the Russians attempt to remove political opponents from public life by defamation of character. For this they find the free institutions of this country especially suitable for their malignant purposes.

Fourthly, I would mention the Bossard affair. This, which is in the recent memory of all hon. Members, was a clear illustration on our very doorstep of the continuing activities of Soviet espionage here in this country operating with the connivance and assistance of the Soviet Embassy in London under the cloak of diplomatic immunity.

Finally—this is the only welcome development to which I can point—we have the first timid reaction by Her Majesty's Government to this what some of us would describe as an intolerable state of affairs.

We have an excellent booklet to which I have previously drawn attention—*Their Trade is Treachery*—a booklet which has been given a limited circulation and which describes in detail, with factual personal cases, the mediaeval methods of blackmail and subversion carried out by the representatives of Communist embassies in this country. In particular, this booklet refers in the main to the activities of the two Russian intelligence services which I have mentioned, operating from within the Soviet Embassy.

I should like to ask the Government three questions here. Why is this booklet not available to the public? It is important, it is factual, and it is of the greatest interest to national security. Why do the Government refuse to put it in the Library of the House so that it can be looked at by hon. Members. What are they afraid of?

I believe that my Bill would go a little way towards neutralising the threat to national security of which I believe we have abundant evidence before us today, evidence which has been greatly added to since our discussion of the Diplomatic Privileges Bill in July, 1964. On the one hand, the Bill would seek to ensure that legitimate diplomatic machinery should continue to operate without let or hindrance. On the other, it would attempt to see that abuses of the diplomatic machinery can be kept within bounds which can be dealt with by our small but efficient Security Service.

The Bill would attempt, I hope successfully, to draw a distinction between two clear categories of diplomatic representation, which I call for the moment categories A and B. Category A consists of the vast majority of normal foreign embassies which we are glad to welcome and give hospitality to in this country and which conduct normal diplomacy by normal means. These are the great majority of bona fide diplomatic representatives. I would put into category B, however, the small minority which demand and which are accorded privileges and immunities greater than those laid down in the Vienna convention on diplomatic relations to which they and we and the great majority of States have subscribed.

It is no coincidence that the principal country which demands these extraordinary degrees of diplomatic immunity—the Soviet Union—is precisely that which is the greatest offender against the laws of diplomatic hospitality. I have endeavoured, in the Bill, to provide a separate scale of representation in the case of category B nations, as allowed for by the terms of the Vienna convention. I believe that this scale of representation, with certain conditions which I have added—I am not an expert on these matters and this can be considered only as a first tentative draft of the Bill—should take into consideration primarily the interests of national security. This is contained in Schedule I of the Bill.

It was argued in July, 1964, by the Government of that day, that special immunities were necessary in the case of the four nations to which I have referred because of the urgency of safeguarding the interests of our own diplomatic representatives in the capitals of those four countries.

If this is true—and I myself do not accept it—I ask, and I think that the House should ask, why it is not necessary to have similar special arrangements in the case of countries such as Poland and Roumania? This booklet contains references to both Poland and Roumania in the conduct of espionage in this country, but, apparently, it is not necessary to make any special arrangements such as those which exist for the other four Communist countries to which I have referred, and it does not seem that ordinary diplomatic procedures are in any way handicapped by the lack of such special arrangements.

If we think of the appalling 20 year security record in this country, and we think, again, of the Soviet Union as the main recipient of these extraordinary immunities, is there anyone in the House so naïve as to believe that it is not at least possible that it is deliberate Soviet policy to make the lives of our representatives in Moscow sufficiently intolerable for special immunities to be asked for by us and for the corresponding reciprocal extraordinary immunities to be demanded and accorded in this country?

It is a curious historical fact that the first statutory mention of diplomatic privilege and immunity comes in an Act in the reign of Queen Anne, introduced because of the action of certain turbulent and disorderly persons who insulted the person of Andrei Artamanovich Matveev, the Ambassador Extraordinary of His Tsarist Majesty, Emperor of Great Russia, by taking him by violence out of his coach in the public street. The wheel has turned full circle since those days, and it is a sad commentary on the present state of our relations with the Soviet Union in particular that an attempt to introduce this Bill should be made by a Member of the House of Commons who has spent many years of his working life attempting to improve Anglo-Soviet relations.

The Bill would go some way towards remedying a situation which, surely, we should no longer tolerate. There is a continuing abuse of our hospitality which cannot go on much longer without action by this House of Commons."

APPENDIX E

Diplomatic Privileges

A
BILL

To make further provision with regard to
diplomatic privileges and immunities.

Ordered to be brought in by

Commander Anthony Courtney,
Sir Rolf Dudley Williams, Viscount Lambton,
Mr. Iremonger, Dr. Wyndham Davies,
Sir Harry Legge-Bourke,
Sir Godfrey Nicholson, Mr. Edward Gardner,
Sir George Sinclair, Mr. John Page,
Mr. Anthony Grant and
Dame Patricia Hornsby-Smith.

Ordered, by The House of Commons,
to be Printed, 26 January 1966

LONDON
PRINTED AND PUBLISHED BY
HER MAJESTY'S STATIONERY OFFICE
Price 6*d.* net

[Bill 57]   (38130)   43/2

A

B I L L

T O

Make further provision with regard to diplomatic A.D. 1966
privileges and immunities.

B E IT ENACTED by the Queen's most Excellent Majesty, by and
with the advice and consent of the Lords Spiritual and
Temporal, and Commons, in this present Parliament
assembled, and by the authority of the same, as follows:—

5   **1.**—(1) In any case where under section 7(1) of the Diplomatic Provisions
Privileges Act 1964 (hereinafter referred to as " the principal relating to
Act ") a special agreement or arrangement is in force between bilateral
the Government of any state and the Government of the United arrangements.
Kingdom then so long as that agreement or arrangement 1964 c. 81.
10 continues in force—

(*a*) no commercial attaché or member of the mission
performing similar functions or a chauffeur being in any
of these cases a member of the mission of the State with
whom the agreement or arrangement is made shall be
15   entitled to any diplomatic immunity or privilege;

(*b*) the members of any class of persons who under that
agreement or arrangement are entitled to any diplomatic
privilege or immunity shall not exceed the number
specified in paragraph 1 of the Schedule to this Act in
20   relation to that class and no person who is not a member
of any such class shall be entitled to any such privilege
or immunity; and

(*c*) Article 22 of the Vienna Convention on Diplomatic
Relations signed in 1961 shall not apply to any premises
25   of the mission other than those specified in paragraph 2
of the Schedule to this Act.

[Bill 57]   43/2

Appendix E

Diplomatic Privileges

(2) The Secretary of State may by order from time to time alter, add to or otherwise amend the Schedule to this Act and any such order may relate to any one or more of the states with whom agreements or arrangements under section 7 of the principal Act are then in force. 5

(3)—(a) The power conferred by the foregoing subsection on the Secretary of State shall be exercisable by statutory instrument.

(b) Any statutory instrument made under this section shall be of no effect unless approved by a resolution of each House of Parliament. 10

Short title, interpretation and commencement. 2.—(1) This Act may be cited as the Diplomatic Privileges Act 1966.

(2) Words and expressions to which meanings are assigned in the principal Act, shall in this Act have the same respective meanings. 15

(3) This Act shall come into force on 1st January, 1967.

Diplomatic Privileges 3

SCHEDULE

Provisions with respect to Missions referred to in Section 1 of this Act.

1. Staff of the mission entitled to any diplomatic privilege or immunity:—

5 Head of the mission	one
Members of the diplomatic staff of the mission ...	six
Members of the administrative and technical staff of the mission	ten
Members of the service staff of the mission ' ...	fifteen

10 2. The premises of the mission shall comprise the residence of the head of the mission and not more than one other building specified in a notice given by him to the Secretary of State.

IN THE HIGH COURT OF JUSTICE

QUEEN'S BENCH DIVISION

BETWEEN : -

ANTHONY TOSSWILL COURTNEY   Plaintiff

and

SIR THEODORE CONSTANTINE   Defendant

Dated and entered the 20th day of March 1968.

This action having been tried before the Honourable
Mr.Justice.Hinchcliffe with a Jury at the Royal Courts of
Justice and the said Jury having found answers as set out
hereunder to the following questions:-
- (1) Do you find for the Plaintiff or the Defendant ?
     Answer:- For the Plaintiff.
- (2) If you find for the Plaintiff what sum of damages
     do you award him ?
     Answer:- £200.0.0.

The said Mr.Justice Hinchcliffe having on the 20th day
of March ordered that Judgment as hereinafter provided be
entered for the Plaintiff,it is adjudged that the Defendant
do pay the Plaintiff the sum of £200.0.0. and his costs of
the action to be taxed.

The above costs have been taxed and allowed at £   :
    :   as appears by the Taxing Officer's Certificate
.dated the   day of   1968

....
Plaintiff's Solicitors

247

INDEX

Abel, Colonel, R.I.S. Agent, 120, 156
Addie, Robin, 84
Aden, 16
Adjournment Debate, 173, 185
Admiralty, 26, 29, 46, 47, 55, 98
Aeroflot, 95, 114
Agent, Harrow East Constituency, 100,
110, 159, 169, 178, 187, 209, 217
Agincourt, 200
Akkerman, 22
Alafuzov, Admiral, 46
Albany, 150
Alexandria, 28
Alexandrov, Commissar, 32; Contact-
man, 38
Alexandrovsk, Port, 31
Alexandrovskaya, street in Kishinev, 21
All-Union Chamber of Commerce,
Moscow, 60
Almeria, 27
Ambassador in Moscow, British, 71, 88,
99, 155
Anchors and Chain Cables Bill, 119
Anchors and Chain Cables (No. 2)
Bill, 119
Andropov, Yuri, Head of K.G.B., 225
Anglican Church, 88
Anglo-German Conference, 79
Anglo-Russian Business Consultants, 58
Anglo-Russian Cypher, 45
Anglo-Soviet Alliance, 85
Anglo-Soviet Consular Convention, 232
Anglo-Soviet Parliamentary Group, 74
Anglo-Soviet Trade, 89
Anglo-Soviet Visual Tactical Code, 45
Ankara, British Embassy in, 37
Ann Mills, 135, 137, 138
Antsipo-Chikunsky, Engineer-Flagman,
26
Arad, 113
Aragvi restaurant, 41, 105
Arajs, Bob, 133, 207
Arbat Square, Moscow, oo
Archangel, 30, 31, 32, 33, 46
Archbishops, 88
Arethusa, H.M.S., 27, 28
Argyll and Sutherland Highlanders, 85,
90
Askanas, Director, Poznan Fair, 59
Associated British Engineering, 58, 59
Associated Television, 204
Astakhov, Georgi Alexandrovitch, 26
Astoria Hotel, Leningrad, 25
Athenée Palace Hotel, Bucharest, 20
Atlantic Fleet, 17
Attorney-General, 120
Aubretia, H.M.S., 36
Auster Aiglet, 92

Australia, 16, 168
Aviation, 127

Bad Oeynhausen, H.Q. Rhine Army, 54
Bahamas, 100, 116
Baidukov, Lt.-Colonel, 28
Baikal, Lake, 77
Bakaritsa, 32
Bakhchisarai, Fountain of, 78
Baltic, 55
Bandera, Victim of R.I.S., 227
Barnes-Wallis, Dr., 127
Battet, Capitaine de Vaisseau, 28
Battle of the Atlantic, 28
Battle Cruiser Squadron, 16
Battle Squadron, 2nd, 17
Battle Squadron, 3rd, 28
B.B.C., 170, 177; Russian Service, 58
Beagle Airedale, 92, 110, 112, 127, 184
Bear Island, 46
Bednyakov, 80
Belgrade, 113
Belin, Cmdr. Peter, U.S.N.R., 51
Belmont Ward (Harrow East), 100, 110,
194, 195, 201, 212
Bennett, Reggie, 119
Beria, Lavrenti, 44, 45, 223
Berlin, 54, 92; Blockade, 54
Bessarabia, 20, 46
Bevan, Aneurin, 73
Blackett, Patrick, 24
Black Rod, 67
Black Sea, 28; Intelligence from, 53
Blake, George, R.I.S. Agent, 52, 97,
100, 165, 231, 234
Board of Trade, 63, 226
Bolshoi Theatre Company, 38, 43, 103,
105
Bordeaux, 190
Borvikha-Zhukovka, 92
Bossard, 121, 124, 148
Bow Group, 220
Brighton, 1965, Tory Conference at,
163
British Aircraft Corporation, 127
British Industrial Exhibition in Moscow,
85, 86, 89
Brooke, Gerald, 121, 153, 156, 232
Brown, Hubert, Master at Dartmouth,
16
Bucharest, 19, 113, 114
Budapesth, 113, 167, 231
Bulgaria, 111, 114, 232
Burgess, Guy, R.I.S. Agent, 56, 71, 234
Burrough, Rear-Admiral Harold, 29,
31, 47, 50
Burrough, Stephen—also Burrough
Strait, 29

Index

Index